Gender, Power and Management

Also by Barbara Bagilhole

UNDERSTANDING EQUAL OPPORTUNITIES AND DIVERSITY:
The Social Differentiations and Intersections of Inequality

WOMEN IN NON-TRADITIONAL OCCUPATIONS: Challenging Men

WOMEN, WORK AND EQUAL OPPORTUNITIES

THE EVALUATION OF POLICIES IN RELATION TO THE DIVISION
OF UNPAID AND PAID WORK BETWEEN WOMEN AND MEN
(*with C. Dugmore*)

EQUAL OPPORTUNITIES AND SOCIAL POLICY:
Issues of gender, 'race' and disability

TOMORROW'S TEAM: Women and Men in Construction
(*with S. Rhys-Jones, A. Dainty and R. Neale*)

UNDERSTANDING INTERSECTIONALITY: Keeping Gender at the Centre
(*with M. Franken, A. Cabo and A. Woodward*)

THE MAKING OF EUROPEAN WOMEN'S STUDIES, VOLUME I
(*with M. Franken*)

PEOPLE AND CULTURE IN CONSTRUCTION (with *A. Dainty and S. Green*)

STATE OF THE ART IN WOMEN'S STUDIES IN EUROPE:
Some Bad News But More Good (*with T. Levin and A. Visser*)

Also by Kate White

A POLITICAL LOVE STORY: Joe and Enid Lyons

JOHN CAIN AND VICTORIAN LABOUR 1917–1957

BARNEY: The Story of Rees D Williams, Architect of the White-Collar
Union Movement

AN OPEN ACCOUNT: 72 Years of Unionism in the State Bank of Victoria

WOMEN IN AUSTRALIAN POLITICS (*with J. Clarke*)

INTERNATIONALISING EDUCATION: Risks and Returns
(*co-edited with R. Adams*)

RESEARCH FOR WRITERS (*with R. Murray*)

STATE OF FIRE (*with R. Murray*)

A BANK FOR THE PEOPLE (*with R. Murray*)

THE FALL OF THE HOUSE OF CAIN (*with R. Murray*)

DHARUG AND DUNGAREE (*with R. Murray*)

THE GOLDEN YEARS OF STAWELL (*with R. Murray*)

THE IRONWORKERS (*with R. Murray*)

Gender, Power and Management

A Cross-Cultural Analysis of Higher Education

Edited by

Barbara Bagilhole
and
Kate White

palgrave
macmillan

First published 2011 by
PALGRAVE MACMILLAN

Palgrave Macmillan in the UK is an imprint of Macmillan Publishers Limited,
registered in England, company number 785998, of Houndmills, Basingstoke,
Hampshire RG21 6XS.

Palgrave Macmillan in the US is a division of St Martin's Press LLC,
175 Fifth Avenue, New York, NY 10010.

Palgrave Macmillan is the global academic imprint of the above companies
and has companies and representatives throughout the world.

Palgrave® and Macmillan® are registered trademarks in the United States,
the United Kingdom, Europe and other countries.

ISBN 978–0–230–23225–9   hardback

This book is printed on paper suitable for recycling and made from fully
managed and sustained forest sources. Logging, pulping and manufacturing
processes are expected to conform to the environmental regulations of the
country of origin.

A catalogue record for this book is available from the British Library.

Library of Congress Cataloging-in-Publication Data
Gender, power and management : a cross-cultural analysis of higher
education / edited by Barbara Bagilhole and Kate White.
p. cm.
Includes index.
ISBN 978–0–230–23225–9 (hardback)
1. Women executives. 2. Sex discrimination in education. 3. Education,
Higher. I. Bagilhole, Barbara, 1951 Feb. 3– II. White, Kate, 1949 Aug. 3–
HD6054.3.G38 2011
378.1'11082—dc22   2011007018

10   9   8   7   6   5   4   3   2   1
20 19 18 17 16 15 14 13 12 11

Printed and bound in Great Britain by
CPI Antony Rowe, Chippenham and Eastbourne

This book is dedicated to the senior managers who participated in this research and to women who are still challenged in universities worldwide

Contents

List of Tables

Acknowledgements

We would like to acknowledge the contribution of a number of organisations and individuals to this project. The Center for Research in Higher Education Policies (CIPES) at the University of Porto hosted the first project meeting of the Women in Higher Education Management (WHEM) Network and the support of its former Director, Professor Alberto Amaral and its current Director, Professor Pedro Teixeira, has been important.

We also acknowledge financial support for the WHEM Network from The Bank of Sweden Tercentenary Fund and the Swedish Research Council that enabled the Network to meet in Stockholm in August 2008 and Uppsala in April 2009, and the coordinator to work on the project as a visiting researcher at Uppsala University and the Centre for Gender Excellence at Linkoping University.

Finally we would like to thank the university senior managers in eight countries who agreed to be interviewed and share their experiences of working in management teams.

Notes on Contributors

Barbara Bagilhole is Professor of Equal Opportunities and Social Policy, in the School of Social Sciences, Loughborough University, UK. She has researched and published extensively in the area of equal opportunities and diversity across gender, race, disability, sexual orientation, religious belief, age and intersectionality. Her most recent book was *Understanding Equal Opportunities and Diversity: The social differentiations and intersections of inequality*. She is currently part of a European Union funded research group 'HELENA' exploring how to encourage women engineering students, and is the Treasurer of 'ATGender', the European Women's Studies Association.

Teresa Carvalho is Assistant Professor at the University of Aveiro and senior researcher at the Center for Research in Higher Education Policies (CIPES). Her main research interests are institutional governance and management, the academic profession and gender in higher education. Recent publications include articles in: *European Journal of Education, Higher Education Quarterly, Tertiary Education and Management, Equal Opportunities International, Higher Education, Higher Education Policy, Journal of Higher Education Policy and Management* and *Journal of Management Research*.

Anita Göransson is guest Professor at Uppsala University with special reference to economic change and organisations. Her general research interest is how the gender order and other social hierarchies affect and interact with the formation of societies and their power orders. She has worked with extensive empirical material and used the results in developing a theoretical approach that combines post-structural and materialist elements and stresses the analytically primary role of masculinity. Her most recent research focusses on the Swedish power elite and how different combinations of class, gender and ethnicity affect access to power in various social fields.

Maria de Lourdes Machado is a Senior Research Associate at the Center for Research in Higher Education Policies in Portugal. Her research interests include gender studies, governance and management, strategic planning, the non-university sector, student success, diversity and faculty satisfaction. She is the author of several books on higher education legislation and other publications in European and American journals such as *Diálogo Educacional, European Higher Education, Higher Education Policy, Planning for Higher Education* and *Tertiary Education and Management.*

Jenny Neale is currently a Senior Research Fellow in the Health Services Research Centre at Victoria University of Wellington. She was formerly Head of the School of Social and Cultural Studies and Deputy Dean in the Faculty of Humanities and Social Sciences. She has had a long-term involvement in evaluation and research with a particular emphasis on gender analysis.

Pat O'Connor is Professor of Sociology and Social Policy at the University of Limerick in Ireland, and has been Dean of the Faculty of Arts, Humanities and Social Sciences there for ten years. Her research interests revolve around gender: its structural and cultural reality as reflected, for example, in organisational cultures in academia. She has published five books, over 45 refereed journal articles, 15 book chapters and roughly 30 other publications. She has worked in a number of other academic organisations, including Bedford and Royal Holloway College, NISW London, the Economic and Social Research Institute in Dublin and at WIT, and has been a reviewer for the European Science Foundation and Chair of the Linnaeus International Expert Panel.

Özlem Özkanlı is Professor and Head of Management in the Faculty of Political Sciences and Organisation Chair at Ankara University. She teaches Management and Organisation, Human Resources Management, Enterprise Policy and Strategic Management, Modern Organisational Theory, Managerial Behaviour, Management of Multinational Enterprises and Women in Management. She is the author of three books and many academic articles. She worked at the National Productivity Centre as a specialist between1988 and 1996 and has led a number of training/consulting missions in public and private sector enterprises. She specialises in women's studies, productivity improvement techniques and HRM.

Sarah Riordan is a registered organisational psychologist in South Africa, where she is self-employed. She balances teaching at the University of Cape Town and the University of Stellenbosch with consulting to businesses. Until recently, she was a managing member of HERS-SA, a non-profit organisation dedicated to the advancement of academic women. Her particular research interests include career psychology and career management.

Kate White is Adjunct Research Associate, at the Centre for Women's Studies and Gender Research, Monash University. She is the coordinator and co-founder of the Women in Higher Education Management Network. She is the author/co-author of 12 books. Her current research interests are gender and higher education and women's academic careers. Recent publications include articles in: *Tertiary Education and Management, Equal Opportunities International, Journal of Higher Education Policy and Management, South African Journal for Higher Education, International Journal of Knowledge, Culture and Change Management* and *Gender and Education.*

Introduction: Building a Feminist Research Network

Barbara Bagilhole and Kate White

1 Outline

This introduction explores the potential significance of women being part of, rather than excluded from, university senior management. It outlines the background to a study undertaken by an international collaborative network: how the eight-country network was developed, the selection of countries, and the logistics of the project.

Women are now part of senior management in higher education (HE) to varying degrees in most countries, and they actively contribute to the vision and strategic direction of universities. This book attempts to analyse their impact and potential impact on both organisational growth and culture. Nevertheless, roles within HE senior management tend to be gendered, reflecting the gendering of academic careers, in which in most countries the traditional male academic career model continues to be considered the only path into senior management. Even though women are no longer excluded from senior management in universities, this gendered segregation of management roles required exploration and analysis and is examined, compared and contrasted across the eight countries.

The aim of this book is to provide a comprehensive analysis of gender and power in universities and their impact on the representation of women in university senior management.

The objectives are

- To gain an understanding of women's representation in, experience of and influence on senior management in the eight countries in this study; and
- To explore the feasibility of developing interventions for women who wish to apply for HE senior-management positions.

1

This is the first multi-country study to examine the dynamics of men and women working together in HE senior-management teams. Key concepts include: career paths in higher education; support and mentoring; gate keeping; management skills; gendered management and leadership styles; gendered organisational cultures; structural and cultural barriers; hegemonic masculinities in academia; and policy and practice in higher education.

The book provides a comprehensive analysis of gender, power and university management across Australia, Ireland, New Zealand, Portugal, South Africa, Sweden, Turkey, and the United Kingdom. The research explores pathways into university leadership, the dynamics of men and women working together in senior-management teams and the broader organisational context. It analyses whether or not women can and do make a distinctive contribution to university decision-making, and the impact of organisational cultures on their effectiveness as managers and leaders. This is an innovative study that analyses the data of all countries in each chapter rather than allocating each chapter to analysing the data of one particular country. It therefore enables the analysis of particular themes using the total data set.

Chapter 1 provides the broad societal context for the study. It examines economic participation and opportunity in each country, educational attainment, health and survival, and political empowerment. It then explores the national policies and legislative framework supporting labour force participation of women, including parental leave provisions, flexible work arrangements and pay equity.

Chapter 2 explores the role of HE in society in these countries, and the move from collegial to managerial models. It surveys the historical development of HE, comparing those countries that developed on the British model with others where mass HE has been a more recent development. It explores the nature of power within universities, focussing particularly on the extent, nature and implications of a shift from collegial to managerial models. It then examines the trends in the participation of women in academia and management. Finally, it analyses Equal Opportunity and Affirmative Action policy frameworks in HE within each country.

Chapter 3 sets out the research design of the project and critically explores and analyses the academic and practical reasons for it. The research project addresses the following questions regarding women in HE senior management:

- What are the factors in women's under-representation in HE senior management? Is discipline an important factor?

- Do recruitment and selection processes discriminate against women who apply for senior-management positions? If so, how?
- Is support and mentoring critical to getting into and getting on in senior management?
- What are the skills required for effective HE leadership and management?
- Do women and men in HE have different management styles?
- Do gender and leadership styles impact on senior management?
- Does having women in senior management impact on decision-making in, and the organisational culture of, HE?
- How powerful are Rectors/VCs/Presidents and do they have an impact on the gender composition of senior-management teams?
- Do collegial and managerial models differently impact on the opportunities for female managers and leaders in universities?

These questions will be addressed in Chapters 4, 5, 6 and 7 and form the framework for Chapter 8, the discussion and conclusion chapter.

Chapter 3 also details the two stages of the research. In the first stage investigators in each country, where statistics were available, analysed the representation of women in senior management. This representation was examined in relation to the participation of women as undergraduates and as academics by level, given the importance of women as senior managers acting as role models. The second stage involved open-ended, qualitative interviews with a sample of female and male senior managers, including current and former Rectors/Vice-Chancellors/Presidents. The chapter explains how interview subjects were selected across the eight countries, how the interviews were conducted, how interview summaries were developed, and how these de-identified summaries were analysed by the project team.

Chapter 4 explains the various historical models of HE, recent changes in HE in each country, and definitions of university senior management. It then explores power in universities and the traditional male model of management. It also analyses the impact of the shift from collegial to managerial models on women in university management.

Chapter 5 analyses data from the eight countries, focussing on how one becomes a senior manager, and explores typical career paths into senior management. It then explores the experience of being appointed to senior management, the factors or people that were most supportive or not, and how being in senior management affects work/life experience. Next it examines the skills that senior managers consider are required to operate effectively. Finally, the chapter analyses the appointment processes and management and leadership styles of Rectors/VCs/Presidents, and how they influence faculties and university operations both internally and externally.

Chapter 6 investigates the dynamics of women and men working together in university senior-management teams: how they carry out their roles, perceptions of how their colleagues regard them, and whether women have a different management style. It also tries to tease out whether university leaders believe that women in management tend to modify their behaviour to fit in with the predominantly male management culture.

Chapter 7 explores who has key influence in universities, who influences the selection process for appointment of senior managers, and who within management teams has most power both internally and externally. It questions whether women as managers can impact on entrenched organisational cultures. It then explores whether or not Rectors/VCs/Presidents believe they should – and in fact do – have an impact on the gender composition of senior-management teams.

Chapter 8, based on the analysis of the data from Chapters 4 to 7, explores the nexus between gender and power in universities, through the lens of senior management. It questions whether or not collegial and managerial models impact on the opportunities for female leaders in universities. It also analyses the impact of career paths, changes in leadership roles, the dynamics of gendered management teams, gendered stereotypes of leadership, and demands of the job on women becoming – or being effective as – senior managers.

2   Scope

The title of this book is *Gender, Power and Management: A Cross-Cultural Analysis of Higher Education.* The approach taken is centrally one of feminist standpoint theory. As feminist researchers we consider that it is important to locate ourselves within this research. Anderson (2009) emphasises that dominant knowledge practices can disadvantage women by producing theories of social phenomena that render gendered power relations invisible. Standpoint theory endeavours to develop a feminist epistemology, or theory of knowledge, that delineates methods for building effective knowledge from women's experience (Harding 1986). This research adopts a feminist standpoint that foregrounds women's experiences in university senior management.

Given the broad spread of disciplinary backgrounds of the researchers in this Network, we have adopted an interdisciplinary negotiated approach to our understanding of concepts such as gender, power, leadership and management. This entails moving beyond a strictly sociological theoretical position and incorporating other disciplinary perspectives.

2.1 Gender

Gender and power are issues in HE management, and leadership particularly, in terms of gendered styles of leadership and management – often characterised by women's preference for transformational in contrast to transactional leadership. As these terms will be used extensively in the book, they need to be defined.

Transformational leadership is often regarded as a defining characteristic of women managers. Rosener (1990) noted women's preference in leadership to be transformational; that is, to use an interactive style, share power and information, use personal power, enhance people's self worth, and make them feel part of the organisation. Alimo-Metcalfe (2005) outlined a UK transformational leadership model characterised by demonstrating genuine concern, enabling, being accessible, encouraging questioning and curiosity, integrity, networking, building shared vision, self development, creating cultures of learning and developing others' sense of leadership. This focus on encouraging participation and team work, in transformational leadership (Miller 2006), enables the leader to become a role model through establishing trust and confidence and by empowering staff (Eagly & Carli 2007). However, according to Doherty and Manfredi (2005), the evidence is unclear about the extent to which adopting a transformational management style helps career progression for women in universities. Barker and Monks (2003, p. 6) observed in a university context that 'it may be that only those female managers who are transactional in approach [rather than transformational who] are admitted by the mainly male "gatekeepers" to top management positions'.

Unchallenged authority is generally identified with a masculine, or transactional, view of university leadership. Currie, Thiele and Harris (2002) reported that male university managers identified characteristics of successful university senior managers as including: executive attributes (as opposed to scholarly attributes), common sense, flexibility, motivation, tact, firmness, delivery, aggression, thinking before speaking, knowing how to play the committee game, getting the ear of management (i.e., the VC), being prepared to sacrifice collegiality, leisure, and family life, and accepting that the workload is continuous. This transactional model is often problematic for women. Eveline

(2004, p. 100) commented that if 'the criteria for senior management include the ability to avoid "going limp", and if women are stereotyped as lacking that ability, then men are more likely than women to be seen as meritorious'.

Another similar interpretation of gendered styles of leadership and management sees men as agenic, the 'doers', while women are seen as 'communal' and relating to people (Eagly & Sczesny 2009, p. 23) and there is an assumption that men are agenically competent (Eagly & Carli 2007) (see Chapter 6 for a full discussion).

2.2   Power

The concept of power is controversial and well discussed in the literature. In this work power is considered, according with Weber's (1995) famous definition, as the capacity to enforce someone to do something even if it is against their own will. To be able to do this people may rest on different sources of power legitimacy, based on three different types of authority: charismatic, emotional responses to the qualities of an individual; traditional, detailed institutionalised traditions; and legal-rational, formalistic belief in the content of the law and uniform principles. In the HE context power legitimacy rests on legal-rational authority and, more specifically, on expertise, both in collegial and managerial models (see discussion in Chapters 4 and 7). As O'Connor and White (2009) argue:

> Expertise is an important source of power in both the collegial and managerial models and is arguably the most acceptable form of power within a knowledge generating organisation such as a university, although the kind of expertise that is valued may vary.

In addition, positional power (Handy 1985), that is, power as vested in the position of Rector/VC/President, is an important source of power in universities particularly as that role in the managerial model increasingly moves to being a Chief Executive Officer (CEO), as in the private sector (as discussed further in Chapter 4).

2.3   Management and Leadership

While universities have different governance structures, the scarce number of women at the top seems to be a persistent pattern in all countries in this study. Historically, women have been predominantly excluded from leadership and managerial roles (O'Connor & White 2011).

In higher education an important distinction has to be made between leadership and management. While the concepts of leadership and management of HE institutions are often confused and misunderstood (Bergquist 1992; Cohen & March 1983), they are two entirely different, yet intimately intertwined aspects of the overall effective functioning of a higher education institution: 'Each depends on the other for support and to provide the institution with the multifaceted decision-making, policy development and administrative roles necessary to function effectively' (Taylor & Machado 2006, p. 138; see also Cohen & March 1983). Taylor and Machado (2006, p. 142) differentiate the concepts as follows: 'management is often seen as a relatively structured process for achieving organisational objectives within the parameters of prescribed roles. Leadership is more often viewed as an interpersonal process of inspiring and motivating followers with a focus on long term institutional aspirations and changes'.

Leadership is therefore a process for influencing decisions and guiding people, whereas management involves the implementation and administration of institutional decisions and policies (Bennis & Nanus 1985; Gayle, Bhoendradatt & White 2003; Peterson 1995; Taylor & Machado 2006). There are, however, many other less universally accepted attributes of each concept that can militate against their effective co-existence (Cohen & March 1983; Larsen 2003; Yammarino & Dansereau 2001). It can be argued that leadership and management cannot be addressed as discrete and autonomous entities. A meaningful understanding of both concepts can only be reached when they are examined in relation to one another. The symbiotic interdependence of leadership and management in higher education is an important element in understanding either concept (Clark 1998; Millett 1989; Peterson & Mets 1987). Each depends on the other for support and to provide the institution with the multifaceted decision-making, policy-development and administrative roles necessary to function effectively. To achieve this compatibility both concepts must be clearly understood by all parties, and those individuals engaged must possess the personal skills and tools necessary to implement their contributing roles as leaders and managers (Moore 2001; Nanus 1992). Assuming this perspective throughout the book, leadership and management are often used here interchangeably.

Early studies of leadership and management did not include gender perspectives. Only in the beginning of the 1970s did such research start to include woman (Terborg 1973; Veiga & Yanouzas 1978; Nieva & Gutek 1980 in Kovalainen 1988). These first studies concentrated on the dichotomy perspective based on 'leadership trait theory' and 'leadership style theory' and tended to reproduce the popular stereotypes that there were differences in personality traits and leadership styles between female and male leaders (Kovalainen1988). The first empirical results supported the idea that women had less leadership potential than men (Chapman, Brad & Luthans 1975). However, further developments demonstrated the existence of more complex relations between gender and management. Several studies acknowledge the importance of more or less explicit cultural mechanisms creating obstacles for women to gain and develop managerial roles (Hearn & Parkin 1987; Collinson 1992; Kerfoot & Knights 1993; Connell 1993, 1995; Collinson & Hearn 1996; Marshall 1984). The increasing interest in this topic creates a new research field known as women in management.

Universities have been characterised as 'ivory towers', somehow removed from the wider societal context in which they operate. Normative values underlying the organisational behaviour of universities are those of merit and universalism, which are assumed to ensure equal opportunities for everyone. However, several studies have demonstrated that even in this sort of environment one can find gender differences in career attainment, with the persistent phenomena of horizontal and vertical segregation (Rees 2001; Kloot 2004; Fiona 2005; Stromquist et al. 2007; Amâncio 2005; Harman 2003; Bagilhole 2000; Krais 2002; Saunderson 2002; Benschop & Brouns 2003).

It is clear that universities have some relevance in the analysis of the international phenomenon of women's under-representation in senior management. One of the main features of universities, resulting from their traditional bureau-professional system, has been the coexistence, and even the intersection, of administrative/managerial and professional (academic) roles under the same category (Clarke & Newman 1997; Deem, Hillyard & Reed 2007).

Practising academics are only involved in professional roles. But even among this group there are some whose roles include direct supervision, described as the *quasi-managerial*. The managing professional is the term used to describe professionals whose main responsibility is to manage the daily work of other colleagues and the resources used in their performance. General managers are those who have responsibilities for managing professionals but are not involved in daily practices. These general managers may or may not have the same professional background. Freidson (1994) argues that as managers have often been professionals, it is inadequate to treat them in a dichotomised way.

To avoid this dichotomy, and based on Pritchard and Deem (1999), the manager can better be understood 'not as a particular person, or organisational role, but as a subject position. A subject position is that point where the multiple lines of force embedded in the language and practices of the managerial mode come together' (Prichard & Deem 1999, p. 327).

Gender, power, leadership and management form a continuous narrative in this book. Before examining the broader country context for the study, the processes of developing this international collaboration will be outlined.

3   Developing an international collaborative network

The origins of the book go back to a research collaboration developed by the editors in 2003. They had first met at a European Gender Equality in Higher Education Conference in Zurich three years earlier. After subsequently presenting a joint invited paper on women in university management at an Australian Technical Network Women's Executive Development (WEXDEV) conference in Perth in 2003, they then undertook a quantitative analysis, drawn from university websites, of all senior managers in UK and Australian Universities. That analysis indicated that while the percentage of women at VC and Deputy Vice-Chancellor (DVC) level was higher in Australia than the UK (26 per cent and 18 per cent in Australia compared to 8 per cent and 6 per cent in the UK), the worrying trend in both countries was that women were still only between a quarter and one-fifth of Pro Vice-Chancellors, Deans and Deputy-Deans, an important pool from which VCs and DVCs are recruited. Moreover, there was a difference in the success of women attaining senior-management positions in 'old' (most prestigious) versus 'new' universities, and men in the science, engineering and technology disciplines predominated as VCs in both countries (Bagilhole & White 2005).

The next stage of their research was to gain an understanding of the skills required for effective university management. Given the lack of transparency in recruitment and selection processes, senior women academics often lacked the knowledge of what was required to successfully compete for senior-management positions. This involved qualitative research with current and former VCs, senior managers and recruitment firms that Australian and UK universities engage to identify skill requirements for effective leadership and management, approach suitable candidates and provide short-lists. This study, which eventually became the pilot for the present study, undertook qualitative interviews with 26 male and female senior managers and several recruitment consultants.

Bagilhole and White's (2008) research identified a spectrum of skills required for effective university management, from soft skills through to hard skills (similar to Currie, Thiele and Harris's list mentioned above). At one end of the spectrum were the hard-edged skills such as competitiveness, aggression and entrepreneurialism often identified with male authority and at the other end collaborative, cooperative people skills, which were considered part of women's management style. In between these extremes were skills such as integrity, emotional intelligence, confidence, and resilience that had less obvious gender dimensions (Bagilhole & White 2008, p. 10).

The findings of this research were presented at two conferences in 2006:

- Australian Technical Network Women's Executive Development (ATN WEXDEV) Conference in Adelaide in April (see Bagilhole and White (2006)).
- European Association for Institutional Research Forum in Rome in September (see Bagilhole and White (2008)).

As a result of these and subsequent presentations, participants from other countries expressed interest in replicating the research. It was clear from initial conversations and analysis of the relevant literature that the findings of Bagilhole and White's research resonated with women in several other countries. Common challenges for women in senior management were identified. These included the under-representation of women in senior-management positions which resulted in academic colleagues and students not being provided with role models of successful women managers; lack of information and support for women about the process of applying for management and the skills and personal values required to be an effective manager; lack of information about effective management styles in a university context; little mentoring support for women to work successfully with colleagues in senior-management teams; and lack of effective networks for women in senior management in each country both nationally and internationally. Women in several other countries were therefore interested in working together to be part of an international project that explored the similarities and differences of their experience of women working in senior management in universities.

Over 2006 and 2007 the editors of this book built the Women in Higher Education Management (WHEM) Network, as additional gender researchers in appropriate and relevant countries were invited to join in the study.

Table I.1 Country/participating researchers

Country	Original participating researchers
Australia	Dr Kate White, Monash University
UK	Professor Barbara Bagilhole, Loughborough University
	Additional researchers
Ireland	Professor Pat O'Connor, University of Limerick
New Zealand	Associate Professor Jenny Neale, Victoria University Wellington
Portugal	Dr Maria de Lourdes Machado, Center for Research in Higher Education Policies (CIPES)
Portugal	Professor Teresa Carvalho, University of Aveiro and CIPES
South Africa	Dr Sarah Riordan, HERS-SA
Sweden	Professor Anita Göransson, Linkoping University
Turkey	Professor Özlem Özkanlı, Ankara University

In 2007 Kate took on the coordination of the project and the following international researchers agreed to join the Network (see Table I.1).

Each of the Network members has a strong interest in gender and HE as well as extensive research and publications in the area. The researchers collectively have broad disciplinary backgrounds – from management, sociology and social policy to political science and organisational psychology. As the Network expanded it included a grouping of several current and former British Commonwealth countries (Australia, New Zealand and South Africa), as well as two southern European countries (Turkey and Portugal). In late 2007 it was resolved to broaden the representation to include one Scandinavian country, given that women in academia and university management have generally fared better there than in the UK, for example.

The Network began to take substantive shape in May 2007 when the Center for Research in Higher Education Policies (CIPES) at the University of Porto hosted the first project meeting. Over three intensive days the researchers who were able to be present (from Australia, Portugal, Turkey, and the UK) examined the context for the study and some of the broad issues impacting on women's participation in HE in a global context. They also analysed the statistics on the representation of women at each level of management in each country (this updated analysis is included in Chapter 4). Another important decision at the meeting was to provide a name for the Network. The Porto meeting was critical to the subsequent development of the Network. It provided a unique opportunity to explore the parameters of this emerging international research consortium. The researchers appreciated the benefits of intensive, stimulating discussion and debate where each contributed information and different perspectives and ideas that enabled a broader understanding of the literature and of the specific country contexts for the study. Even at this early stage there emerged clear differences between the southern European countries – Portugal and Turkey – and the UK and Australia (where HE developed on the British model) in relation to legislative frameworks for HE, the impact of Equal Opportunity and Affirmative Action legislation, and academic career paths.

The subsequent research project of the WHEM Network, while using the research of Bagilhole and White as a starting point, developed further with a stronger emphasis on the dynamics of men and women working together in senior-management teams. An additional further meeting of several of the researchers in the Network was held in Berlin in early September 2007 (from Australia, New Zealand, UK and Ireland) and coincided with the 5th European Conference on Gender Equality in Higher Education.

During late 2007 the network spent considerable time developing a common interview schedule for the project, to ensure that the schedule captured a comprehensive and comparable range of information. We decided not to collect demographic data such as age, marital status, number of children, and educational history because the key explanatory variables, considered interesting and innovative for the project, are by academic experience not personal background. This privileges the institutional focus of the research, and also steered the research in a unique direction.

We wanted to capture three clusters of information about senior managers and their organisation. The first cluster was loosely entitled 'getting into and on in HE senior management'. It explored typical career paths, support or barriers to move into these positions, balancing paid and unpaid work, and aspirations and ambitions. The second cluster explored in detail the dynamics of men and women working together in senior-management teams. It asked respondents how they thought either women or men in the team perceived them; and probed their awareness of the position of academic women within their own university. The final cluster focussed on organisational culture and the pivotal role of Rectors/VCs/Presidents.

The next project meeting was in Madrid in July 2008 and coincided with the 11th International Interdisciplinary Congress of Women's Worlds where WHEM hosted a well attended Roundtable and five members presented papers. The Network received some valuable feedback. Immediately prior to the Conference the coordinator spent two weeks at CIPES as a Research Fellow. By this stage some of the Network members were undertaking their interviews.

The following indicates some of the issues with which the Network grappled in this early phase of the project in Madrid:

1. *Labour force participation*: we agreed that there needed to be robust discussion of women's labour force participation in each country and national policies supporting women in the labour market, including paid-unpaid work, work-life balance policies and Equal Employment Opportunity and Affirmative Action.
2. *Higher Education System*: the legal context for each country was important and needed to be addressed; that is, the national legislative framework for HE.
3. *Career paths into HE senior management*: early data was unclear on whether or not the perception of the traditional academic model prevailed, despite some managers having had a different career path.
4. *Importance of professorial rank to becoming a senior manager*: while investigators noted the common assumption that senior managers needed to be at professorial level, there were examples where some senior managers were not. However, some women considered that to have credibility senior managers needed to be professors.
5. *Life after being a Rector/VC/President*: it was noted that in some countries there was no provision for what people in these positions would do once they completed their term; contracts were generally for five years and in Ireland, Portugal and Sweden Rectors, VCs/Presidents were generally 'home grown'; that is, Universities tended to recruit senior managers from within the organisation.
6. *Interviewing senior managers in polytechnics*: the Network explored the status of polytechnics/technical/new universities in relation to old universities and the pattern for a higher proportion of women to be academics in polytechnics and more women senior managers. The meeting agreed that interviews would be conducted only in public universities in each country.
7. *Definitions of HE senior management*: the meeting discussed what constitutes senior management and what was meant by academic versus administrative management, and whether it referred to the portfolio held by the senior manager or whether or not they had come from an academic background. For example, Portugal and Turkey only have academics in senior management, whereas in Ireland and the UK women were more likely to be appointed to senior administrative

roles. Discussion then focussed on whether or not this was an issue of obfuscation in universities and the difficulty of understanding who has power. It was also acknowledged that universities were becoming more line-managed, and it was therefore important to uncover the impact of the culture of collegiality on women's career progression. It was further acknowledged that opportunities in senior management may open up for women if men prefer to move to research institutes rather than take on senior-management roles.

At the Madrid meeting a protocol for sharing data and material was drafted (see Appendix 1).

The WHEM Network also discussed in Madrid the publication of the research and securing funding. In the early stages of the project members had cross-subsidised their participation from other sources. The coordinator suggested that Palgrave Macmillan should be approached to publish the results of the WHEM project as an edited book. A draft book proposal was circulated for comment by the end of August 2008 and then submitted to the publisher in November 2008.

Discussion on possible funding sources led to a decision that:

- An application to The Bank of Sweden Tercentenary Fund for the 2009 WHEM Network Meeting should be made; and
- The coordinator would apply for a Visiting Fellowship from the Irish Research Council for Humanities and Social Sciences (IRCHSS) (this was successful).

The coordinator subsequently spent two weeks in December 2008 working with Professor Pat O'Connor at the University of Limerick. At the same time the original two members of WHEM were offered a book contract with Palgrave Macmillan. Then in early 2009, the application submitted by Professor Anita Göransson to The Bank of Sweden Tercentenary Fund was successful. This enabled travel and accommodation expenses to be met for all Network members to attend the next project meeting in Stockholm in August 2009.

WHEM continued to explore further funding opportunities and in May 2009 Professor Göransson coordinated an application for funding for the Network to the Swedish Research Council.

The 2009 WHEM Network project meeting coincided with the 6th European Conference on Gender Equality in Higher Education in Stockholm. This was the first occasion when all the researchers were able to attend and contribute on a face to face basis to the development of the project. WHEM presented four papers by a total of eight authors on various aspects of its research at a well attended Roundtable. Discussion at project meetings on 6th and 7th August 2009 focussed and built on feedback received at the Roundtable and included:

- The methodology was valued, as interviews in each country were conducted by the Network expert researcher in that country;
- Identifying various clusters of countries, for example, in relation to the power of Rectors/VCs/Presidents; gatekeepers; the tension between systems being gender neutral and competing with meritocracy;
- It was agreed that the research question would vary from chapter to chapter of the edited book, and that the collegial versus managerial model, for example, may vary from university to university;
- The dimensions of the research would be around the original three clusters of questions in the interview schedule, but would depend on the independent variables and how we explained variables between each country;
- It was agreed that once the book had been completed future collaboration should be planned and would be important;
- The Network finalised allocation of chapters; and editorial responsibilities and powers: the editors took responsibility for drafting the introduction, chapter one, and the discussion/ conclusion chapter; and editing other contributors' chapters;
- In the interest of confidentiality it was agreed not to use pseudonyms to identify interviewees in the book. Instead quotes would be identified by gender and country code as discussed in Chapter 3; and
- Sustainability of the project: the meeting also discussed securing future funding for the Network – including funding for the coordinator to work on the project for a three month period, extending the Network and developing a marketing plan.

The application to the Swedish Research Council was successful and provided funding for the project researchers to meet in Uppsala and three month's funding for the coordinator to work full-time in Sweden on the project. The Uppsala meeting from 9th to 11th April 2010 provided an opportunity for feedback on the draft chapters and overlap and gaps to be identified. Again all researchers were able to attend. Several important dimensions of the book were discussed, including definitions of management, leadership and power, the implications for senior women of the shift from collegial to managerial models, and the skills and values required for effective university management. It was an intensely collaborative process where researchers were able to provide critical feedback on each chapter as well as useful advice to the editors.

4 Sustainability of the WHEM Network

The collective passion of the Network has been demonstrated in the huge time commitment of members and the strategic focus on securing funding to enable the research to continue. It has also been demonstrated in the energy devoted to writing and presenting conference papers, publication of articles, and drafting book chapters and offering comment on other chapters.

Building an international research collaboration is a major undertaking. The critical role of the coordinator has been to provide information, encourage communication across the Network, and to be the continuing rallying call to us all. The coordinator circulated a monthly project update and, with WHEM colleagues, developed a project timeline in order to make the tasks and deliverables transparent.

This book is a testament to the research expertise and experience of the Network members but also importantly their growing respect and friendship. What shines through is their shared passion and commitment to improving the representation and effectiveness of women in HE senior management. Each of us has her own personal story of building an academic career in often challenging circumstances. The common thread of these stories is around gendered organisational cultures in universities in which we have worked. Gender has often not been on the agenda for many university managers because gender has been rendered invisible, even though paradoxically particular academic and non academic positions, disciplines and even management positions are highly gendered. If one believes that management is responsible for the vision and strategic direction – and in turn organisational culture – of universities, then careful analysis of the dynamics of senior-management teams might throw light on management's role in shaping and perpetuating – or changing – gendered organisational cultures.

References

Alimo-Metcalfe, B. (2005). Developments in leadership: A masculine past, but a feminine future, presentation to Women to Management Conference, Leeds.

Amâncio, L. (2005). 'Reflections on science as a gendered endeavour: Changes and continuities', *Social Science Information*, 44, 1, 65–83.

Anderson, E. (2009). 'Feminist epistemology and philosophy of science', *Stanford Encyclopedia Philosophy*, http://plato.stanford.edu/entries/feminism-epistemology, accessed 20 April 2010.

Bagilhole, B. (2000). 'Too little too late? An assessment of national initiatives for women academics in the British university system', *Higher Education in Europe*, 23, 2, 139–45.

Bagilhole, B. and White, K. (2008). 'Towards a gendered skills analysis of senior management positions in UK and Australian universities', *Tertiary Education and Management*, 14, 1, 1–12.

Bagilhole, B. and White, K. (2006). 'Making it to the top? Towards a gendered skills analysis of senior leadership and management positions in UK and Australian Universities', in C. Chesterman (ed.), *Change in Climate: prospects for gender equity in Universities. Proceedings of ATN WEXDEV Conference* (Adelaide: WEXDEV), 1–14.

Bagilhole, B. and White, K. (2005). Benign burden: gender and senior management in the UK and Australia, paper presented to the 4th European Conference on Gender Equality in Higher Education, Oxford.

Barker, P. and Monks, K. (2003). Women in senior academic positions: Two case studies, paper presented to 3rd European Conference on Gender Equality in Higher Education, Genoa.

Bennis, W. and Nanus, B. (1985). *Leadership: The Strategies for Taking Charge* (New York: Harper and Row).

Benschop, Y. and Brouns, M. (2003). 'Crumbling ivory tower: Academic organizing and its gender effects', *Gender, Work and Organisation*, 10, 2, 194–212.

Bergquist, W. (1992). *The Four Cultures of the Academy* (San Francisco: Jossey-Bass Publishers).

Clark, B. (1998). *Creating Entrepreneurial Universities: Organisational Pathways of Transformation* (Oxford: IAU Press Pergamon).

Clarke, J. and Newman, J. (1997). *The Managerial State* (London: Sage).

Chapman, J., Brad, F. and Luthans, F. (1975). 'The female leadership dilemma', *Public Personnel Management*, 4, 3, 173–9.

Cohen, M. and March, J. (1983). *Leadership and Ambiguity: The American College President* (2nd edn) (New York: Mc-Graw Hill).

Collinson, D. (1992). *Managing the Shopfloor: Subjectivity, Masculinity, and Workplace Culture* (Berlin: Walter de Gruyter).

Collinson, D. and Hearn, J. (eds) (1996), *Men as Managers, Managers as Men: Critical Perspectives on Men, Masculinities and Managements* (London: Sage).

Connell, R. W. (1995), *Masculinities* (Sydney: Allen & Unwin).

Connell, R. W. (1993), 'The big picture: Masculinities in recent world history', *Theory and Society*, 22, 5, 597–623.

Currie, J., Thiele, B. and Harris, P. (2002). *Gendered Universities in Globalized Economies* (Lanham: Lexington Books).

Deem, R., Hillyard, S. and Reed, M. (2007). *Knowledge, Higher Education, and the New Managerialism. The Changing Management of UK Universities* (Oxford: Oxford University Press).

Doherty, L. and Manfredi, S. (2005). Women's progression in English universities, paper presented to 4th European Conference on Gender Equality in Higher Education, Oxford.

Eagly, A. H. and Carli, L. L. (2007). *Through the Labyrinth: The Truth about How Women Become Leaders* (Boston: Harvard Business School Publishing Corporation).

Eagly, A. H. and Sczesny, S. (2009). 'Stereotypes about women, men and leaders: Have times changed?' in M. Barreto, M. K. Ryan and M. T. Schmitt (eds), *The Glass Ceiling in the 21st Century: Understanding Barriers to Gender Equality* (Washington: American Psychological Association), 21–48.

Eveline, J. (2004). *Ivory Basement Leadership: Power and Invisibility in the Changing University* (Perth: University of Western Australia Press).

Fiona, W. (2005). 'Caught between difference and similarity: The case of women academics', *Women in Management Review*, 20, 4, 234–48.

Freidson, E. (1994). *Professionalism Reborn* (Cambridge: Polity Press).

Gayle, D., Bohendradatt, T. and White, A. (2003). 'Governance in the twenty-first century university', *ASHE-ERIC Higher Education Report*, 30, 1.

Handy, C. (1985). *Understanding Organisations*. 2nd edn. (Harmondsworth: Penguin).

Harding, S. (1986). *The Science Question in Feminism* (Cornell University Press: Ithaca).

Harman, G. (2003). 'Australian academics and prospective academics: Adjustment to a more commercial environment', *Higher Education Management and Policy*, 15, 3, 105–22.

Hearn, J. and Parkin, W. (1987). *'Sex' at 'work'* (New York: St. Martin's Press).

Krais, B. (2002). 'Academia as a profession and the hierarchy of the sexes: Paths out of research in German universities', *Higher Education Quarterly*, 56, 4, 407–18.

Kerfoot, D. and Knights, D. (1993), 'Management, masculinity and manipulation: From paternalism to corporate strategy in financial services in Britain', *Journal of Management Studies*, 30, 4, 659–77.

Kovalainen, A. (1988). 'Towards a new research model of gender in management and leadership studies', *International Journal for the Advancement of Counselling*, 11, 305–11.

Larsen, I. (2003). 'Departmental leadership in Norwegian universities – in between two models of governance?' in A. Amaral, L. Meek and I. Larsen (eds), *The Higher Education Managerial Revolution?* (Dortrecht, NE: Kluwer Academic Publishers), 71–88.

Kloot, L. (2004). 'Women and leadership in universities. A case study of women academic managers', *The International Journal of Public Sector Management*, 17, 6, 470–85.

McGauran, A. M. (1996). 'The effects of EU policy on women's employment: the case of women in Irish and French retailing', *Irish Journal of Feminist Studies*, 1, 2, 83–102.

McGinnity, F., Russell, H., Williams, J. and Blackwell, S. (2005). *Time Use in Ireland 2005* (Harmondsworth: Penguin, 2nd edn).

Marshall, J. (1984). *Women Managers: Travellers in a Male World* (Chichester: John Wiley & Sons).

Miller, K. (2006). 'Introduction: Women in leadership and management: Progress thus far?' in D. McTavish and K. Miller (eds), *Women in Leadership and Management* (Cheltenham: Edward Elgar), 1–10.

Millett, J. (1989). 'Relating to governance and leadership', in P. Jedamus and M. Petersons & Associates (eds), *Improving Academic Management* (San Francisco: Jossey-Bass), 495–510.

Moore, J. (2001). 'Planning, politics and presidential leadership', in R. Rose (ed.), *Connecting the Dots ... the Essence of Planning* (Ann Arbor, MI: Society for College and University Planning).

Nanus, B. (1992). *Visionary Leadership Creating a Compelling Sense of Direction for your Organization* (San Francisco: Jossey-Bass).

O'Connor, P. and White, K. (2009). Universities – change or continuity? Collegial/managerialist? Gendered?, paper presented to the 6th Gender Equality in Higher Education Conference, Stockholm.

O'Connor, P. and White, K. (2011). 'Similarities and differences in collegiality/ managerialism in Irish and Australian universities', *Gender and Education* (forthcoming).

Peterson, M. (1995). 'Images of university structure, governance and leadership: adaptative strategies for the new environment', in D. Dill and B. Sporn (eds), *Emerging Patterns of Social Demand and University Reform: through a glass darkly* (Paris: IAU Press Pergamon), 140–58.

Peterson, M. and Mets, L. (1987). 'An evolutionary perspective on academic governance, management and leadership', in M. Peterson (eds), *Key Resources on Higher Education Governance, Management and Leadership* (San Francisco: Jossey-Bass), 1–20.

Pritchard, C. and Deem, R. (1999). 'Wo-managing further education; gender and the construction off the manager in the corporate colleges of England', *Gender and Education*, 11, 3, 323–42.

Rees, T. (2001). 'Mainstreaming gender equality in science in the European Union: The "ETAN report"', *Gender and Education*, 13, 3, 243–60.

Rosener, J. (1990). 'Ways women lead', *Harvard Business Review*, 68, 119–25.

Saunderson. W. (2002). 'Women, academia and identity: Constructions of equal opportunities in the "New Managerialism" – A case of lipstick on the gorilla?', *Higher Education Quarterly*, 56, 4, 376–406.

Stromquist, N., Gil-Antón, M., Balbachevsky, E., Mabokela, R., Smolentseva, A. and Colatrella, C. (2007). 'The academic profession in the globalisation age: Key trends, challenges, and possibilities', in P. Altbach and P. Peterson (eds), *Higher Education In the New Century. Global Challenges and Innovative Ideas* (Massachusetts: The Boston College Center for International Higher Education).

Taylor, J. and Machado, M. (2006). 'Higher education leadership and management: From conflict to interdependence through strategic planning', *Tertiary Education and Management*, 12, 2, 137–60.

Terborg, J. (1973). 'Women in management: a research review', *Journal of Applied Psychology*, 62, 6, 647–64.

Veiga, J. and Yanouzas, J. (1978). 'What women in management want: the ideal versus the real', *Academy of Management Journal*, 19, 1, 137–43.

Weber, M. (1995). *Économie et Société/1. Les catégories de la sociologie.* [Economy and Society: Categories from sociology] (Paris: Plon/Pocket).

Yammarino, F. and Dansereau, F. (2001). 'A multi-level approach for understanding the nature of leadership studies', in S. Outcalt, K. Faris and K. Macmohan (eds), *Developing Non-Hierarchical Leadership on Campus: Case Studies and Best Practices in Higher Education* (Westport CT: Greenwood Press).

1
Legislative Frameworks for Equal Opportunities

Kate White

1.1   Introduction

This chapter provides the broad context for the study. It examines the gender profiles of each country, including economic participation and opportunity, educational attainment, health and survival and political empowerment. It then examines the influence of the European Union (EU) on the legislative framework for labour force participation of women, given that four of the eight countries in the study are member states. Next, it analyses how legislative frameworks for Equal Opportunities (EO) and Affirmative Action (AA), including parental leave provisions, have impacted on women's participation in the workforce. Finally, it examines the impact of legislative frameworks on the careers of women within and across these eight countries, with particular attention to occupational segregation, and the reasons for and effects of gender pay equity gaps.

The Global Gender Gap Index compiled by the World Economic Forum (WEF) provides a useful snapshot of where the countries in this study are ranked on key employment, educational, health and political empowerment indicators (see Table 1.1).

Before comparing the ranking of each of the eight countries in this research, it is necessary to clarify what each of the Global Gender Report groupings imply.

- *Economic participation and opportunity*: this includes the participation gap, the remuneration gap and the advancement gap.
- *Educational attainment*: the gap between women's and men's current access to education is captured through ratios of women to men at primary, secondary and tertiary-level. A longer-term view of the country's ability to educate women and men in equal numbers

Table 1.1 Global Gender Gap Index 2009

Country	Global Gender Gap Index Ranking	Economic participation and oppor- tunity (f/m ratio)	Educational attainment (f/m ratio)	Health & survival (f/m ratio)	Political empower- ment (f/m ratio)
Sweden	4	.78	.99	.97	.49
New Zealand	5	.78	1	.97	.39
South Africa	6	.66	.99	.96	.44
Ireland	8	.69	1	.97	.37
United Kingdom	15	.70	1	.97	.28
Australia	20	.74	1	.97	.19
Portugal	46	.68	.98	.97	.16
Turkey	129	.40	.89	.97	.06

Source: WEF, *Global Gender Report* (2009).

is captured through the ratio of the female literacy rate to the male literacy rate.

- *Health and survival*: this category attempts to provide an overview of the differences between women's and men's health using two vari- ables: first, the gap between women's and men's healthy life expec- tancy, calculated by the World Health Organisation. The second variable is the sex ratio at birth, which aims specifically to capture the phenomenon of 'missing women' prevalent in many countries with strong son preference.
- *Political empowerment*: this includes mainly measures of the gap between men and women in political decision-making at the high- est levels.

Interestingly four of the eight countries in this research – Sweden, New Zealand, South Africa and Ireland – are in the top eight countries in the Global Gender Gap Index, while the UK is at 15 and Australia 20. The two southern European countries in the study – Portugal and Turkey – are at 46 and 129 respectively.

There is significant variance in economic participation and opp- ortunity, with the female/male ratio highest in Sweden and New Zealand at .78, followed by Australia .74 and the UK .70, and lowest in Turkey at .40. There is much less variation across the countries in relation to educational attainment, which is equal for females and males in New Zealand, Ireland, United Kingdom and Australia, and only just below 1 in Sweden and South Africa (.99), and Portugal (.98). In Turkey the ratio is .89. All countries in this research have a female/male health and survival ratio of .97, except South Africa at .96.

There are two main observations about the political empowerment category: the ratio is low in all eight countries and there is wide variation in the ratio between these countries. This suggests that women have historically been greatly under-represented in political decision making and this trend continues. The highest female to male ratio is in Sweden (.49), followed by South Africa (.44), New Zealand (.39), Ireland (.37) and UK (.28). The ratio is particularly low in Australia (.19), Portugal (.16) and Turkey (.06).

It is noted that generally those countries that have a stronger regulatory approach for EO in practice are better ranked in key international indicators than those countries that do not (however, the US has EO legislation but is ranked 31st). It is likely that employment outcomes for women are influenced by a combination of regulatory frameworks, economic participation and opportunity, educational attainment, health and survival and political empowerment (KPMG 2010, p.11).

1.2   Legislative frameworks for EO in this study

There are some similar and some different imperatives for legislation for EO in the eight countries in this study: Australia, Ireland, New Zealand, South Africa, Sweden, Portugal, Turkey and the UK. EU Directives have formed an influential recent framework for EO legislation in Ireland, Portugal and the UK. Sweden, although an EU member state, has a different approach to EO, formed along the Nordic model before entry to the EU. In Australia, New Zealand, and South Africa EO legislation was developed consistent with international conventions related to pay and employment equity, the most important being the UN Convention on the Elimination of All Forms of Discrimination against Women. In South Africa, employment equity is aimed at redressing past injustices and targets the majority of the population. Therefore, as part of a wider social justice framework it is compulsory for employers to address equity. Turkey does not have any specific EO legislation.

1.3   Impact of EU baseline legislation on Equal Opportunities

Because of the major influence of the EU on EO across and beyond Europe, this section will outline its pivotal role in developing and strengthening legislative frameworks for EO. The EU has been a catalyst for EO legislation among member states and 'gender equality policy has been considered one of the EU's major success stories' (Bagilhole 2009, p. 166). It has been argued that the introduction of European Community (EC)[1] legislation was at the insistence of France who already had such legislation, and who did not wish to be at an international disadvantage within an increasingly economically integrated Europe (McGauran 1996).

Importantly, 'the aims and principles of the EU dictate that its laws must be applied uniformly and have supremacy over conflicting national legislation' (Bagilhole 2009, p. 166). The legal framework of EU law regarding equal treatment of women and men consisted of several directives, treaty terms and European Court of Justice decisions, as well as the general principle of the removal of sex discrimination as a fundamental right (Bagilhole 2009). The framework originated in Article 119 of the 1957 Treaty of Rome, which established the principle of equal treatment for women and men workers in relation to pay. But it was not until the influence of the women's movement in the 1970s that the EU issued five important directives:

- Equal Pay Directive in 1975;
- Equal Treatment Directive in 1976;
- Directive on equal treatment of men and women in matters of social security 1979;
- Directive on equal treatment for men and women in occupational social security schemes 1986; and
- Directive on equal treatment for men and women in self-employment in 1986.

Bagilhole (2009) asserts that the EU's gender policy agenda has shifted from equal treatment to positive action; from 'hard' directives on equality to 'softer' legislation reconciling the competing demands of paid work and family life, which has in turn affected policies of member states. The EU concentrated its effort on action programmes designed to allow for subsidiarity and exhorted member states to take their own initiatives to realise common goals. Moreover, since the late 1990s the EU has begun to accept and enforce its competency in other areas of EO, with the introduction of additional legislation on race, disability, religion or belief, sexual orientation and age.

2007 was designated by the EU as the European Year of Equal Opportunities for All. Member states were encouraged to undertake awareness-raising initiatives to:

- challenge discriminatory attitudes and behaviour that still existed; and
- inform people about their legal rights and obligations.

In launching 2007 European Year of Equal Opportunities for All, the EU identified two major political challenges for Europe (Bagilhole 2009). These were:

- To tackle resistant inequalities and discrimination: women were still paid on average in the EU 15 per cent less than men for comparable work, and most leading roles in society, where policy decisions affecting women were made, were filled by men; and
- To work on social cohesion because of the ageing of society and bigger migration movements in the labour market.

The EU identified four specific goals for the year:

- Rights: raising awareness on the right to equality and non-discrimination, and the problems with multiple discrimination;
- Representation: stimulating debate on the ways to increase participation in society of under-represented groups, in particular those that are victims of discrimination;
- Recognition: celebrating and accommodating diversity and equality; and
- Respect and tolerance: promoting a more cohesive society.

The EU continues to have an impact on EO throughout the member states, both through its directives on equality and through legislation.

1.3.1 EU countries

The impact of the EU Directives on member countries will be examined, followed by an overview of how the remaining four countries have developed their EO frameworks.

1.3.1.1 Ireland

Gender as an issue in Irish society includes the difficulties experienced, particularly by women, in combining paid work and family responsibilities in a society where women still carry the main responsibility for housework and child care (Lynch & Lyons 2008). Women experience 'glass ceilings' and homosocial organisational cultures in male-dominated organisations, with sizeable proportions of those who have been successful in such organisations reporting discrimination and prejudice (Humphreys, Drew & Murphy 1999; O'Connor 2000 and 2010).

The legal and constitutional framework provided by the Irish State as regards women's position in Irish society came under a great deal of scrutiny initially in the context of entry to the European Community in 1973. Thus, in 1973 the *Civil Service (Employment and Married Women) Act 1973* was passed, and it removed the ban on married women working in the Civil Service, Local Authorities and Health Boards. As signatories of the Treaty of Rome, Ireland was bound by a series of Directives regarding equal pay and equal treatment in the area of access to employment and vocational training, including ending different pay rates for men and women. Legislation enacted round that time included the *Anti-Discrimination (Pay) Act 1974; the Employment Equality Act, 1977;* and the *Maternity (Protection of Employees) Act, 1981.* It has been suggested that pressure for legal change was most effective when it came from outside Ireland and was followed up by individual legal action and/or group pressure within Ireland (O'Connor 2008b).

The duration of maternity leave has improved a great deal in recent years. The *Maternity Protection Act 1994* and the *Maternity Protection (Amendment) Act 2004* provides up to 26 weeks' maternity leave together with 16 weeks additional unpaid maternity leave. It is important to note that employers are not obliged to pay women on maternity leave. If they do not do so, a woman may qualify for maternity benefit, which is a state payment, if she has sufficient pay-related social contributions (fathers are only entitled to maternity leave if the mother dies within 24 weeks of the birth). After maternity leave women are entitled to return to work to the same job and if it is not practicable, then they must be provided with suitable alternative work, which should not be on terms substantially less favourable than their previous job (http://www.citizensinformation.ie/categories/employment/employment-rights-and-conditions/leave-and-holidays/maternity_leave). Nevertheless Crowley (2010, p. 17) noted that 'pregnancy-related discrimination is widespread', and has now become 'one of the biggest issues in the casework of the Equality Authority under the gender ground of the Employment Equality Acts'.

It is widely accepted that parental leave legislation was introduced to comply with the 1995 EU Directive. The *Parental Leave Act 1998,* as amended by the *Parental Leave (Amendment) Act 2006,* allows parents in Ireland to take unpaid parental leave from employment in respect of certain children. Since 2006 leave can be taken in respect of a child up to 8 years of age (previously 5 years). Parental leave amounts to a total of 14 weeks per child. Both parents have an equal separate entitlement to parental leave (http://www.citizensinformation.ie/categories/employment/employment-rights-and-conditions/leave-and-holidays/parental_leave). Similar entitlements and issues arise on return from parental leave as on return from maternity leave.

The *Employment Equality Act (1998)* prohibited discrimination in the workplace and in vocational training in relation to selection, promotion or training on nine grounds (including not only gender and marital status, but also family status, sexual orientation, age, disability, race, religion and membership of the travelling community) (http://www.irishstatutebook.ie/1998/en/act/pub/0021/print.html). The *Equal Status Acts* (2000 and 2004) prohibited discrimination on the same nine grounds in the context of providing a range of services or goods (http://www.equality.ie/index.asp?docID=234).

Furthermore, in 1999 legislation was introduced that established the Equality Authority on a statutory basis with a brief to 'combat discrimination and promote equality of opportunity'; 'to provide information to the general public'; and to 'keep the equality legislation under review' (Crowley 2010, p. 7). Although the legislative focus was on equality of opportunity, and excluded economic opportunity, some progress was evident (but much of that has now been effectively neutralised).

The persistence of occupational segregation in Ireland, as elsewhere in Europe, has made progress on equal pay difficult. Furthermore, in the case of equal pay, an actual comparator must be found with which claimants must compare themselves. At the level of average weekly income, women are paid 67 per cent of men's average weekly income (CSO 2009). This partly reflects the fact that they work shorter hours of paid work (not unrelated to the larger number of hours of unpaid work that they undertake); and partly the fact that activities and occupations which are predominantly female are paid less than those which are predominantly male, reflecting a patriarchal dividend (Connell 1987; see also O'Connor 2000). The gap between men's and women's hourly earnings in Ireland is 17 per cent, broadly similar to the EU 27 (http://www.cso.ie/newsevents/pr_womenandmen2009.htm).

However we know that even among young graduates in the public sector, patterns of differential privileging of men and women are apparent within the first five years (McGinnity et al. 2005). McGinnity et al. found no difference in hourly pay in the public sector (arguably reflecting the successful number of equal pay cases against the state), but in the private sector these young women graduates earned 8 per cent less than men per hour. They found that a higher proportion of men than women received bonuses (and higher bonuses) and other kinds of privileges, including employer-funded training.

It has been suggested that the inclusion of definitions of indirect discrimination, and in particular of a definition of indirect discrimination on the grounds of gender, brings Ireland in line with decisions of the European Court of Justice (*Employment Equality Act, 1998*) (http://www.citizensinformation.ie/categories/employment/employment-rights-and-conditions/employment-rights-and-duties/employment_law_update). It is questionable to what extent either the *Employment Equality Act (1998)* or *Equal Status Acts (1997)* or the *Equality Act (2004)* are concerned with actively promoting gender equality, since certain kinds of positive action are allowed, but not required. However a number of attempts have been made by the State to reduce the impact of equality legislation. Thus the State fused the Department of Equality and Law Reform with the very much larger and more conservative Department of Justice in 1997 (O'Connor 2008 a and b) and in 2008 imposed a cut of 42 per cent in the Equality Authority's budget at a time when cuts of 2–9 per cent were being imposed on broadly similar structures (Crowley 2010). The latter has greatly reduced its ability both to take legal cases and to encourage a proactive approach to gender, including encouraging employers to carry out regular pay audits and action plans to deal with gender differences in pay. Furthermore, these cuts were linked with an attempt to reduce the autonomy and independence of the Equality Authority in a context where, for example, roughly half of their case files related to allegations of discrimination by employees of public sector bodies (Crowley 2010). Lester (1997) has suggested that contract compliance, which has been widely used in Northern Ireland to combat discrimination, constitutes one of the most effective ways of combating discrimination (and one which is compatible with EU law). No interest has been evinced in introducing this in Ireland. Indeed despite the 1998 Belfast Agreement which requires the Irish Government to ensure at least an equivalent level of protection of human rights as in Northern Ireland, there is no requirement for public bodies in Ireland to have 'due regard to equality in carrying out their functions'. There is no equivalent obligation on designated public sector bodies to produce plans for promoting equality, as exists in Northern Ireland (Crowley 2010, p. 6).

On the other hand legislation that has not been specifically targeted at women has improved their position. Thus for example, the 1991 *Worker Protection (Regular Part-time Employees Act)*; *Protection of Employees*

(Part-Time Work) Act 2001; and *Protection of Employees (Fixed Term Work) Act 2003* protects part-time and fixed-term employees by ensuring that they cannot be treated less favourably than comparable permanent workers. And since women are more likely than men to be in these categories it has improved their position (http://www.categories/employment/employment-rights-and-conditions/employment-rights-and-duties/employment_law_update).

Issues surrounding equality in the university sector have particularly involved a concern with gender imbalances in faculty profile (dating back to the 1980s: HEA, 1987). However the closing by the Higher Education Authority (HEA) of the Access and Equality Unit in University College Cork (UCC) in 2002, and its failure to allocate responsibility for even gender monitoring within its own structure, has not been helpful. Indeed, despite its responsibilities for equality under the *Universities Act* (http://www.irishstatutebook.ie/1997/en/act/pub/0024/index.html), since 2004 it has even stopped collecting data on faculty by level and gender. A HEA Report (2004) did recommend that the universities identify 'explicit and challenging targets and timetables', but no progress whatsoever has been made since then in moving this recommendation forward.

1.3.1.2 UK

The development of EO legislation in the UK has also been within EU frameworks. With accession to the EC in 1973, the British government implemented the *Sex Discrimination Act (SDA) 1975*. However, Bagilhole (2009) argues that the legislation was inspired by domestic, political factors rather than any prompting from Europe, and successive British governments adopted their own conception of EO and their own methods of tackling the issue. Between 1989 and 1997 Conservative governments showed a repeated reluctance to bring the UK into line with other member states (Bagilhole 2009).

When New Labour came to power in 1997 it was committed to a more constructive relationship with the EU and to bringing the country more into line with mainstream EU thinking on EO.

As a result the UK Labour government:

- Agreed to implement EU Directive 93/104/EC on the organisation of working time, which was potentially costly as working hours in the UK were longer than elsewhere in the EU;
- Re-launched the Equality Agenda that called for a national childcare strategy based on a partnership between government, employers and

parents, and for a family policy that would address flexible working for women and men with young children;

- Advocated a mainstreaming approach to EO in line with the new EU agenda, implying that responsibility for EO must be held by all parts of an organisation, and all policies, procedures and practices must be considered and appraised for EO implications;
- Introduced the first ever National Child Care Strategy. This pledged to provide free education places for all four-year-olds and additional funding for pre-school and out-of-school clubs;
- Introduced a Child Tax Credit aimed at improving access to childcare for low-income working families by meeting up to 70 per cent of eligible child care costs depending on the number of children;
- Introduced the Working Family Tax Credit in 1999 (renamed Working Tax Credit in 2003) that guaranteed a minimum income for families on low earnings. Families were able to choose whether the mother or father received the benefit and if couples could not agree, the woman had the final choice;
- Introduced a family-friendly framework of employee rights and practices through flexible work arrangements;
- Signed up to the Parental Leave Directive to encourage family-friendly and flexible working patterns by giving all employees a basic right to three months' paid leave following the birth or adoption of a child (later extended to 26 weeks, plus unpaid leave to 26 weeks, enabling mothers to take a year off work). The right to two weeks' paid paternity leave was introduced in the UK in 2003; and
- Introduced flexible work arrangements: the *Employment Act 2002* gave mothers and fathers of children aged six and under, and working parents with disabled children under 18 years of age, the right to work flexibly, and employers the duty to consider their requests seriously.

The *UK Equality Act 2010* set out both to close the gender gap and to shed more light on it. For instance, if private organisations do not start reporting their gaps voluntarily, the Act enables the government to require disclosure of average pay for men and for women. The Act harmonises and in some cases extends existing discrimination law covering the 'protected characteristics' of age, disability, gender reassignment, marriage and civil partnership, pregnancy and maternity, race, religion or belief, sex, and sexual orientation. It addresses the impact of recent case law which is generally seen as having weakened discrimination protection, and harmonises provisions defining indirect discrimination. It is not clear if the new Conservative–Liberal Democrat coalition government will amend this legislation or how far they will implement it.

1.3.1.3   Sweden

Even as another member state of the EU, Sweden's approach to EO, including parental leave, differs substantially from Ireland and the UK. The Nordic countries have developed a concept of reconciliation of paid employment and private life that is based on equal parenthood and the dual-breadwinner family; family policy is seen as equal opportunity policy, supported by good state sponsored child care facilities and generous monetary transfers for any parent staying at home with a child during parental leave (Zacharias 2006). In 1974 Sweden replaced its maternity leave scheme with that of parental allowances and was the first country in the world to introduce leave rights for fathers. In 1995, the 'father's quota' was implemented. This quota reserved 30 days for each parent which were non-transferable to the other spouse and were lost to the couple if the father did not make use of his leave days. The number of non-transferable parental leave days was increased to 60 days per parent in 2002 (SCB 2004). It has been argued that the intention of the Swedish Government was to actively encourage fathers to take more responsibility in child rearing (Haas et al. 2002 cited in Zacharias 2006).

The current entitlements to paid parental leave for a couple or single parent in Sweden are 480 days, or 16 months. On top of this, ten days of paid paternity leave are available to the father within the first 60 days after the mother returns from hospital. Of the 480 days, mothers and fathers have to take a minimum of 60 each. The first 360 days are compensated at 80 per cent of the prior salary level up to a maximum amount. The remaining days are compensated at a flat rate. Since 2002, 30 sickness benefit days have also been available that can be taken by either parent and for which temporal parental benefits are paid. The *Parental Leave Act 1995* enabled leave to be accessed in highly flexible ways until the child is eight years old or completes the first year of school. All parents are eligible for parental leave and associated benefits after they have been employed with the same employer for six months or for a combined period of at least 12 months during the preceding two years (Zacharias 2006).

Unlike the UK, for example, take-up rates are high. In 2005, virtually all mothers (95.7 per cent) of newborn babies and almost half of the fathers (43.7 per cent) took some share of their parental leave. Paid paternity leave is an uncontested success story in that fathers claimed an average of 9.7 days (out of a possible 10) and almost

79 per cent of men used some share of their 'father days' in 2004. Overall, 561,000 persons used paid parental leave days in 2004 with slightly more women (57 per cent) than men using their entitlements (Forsakringskassan 2005 cited in Zacharias 2006).

Zacharias (2006, p. 37) argues that the overall aim of Sweden's gender equality policy is for women and men to have the same opportunities, rights and responsibilities in all areas of life (see Chapter 2), and adds:

> not only does this charter give strong emphasis on the public sphere of paid employment and equal access to all its benefits for women and men. It also explicitly addresses the private sphere of children and the home for which Swedish men are expected to take active responsibility. Through this political statement and the policies that were developed in its spirit, the Swedish Government consciously addresses the traditional public/private dichotomy, redefines the expectations regarding the place of women and men in society and requests a redistribution of access to privileges and status.

1.3.1.4 *Portugal*

Portugal has also responded to EU Directives on EO. Since 1974 the Portuguese constitution has guaranteed the equal treatment of men and women in the labour market. Other important legal changes have included equality of opportunity and treatment at work in the public sector (1988), establishing a Commission for Equality and Women's Rights (1991) and legislation addressing direct and indirect discrimination in the workplace (1997). The impact of the EU's equal opportunity Directives has been clear in the past ten years in relation to part-time work (Laws 103/99), parental leave (Law 7/2000) applying the principle of equal remuneration for women and men workers, and equal treatment of women and men to access to employment, training, promotions and working conditions.

Parental leave is regulated by the Labour Code (Law 7/2009) and more specific laws (Decree-Law 89/2009 and Decree-Law 91/2009). Portugal has a national paid maternity leave provision, with 100 per cent of the salary paid for 120 days; in some instances paid parental leave is also granted to fathers. In addition, parents can choose to take parental leave for 150 days at 80 per cent of paid salary or 180 days at 83 per cent. Fathers have a right to 10 days of paid leave following the birth of the child. Both the mother and the father have the right to return to their previous jobs after parental leave. Since the intention of the legislation is to ensure that the leave corresponds to a period during which the mother would care for her newborn child, if the mother and/or child are hospitalised immediately after the birth the leave can be interrupted (the intervening period in hospital taken as sick leave) and then resumed afterwards.

The national parental leave scheme not only meets the requirements of the EU directives but goes even further in providing the right to short paid absences to attend medical consultations during pregnancy, and to reduced working hours when breastfeeding. Despite political initiatives to promote father-friendly policies in parental leave, these policies do not really promote the equal sharing of childcare, as men do not spend as many hours as women on domestic responsibilities (Perista & Lopes 1999; Perista 1999, 2002). Portugal's parental leave legislation nevertheless recognises the duty of the state to assist families to balance work and parental responsibilities and is closer to the model developed in Sweden than that in Ireland, for example.

It can therefore be concluded that the influence of EU Directives on member states has been to ensure national anti-discrimination legislation in paid employment and national parental leave schemes. However, the impact of paid parental leave on the ability of couples and individuals to balance work and family responsibilities is influenced by the state's basic notions of the place of women in society. Clearly Sweden, and to a lesser extent Portugal, have moved a good deal further towards addressing the traditional public/private dichotomy (Zacharias 2006) than Ireland and the UK.

1.3.2   Development of EO in non-EU countries

1.3.2.1   *New Zealand*

EO legislation in Australia and New Zealand, both former British colonies, has developed within UN EO frameworks but at a different pace. New Zealand introduced EO legislation at least a decade before Australia. In New Zealand one of the National conservative government initiatives was enactment of the *Equal Pay Act 1972* that made provision for the removal and prevention of discrimination, based on the sex of employees, in the rates of remuneration of women and men in paid employment (www.legislation.govt.nz) and provided for equal remuneration for women when performing work that was substantially similar to men (i.e., work of equal value). However, in practice, only a narrower interpretation was enforced –that of equal pay for women in the same positions as men (see, e.g., Review Committee, 1979 cited in Hyman 1992) – and there was growing alarm about the lack of clear guidelines for assessing equal pay rates or determining exactly which male-dominated professions were deemed comparable to their female counterparts.

In 1990 the Labour government in New Zealand introduced the *Employment Equity Act*, which required employers to develop and implement an Equal Employment Opportunity (EEO) Programme. Although the Act was repealed that same year, due to a change in government, a similar section also appeared in the *State Sector Act 1988* (which has since been amended). Unlike its short-lived predecessor, the *State Sector Act* did not apply to private organisations. It did, however, apply to universities.

Another Act with explicit EEO implications is the *Human Rights Act 1993* (amended 2001) which consolidated and amended both the *Race Relations Act 1977* and the *Human Rights Commission Act 1977*. It was designed to provide better protection of human rights in New Zealand in accordance with United Nations Covenants or Conventions on Human Rights. In relation to employment, the *Human Rights Act* includes provision for an Equal Employment Opportunities Commissioner. The Act also specifies that employers cannot discriminate against current or potential employees on the grounds of: sex (gender); age; colour, race, national or ethnic rights; disability including physical, mental, and presence of organisms that may cause disease (employers must make 'reasonable' accommodation for a disability); marital status; religious or ethical belief; political opinion; employment status; and sexual orientation.

The *Employment Relations Act 2000* extended the personal grievance provisions on discrimination contained in the Human Rights Act. Other legislation, such as the *Public Finance Act 1989* and *Education Acts 1989, 1990*, placed compliance, monitoring and reporting requirements on universities and other educational institutions. For example, the *Education Act 1989* sets out the powers, functions and duties of university Councils that are responsible for appointing, monitoring and evaluating the performance of the Vice-Chancellor (www.vuw.ac.nz/council).

New Zealand has been much more progressive than Australia in implementing parental leave legislation. The right to 12 months unpaid parental leave was established by the *Parental Leave and Employment Protection Act 1987*. The Act was amended from 1 July 2002 to provide for a new state-funded scheme of 12 weeks paid leave. It was amended again on 1 December 2004 to increase this paid entitlement to 13 weeks, and to provide for some entitlements for those who have worked the previous six months. On 1 December 2005 paid leave was increased to

14 weeks. Paid parental leave is a government-funded entitlement paid to eligible working mothers and adoptive parents when they take parental leave from their job(s) to care for their newborn or adopted child (under the age of six). These payments go towards the loss of income that working mothers and adoptive parents experience when they take parental leave to care for a new baby or adopted child (www.legislation. govt.nz/act/public).

1.3.2.2   Australia

Australia did not implement EEO and Affirmative Action frameworks until a decade later than New Zealand. The Australian Human Rights Commission (formerly called the Human Rights and Equal Opportunity Commission) was established in 1986 by the federal government as an independent statutory body. It has responsibility for administering the following federal laws: *Age Discrimination Act 2004, Disability Discrimination Act 1992, Australian Human Rights Commission Act 1986, Sex Discrimination Act 1984*, and *Racial Discrimination Act 1975*. It also has specific responsibilities under the *Native Title Act 1993* (performed by the Aboriginal and Torres Strait Islander Social Justice Commissioner) and the *Workplace Relations Act 1996* – replaced by the *Fair Work Act 2009* – (performed by the Sex Discrimination Commissioner). Individuals can lodge complaints of sex discrimination and sexual harassment with the Australian Human Rights Commission, which undertakes a range of activities to address discrimination, sexual harassment and other barriers to equality, including reviewing laws, conducting research, preparing policy advice and running community education programmes (see http://www.hreoc.gov.au/complaints_information/lodging.html).

The *Sex Discrimination Act 1984 (Cth)* gives effect to Australia's obligations under the Convention on the Elimination of All Forms of Discrimination against Women and certain aspects of the International Labour Organisation (ILO) Convention 156. Its major objectives are to:

- Promote equality between men and women;
- Eliminate discrimination on the basis of sex, marital status or pregnancy and, with respect to dismissals, family responsibilities; and
- Eliminate sexual harassment at work, in educational institutions, in the provision of accommodation and the delivery of Commonwealth programmes.

In response to recommendations made by the Senate Standing Committee on Legal and Constitutional Affairs, following its review of the effectiveness of the *Sex Discrimination Act* in 2008, the federal government announced it intends to introduce a single comprehensive Commonwealth Anti-discrimination Act. Proposed key changes to the *Sex Discrimination Act* include the introduction of breastfeeding as a separate ground of discrimination, a broader test of sexual harassment, the extension of protection from sexual harassment for workers, and protection from family responsibilities discrimination in all areas of employment. As well, the Australian Human Rights Commission released the *Gender Equality Blueprint 2010* setting out recommendations in five priority areas which significantly affect both the public and private lives of women and men (http://www.hreoc.gov.au/sex_discrimination/publication/blueprint/index.html):

- Balancing paid work and family and caring responsibilities
- Ensuring women's lifetime economic security
- Promoting women in leadership
- Preventing violence against women and sexual harassment
- Strengthening national gender equality laws, agencies and monitoring

In addition, the federal government enacted the *Affirmative Action (Equal Opportunity for Women) in the Workplace Act 1986* which covered private sector corporations with more than 100 employees, as well as universities. It was replaced by the *Equal Opportunity for Women in the Workplace Act (1999)* which requires large employers (100 plus staff) to establish a workplace programme to remove the barriers to women entering and advancing in the organisation. The Equal Opportunity for Women in the Workplace Agency (EOWA) is the statutory authority that monitors compliance with the legislation and requires organisations to submit annual compliance reports (EOWA 2008).

Thornton (2008, p. 5) asserts that national EEO and AA legislative mechanisms were 'instrumentally weak', as they assigned no rights to individuals or groups and compliance with the Act was little more than self-regulation, 'while retaining a formalistic commitment to EEO, it [the EOWW Act] embodies the rhetoric of backlash' (Thornton 2008, p. 14). The EOWW Act and the Agency are currently under review (KPMG 2010).

In contrast to New Zealand, which has had a parental leave scheme for some years, Australia passed legislation only in 2010. The *Paid Parental Leave Act (Cth) 2010* established Australia's first national paid parental leave scheme. to operate from 1 January 2011. Payments made under this scheme are in addition to any paid parental leave entitlement an employee has under a contract of employment, industrial instrument or other law. Key features of the legislation are:

- The entitlement of paid parental leave up to 18 weeks at the national weekly minimum wage (currently $569.90) for eligible primary carers;
- Employees must meet certain criteria, including having worked at least 330 hours over the 13 months before the expected birth or adoption of the child, with a break of no greater than eight weeks between two work days (not including periods of paid leave), and earned less than $150,000 (indexed) in the previous full financial year before the claim or birth; and
- The payments will be fully funded by the Government but employers will be responsible for administering the payments.

Previously parental leave provisions had been largely channelled through the industrial relations system rather than national legislation (Zacharias 2006). Consequently many employed women did not have access to paid maternity leave, and the use of unpaid parental leave was low (Whitehouse et al. 2006). Nevertheless, the Australian university sector is a leader in parental leave provisions (EOWA 2010).

Australia's new workplace relations system, Fair Work, came into effect from 1 July 2009 and will significantly impact on flexible work arrangements for families. The system is designed to balance the needs of employees, employers and unions (see www.fwa.gov.au). Fair Work comprises the national tribunal, Fair Work Australia, and the Office of the Fair Work Ombudsman. From 1 January 2010, the Fair Work laws took full effect, as a new safety net of minimum employment conditions and modern awards were put into place. The legislation makes provision for flexible work arrangements for parents. Under the new legislation, which has similarities to the UK *Employment Act 2002*, an employee who is a parent or has responsibility for the care of a child may request a change in their working arrangements. Charlesworth (2009) argues that while the *Fair Work Act 2009* represents a continuation of many aspects of Industrial Relations (IR) regulation and a failure to think outside the traditional standard employment relationship and male breadwinner model, framing of discrimination as 'adverse action' and establishing a discrimination compliance unit within the Office of the Fair Work Ombudsman (OFWO) 'suggest a welcome mainstreaming of the proscription of sex discrimination within the IR jurisdiction, if not the advancement of gender equality'.

In relation to universities, Universities Australia (UA) has released its third Action Plan for Women Employed in Australian Universities. The objectives of the plan (UA 2010, p. 4) are to

- Encourage universities to continue to take responsibility for ensuring equitable work practices and to incorporate equity strategies and targets in their strategic planning, with unambiguous leadership by the Vice-Chancellors;
- Increase the recognition of the contributions of women to the productivity and advancement of Australia's universities (FASTS recommends 'a stronger business case linking diversity and innovation');
- Improve representation of women in HE at all levels to more strongly reflect representation in society, including Indigenous women;
- Increase the proportion of women in senior leadership positions including Deans, Directors and Senior Managers and in a wider range of portfolios and discipline groupings;
- Identify women in middle management and mentor them as the future senior leaders; and
- Test the effectiveness of interventions at critical points in women's careers.

1.3.2.3   *South Africa*

After the first democratic election in South Africa, in 1994, most labour legislation was revisited. The magnitude of this challenge exceeds the scope of this discussion. However, consistent with the overarching 'redress agenda', gender equity as a national priority was articulated in a number of documents. Shackleton, Riordan and Simonis (2006) consider that the following pieces of legislation impact directly on gender equity. The first four apply to all employees in the country and the latter only to those employed in higher education (HE).

The cornerstone of all South African legislation is the *South African Constitution, Act 108/1996*. Within the Constitution, The Bill of Rights refers to gender equity in Section 9, the Equality Clause. Specific references include: that all people shall be equal before the law (9(2)); that the State may not discriminate on the grounds of inter alia, gender and sex (9(3)); that no person may discriminate on the grounds of inter alia, gender and sex (9.4); and that any discrimination on the grounds mentioned heretofore, will be deemed unfair (9(5)).

Secondly, *the Employment Equity Act 55/1998*. In the preamble of the Act, recognition is given to inherited discriminatory practices in employment. The Act therefore is intended, inter alia, to promote the right of equality as it applies in the workplace; to eliminate unfair discrimination in employment; and to redress employment inequity and to achieve a diverse workforce that is broadly representative of the relevant demographics of the economically active population. The Act makes explicit mention of the meaning of 'designated groups'. Broadly speaking, in South Africa, designated groups are delineated on the grounds of race, gender and disability. Therefore, all individuals who are either black, female or disabled are intended to benefit from employment equity. Although not legislated, a hierarchy has emerged within designated groups that places gender equity after racial equity in the 'redress agenda'. In Sections 5 and 6 of the Act, designated employers (i.e., those who employ 50 or more employees or those who employ less than 50 employees but have a total annual turnover equal to or greater than the applicable amount specified in Schedule 4 of the Act) are expressly instructed to take steps to promote equal opportunity in the workplace by eliminating unfair discrimination in any employment policy or practice. Unfair discrimination includes discrimination on the grounds of gender and sex. Furthermore, Section 13 describes implementation and accountability of employers in terms of the Act, including consultation with employees, preparing an equity plan and reporting on progress to the Director General. Section 20 provides specific guidelines to employers with regard to the preparation, submission and monitoring of the employment equity plan. These equity plans must specify numerical targets based on race, gender and disability status and the affirmative action measures that employers intend to take to achieve greater equity in the workforce, such as development plans.

The third piece of legislation in South Africa that impacts on all employer relationships is the *Skills Development Act 97/1998 (SDA)*. The SDA was intended to provide an institutional framework to devise and implement national, sector and workplace strategies to develop and improve the skills of the South African workforce. The implementation of the Act was encouraged through the Skills Development Levies Act which directly funds the training and development of staff. Accountability for the implementation of training and development programmes rests with individual employers and is monitored through the submission of compulsory annual reports, such as the Workplace Skills Plan. The format of the report requires a breakdown of information based on race, gender and disability status.

Finally the *Basic Conditions of Employment Act 75 of 1997* makes provision for four consecutive months unpaid maternity leave (Sec 25) to be taken four weeks prior and at least six weeks after the birth. Depending on income levels, state-funded unemployment benefits are available to some women during this time but academic staff would not qualify for such grants. Men and women are entitled to three days of paid family leave within each annual cycle which may be taken for a range of purposes including caring for a sick child, the death of a relative or similar legitimate reason (Sec 27). The definition of child includes adopted children (www.acts.co.za)

In relation to HE the following pieces of legislation are relevant to the current study.

The Education White Paper 3: A Programme for Higher Education Transformation, 15 August 1997. The White Paper, when addressing the needs and challenges facing HE in SA, identified the following deficiencies: that an inequitable distribution of access and opportunities exists for students and staff along lines of race, gender, class and geography. 'This includes gross discrepancies in participation rates from students from different population groups, indefensible imbalances in ratios of black and female staff compared to whites and males and equally untenable disparities between historically black and white institutions in terms of facilities and capacities' (para 1.4.1). The White Paper envisions a transformed, democratic, non-racial and non-sexist system of HE (para 1.14).

The White Paper furthermore identified fundamental principles that should guide the process of transformation in HE. The principles of equity and redress (para 1.18), democratisation (1.19) and development (1.20), while not explicitly referring to gender equity, nonetheless underpinned the intent of the Ministry in this regard.

Specific reference was made to the replacement of the previously fragmented HE structure with a single, coordinated system, with the purpose of broadening the social base of HE with reference to race, gender, class and age. It was intended that such a system will become increasingly representative of the racial and gender composition of the SA population.

The implementation and accountability for the restructuring rested with the development of an overall national and institutional three-year rolling plan. Such plans facilitated the setting of objectives and implementation targets that are adjusted, updated and revised annually (para 2.9). Institutional plans are expected to include inter alia race and gender equity goals and proposed measures to develop new programmes and human resource development plans.

The Higher Education Act 101/1997: this Act replaced all previous HE legislation and established and regulates a single co-ordinated HE system in South Africa. The Preamble of the Act promotes the redress of past discrimination, ensuring representation and equal access, and promotes the values that underlie an open and democratic society based on human dignity, equality and freedom. Furthermore, it is intended to pursue excellence, promoting the full realisation of the potential of every student and employee, tolerant of ideas and appreciative of diversity. Section 31 of the Act provides for the establishment of an institutional forum which must advise the university council on issues affecting the institution including, inter alia, race and gender equity policies.

The National Plan for Higher Education 2001: this document provides guidance around the implementation of policy in the HE sector in South Africa. The executive summary includes reference that 'participation rate should be increased through recruiting workers, mature students and the disabled, in particular the women'.

One further piece of legislation that impacts on all South African workers has relevance here. Section 2(1)(e) of the *Skills Development Act* (referred to earlier) specifically encourages employers to improve the employment prospects of persons previously disadvantaged by unfair discrimination, and to address the disadvantages through training and education. Frequent mention is made to providing access for women to employment, including HE institutions. But once women are employed, few national policies exist to promote their development specifically. Despite all this legislation and submission of data required by the Department of Education, since the promulgation of the Act no evidence exists of any consequences for institutions that make no progress with respect to their gender equity targets.

Given this legislative context it would be reasonable to expect a transformed and equitable HE landscape. However, 16 years into democracy and equity, gender equity remains a significant challenge in South Africa. Despite all the legislation, good intentions and policy guidelines, women are not equally represented, nor do they participate fully at senior levels in universities. It should be acknowledged though, that 16 years is not a long time to completely overhaul and redress a dramatically imbalanced profile. And some progress has been made. The physical university landscape has been re-engineered. White and black students now attend university together. Almost all universities are led by black academics. However, the professoriate remains largely white and male, and women, although constituting over 50 per cent of the university workforce, continue to dominate the lower paid and administrative departments (Shackleton, Riordan & Simonis 2006);

changing the legislative framework is a necessary, but not sufficient, measure to redress gender equity.

1.3.2.4 Turkey

Turkey does not have specific EO legislation. However at the urging of the European Parliament (1N1/2007/2269), which noted the low rate of employment of women in Turkey (23. 8 per cent in 2007), an Equal Employment Opportunity Commission was established in the Turkish parliament in 2009. Turkey also does not have a national paid parental leave scheme. But women in the public sector (including universities) are entitled to 16 weeks paid maternity leave and an additional one year's unpaid maternity leave. Moreover recent changes in labour laws introduced three days paternity leave. In addition, men who have worked a minimum of ten years in the public sector can take up to six months unpaid leave which some may use as unpaid paternity leave.

1.4 Impact of EO legislation on careers of women: Comparing Ireland and Australia

Despite the rapid integration of women into the workforce, and implementation of EO laws throughout the EU, gender inequality prevails (Bagilhole 2009). Women are still concentrated in a narrow range of occupations. As Anker (1998, p. 3) comments, occupational segregation by sex is 'extensive and pervasive and is one of the most important and enduring aspects of labour markets around the world'. The gender segregation of occupations is both horizontal and vertical; that is, women have different types of occupations, but where women and men are found in the same occupation, even if women predominate, they are most commonly found in the lower levels (Bagilhole 2009). Throughout the EU women remain horizontally and vertically segregated in the labour market in less secure, low-paid jobs, mainly in the service sector which accounts for over 80 per cent of female employment across the EU. Men continue to monopolise jobs in manufacturing and construction. Gender pay gaps persist, and there is a strong relationship between sex segregation and low pay in every member state (Bagilhole 2009). Throughout the EU women's advance into senior management has been very slow. Fewer than 5 per cent of women are in senior management roles and this percentage has hardly changed since the early 1990s (Davidson & Burke 2000).

Comparing participation rates in two countries in this study – Ireland and Australia – is instructive. Traditionally, although women's educational levels were higher than men's in Ireland, the existence of the Marriage Bar and related social and cultural attitudes affected women's participation in paid employment after marriage (O'Connor 2008b). The huge change in women's participation in paid employment in Ireland can be illustrated by the fact that in the thirty years between 1971 and 2001, participation rose by 140 per cent compared to a rise of 27 per cent for men (Coughlan 2002). This increase has been overwhelmingly due to married women's participation in paid employment and was one of the frequently ignored characteristics of the 'celtic tiger'.

Currently 67 per cent of Irish men and 58 per cent of Irish women are in paid employment (CSO 2009), whereas even in 1997 women's participation was significantly below the EU average (CSO 2004). Because of women's high level of educational qualifications, women are just as likely as men to be in professional positions, and one third of those in managerial positions are women, mainly at lower levels (CSO 2009). These dramatic changes in women's labour force participation have occurred despite very low levels of child care provision and a situation in which the state has particularly focussed on grants to facilitate the provision of child care facilities, with child care costs being largely funded from parents' after tax income. Ireland has traditionally had one of the most poorly-developed systems of non-stigmatising, State subsidised, child care in the EU, to help mothers with their responsibilities as regards child care (O'Connor & Shortall 1999). Average full-day child-care costs in Ireland are 20 per cent of average earnings, while the average for other EU countries is eight per cent (O'Hagan 2005).

In Australia women's labour force participation rate has increased at a less dramatic pace than Ireland over the last 30 years from 43.5 per cent in 1978 to 58.7 per cent in 2009. Despite increases in women's workforce participation, women continue to spend less time in the paid workforce than men and to fare less well on a number of indicators while at work. Moreover, the nature of women's work is quite different to that of men (KPMG 2010). Women are much less likely to work full-time than men (54.9 per cent to 84.1 per cent) and comprise over 70 per cent of the part-time workforce. Women's participation rates dip between the ages of 25 and 44 years, which is not evident for men. Australia also has a lower participation rate for mothers with young children than other OECD countries such as Canada, Sweden, the UK and the US (KPMG 2010).

The lower participation rate for women between the ages of 25 and 44 years is linked to a parental leave provision that in the past has been far below international standards: 'because it does not provide mothers with any income and prohibits them from finding alternative sources of income while on leave, is inflexible in its administration, does not offer any incentive to fathers to get involved in the care giving of their very young children and is not accessible for all parents' (Zacharias 2006, p. 40). Not surprisingly, take-up rates of unpaid parental leave are low (Zacharias 2006). While the Australian government, like that in Ireland, sees child care as a family responsibility, in Ireland the EU Directive has ensured women have an entitlement to paid maternity leave to which women in Australia will not be entitled until 2011.

1.5 Impact of EO legislation on careers of women in other countries

Participation rates of women in the workforce in Portugal, compared with other EU states, are relatively high (56.2 per cent) which could be interpreted as an indication of EO in the labour market. However, according to EUROSTAT (European Commission 2007) women were twice as likely as men to work part-time (16.9 per cent to 8 per cent). But this rate is low compared to some other EU states. The unemployment rate has always been higher for women and is increasing: in 2009, 49.4 per cent of those unemployed were men and 50.5 per cent were women (Pordata 2010). Added to this, Portuguese women on average earn 23 per cent less than men, but in the private sector earn 30 per cent less than men (Donnelas 2006).

Participation rates of women in the workforce in Turkey are low. The female to male ratio for economic participation and opportunity in the Global Gender Index is a low .40. Moreover, there is a wider gender pay gap than many EU countries of 30 per cent (Kara 2006, p. 144).

Participation rates of women in the UK show some variation, depending on age, and also between full-time and part-time work. The employment rate for women aged 16–24 is 57 per cent, with 56 per cent in full-time employment and 44 per cent in part-time employment. The employment rate for women aged 25–44 (the peak period for parental responsibilities) rises to 74 per cent, with 60 per cent in full-time work and 40 per cent working part time. This compares with an employment rate for men in the same age group of 88 per cent, with 96 per cent working full-time and only 4 per cent part-time (EOC, 2006). Berthoud and Blekesaune's (2006) analysis of employment rates showed that women as a group faced an employment penalty of about 23 per cent compared to men. However, the employment penalty for mothers with children under 11 years rose to around 40 per cent.

The gender pay gap in the UK in annual earnings for full-time workers is 27.1 per cent which is considerably higher than the EU average. Manning and Swafford (2005) found only small differences between women and men in the early years of their careers. However, a woman working continuously full-time experiences a pay gap of 12 per cent compared to an equivalent male after ten years. About half of this gap was explained by different pay rates in different gendered occupations, but the other half remained unexplained. There was a similar finding in Australia; where the remaining 50 per cent was attributed to discrimination in the workplace (KPMG 2010).

Lower life-time earnings for women mean lower contributions to pensions (Bagilhole 2009). Rake et al. (2000) estimated that the difference in the lifetime earnings of men and childless women was just under £250,000 (British pounds) for mid-skilled workers, which is less than the $900,000 estimated in Australia (KPMG 2010).

In Sweden, despite well-developed legislation against gender discrimination, and policies to facilitate the participation of women in the labour market, the gender pay gap is still 16 per cent at the national level. Occupational segregation is larger in comparison to other EU states (NORDEN 2009): both horizontal as women and men have different occupations and vertical as women do not reach as far in their careers as men. There are three types of wage differences between men and women: structural, as female-dominated professions have lower salaries, positional, as men are over-represented in high positions, and direct, differences that cannot be explained and therefore are considered to be discriminatory (Loven 2009).

In South Africa the participation of women in the paid workforce, and especially at executive level, compares favourably to other countries in this study. In the annual, verified survey conducted by the Business Women's Association of South Africa data is collected from companies listed on the Johannesburg Securities Exchange (JSE), the Alternate Index and their subsidiaries; State Owned Enterprises (SOE's) and from the Department of Labour. Annual reports are analysed, and together with information obtained directly from organisations, they present a clear picture of the race and gender profile of South African organisations. Women make up 51 per cent of the adult population in South Africa, and about 43 per cent of the working South African population. In 2009 a snapshot of corporate South Africa reveals that women constitute 18.6 per cent of executive managers, 14.5 per cent of directors, 5.7 per cent of Chairs of Boards and 3.6 per cent of CEOs in the country (SABWA 2009). Nonetheless, South Africa fares better than most other countries in this study. When looking at the Executive Manager group, the South African JSE, AltX, SOE 2009 figure of 18.6 per cent women representation compares favourably with the 2008 figures from Australia AX200 (10.7 per cent), Canada EP500 (16.9 per cent) and the United States of America Fortune 500 (15.2 per cent) (Women in Business, 2008 as cited by SABWA 2009). In the State sector where 16 salary grades classify employees according to their rank, women constitute 55.5 per cent of the workforce across all levels. The State has made conscious efforts to appoint women into senior positions. Women occupy 34.3 per cent of the most senior management levels (grades 13–16) of which 61.6 per cent are Black African women (Statistics provided by the Department of Labour to SABWA 2009).

1.6   Conclusion

It is clear from the above examination of the countries in this study that those within the EU have more comprehensive EO frameworks than those that are not in the EU. Compliance with EU Directives in relation to equal pay, equal treatment, and parental leave has led to member countries such as Ireland, Portugal and the UK implementing over the last 15 years a robust suite of legislation aimed at removing discrimination in the workplace. The role of the EU as a catalyst for national legislation has been to ensure that member countries focus on reconciling the competing demands of paid work and family life. Some member countries have been more successful than others. For example Sweden, as discussed above, stands out in its development of the concept of reconciling paid employment and private life that is based on equal parenthood and the dual-breadwinner family which it developed prior to joining the EU. Whereas the Irish government considers child care as a family responsibility that it is unwilling to share, and the UK has policies to help the reconciliation of paid work and family that concentrate on women's predominant responsibility in the caring role. This suggests that even within EU member states, the impact of directives on EO is mediated by political imperatives in each country.

In the non-EU countries in this study, especially Australia and New Zealand, the development of EO frameworks has been much more overtly influenced by national politics. For example when Labour governments have been in power there has been more commitment to EO. In New Zealand the Labour government in 1990 introduced the Employment Equity Act and a state-funded parental leave scheme in 2002. In Australia the present Labour government has legislated to introduce a national paid parental leave scheme in 2011. The previous conservative government in Australia channelled parental leave provisions through the more cumbersome industrial relations system rather than national legislation. In contrast South Africa has a much broader EO framework reflecting an intersectional approach to addressing discrimination in the workplace, with the predominance of the race agenda. Turkey remains the least developed in terms of EO policies and legislation.

Note

1. As the European Union was then called.

References

Anker, R. (1998). *Gender and Jobs: Sex Segregation of Occupations in the World* (Geneva: International Labour Office).

Bagilhole, B. (2009). *Understanding Equal opportunities and Diversity: The Social Differentiations and Intersections of Inequality* (Bristol: The Policy Press).

Berthoud, R. and Blekesaune, R. (2006). 'Persistent employment disadvantage, 1974 to 2003', *Institute for Social and Economic Research Working Paper 2006–9* (Colchester: ISER, University of Essex).

Charlesworth, S. (2009). 'The intersections of gender equality and decent work: Progress and prospects in Australia', paper for the Regulating for Decent Work Network Study Group at the 15th World Congress of the International Industrial Relations Association, Sydney http://www.ilo.org/public/english/protection/condtrav/pdf/iiracharlesworth.pdf, date accessed 10 October 2010.

Connell, R. W. (1987). *Gender & Power: Society, the Person and Sexual Politics* (London: Polity Press).

CSO (2004). *Women and Men in Ireland* (Dublin: Government Publications).

CSO (2009). *Women and Men in Ireland* (Dublin: Government Publications).

Coughlan, A. (2002). *Women in Management in Business* (Dublin: Irish Business and Employers Federation (IBEC)).

Cousins, C. and Tang, N. (2004). 'Working time and work and family conflict in the Netherlands, Sweden and the UK', *Women Employment & Society*, 18, 3, 531–49.

Crowley, N. (2010). *Empty Promises: Bringing the Equality Authority to heel* (Dublin: A.A. Farmar).

Davidson, M. and Burke, R. (2000). 'Women in management: Current research issues', in M. Davidson and R Burke (eds), *Women in Management* (London: Sage Publications), 1–7.

Donnelas, A. (Coord.) (2006). *Green Book of Labour Relations* (*Livro Verde das Relações Laborais*), (Lisbon: Ministry of Labour and Social Solidarity).

Equal Opportunities Commission (EOC) (2006). *Women and Men in Britain.* (Manchester: EOC).

Equal Opportunity for Women in the Workplace Agency (EOWA) (2008). *Australian Census of Women in Leadership*, http://www.eowa.gov.au/, date accessed 12 April 2010.

Equal Opportunity for Women in the Workplace Agency (EOWA) (2010). Paid parental leave – EOWA backgrounder (www.eowa.gov.au/Information-Centres/.../PML-Background.doc, date accessed 3 August 2010.

European Commission (2007). *EUROSTAT Statistics* (Brussels: European Commission).

Fynes, B., Morrissey, B., Roche, W., Whelan, B. and Williams, J. (1996). *Flexible Working Lives: The Changing Nature of Working Time Arrangements in Ireland* (Cork: Oak Tree Press).

Hertz, T. (2005). The effect of minimum wages on the employment and earnings of South Africa's domestic service workers. (Working paper), Department of Economics, American University and W.E. Upjohn Institute for Economic Research, www.upjohn.org/publications/wp/05-120.pdf, date accessed 29 July 2007.

Higher Education Authority (HEA) (1987). *The Report of the High Level Group on University Equality Policies* (Dublin: HEA).

Humphreys, P., Drew, E. and Murphy, C. (1999). *Gender Equality in the Civil Service* (Dublin: Institute of Public Administration).

Hyman, P. (1992). 'The use of economic orthodoxy to justify inequality: A feminist critique', in R. Du Plessis with P. Bunkle (eds), *Feminist Voices: Women's Studies Texts for Aotearoa/New Zealand* (Auckland: Oxford University Press).

Kara, O. (2006). 'Occupational wage discrimination in Turkey', *Journal of Economic Studies*, 32, 2, 130–43.

KPMG (2010). *Review of the Equal Opportunity for Women in the Workplace Act 1999 Consultation Report* (Canberra: EOWA).

Lester, A. (1997). Strengthening the legal framework: learning from international experience, paper presented at Employment Equality Authority 1977–1997, Anniversary Conference Programme, Look Beyond 2,000. Dublin: Royal Hospital Kilmainham.

Loven, K. (2009). 'Addressing the Gender Pay Gap: Government and Social Partner Actions in Sweden', *Industrial Relations Observatory Online*: http://www.eurofound.europa.eu/eiro/studies/tn0912018s/se0912019q.htm date accessed 7 June 2010.

Lu, Y. (2005). 'Sibship size, family organization and children's education in South Africa: Black-white variations', *International Sociological Association Research Committee on Social Stratification and Mobility* (RC28) (Los Angeles: RC28) http://www.ccpr.ucla.edu/asp/ccpr_045_05.asp date accessed 29 July 2007.

Lynch, K. and Lyons, M. (2008). 'The gendered order of caring', in U. Barry (ed.), *Where Are We Now?* (Dublin: Tasc Publications), 168–84.

McGauran, A. M. (1996). 'The effects of EU policy on women's employment: The case of women in Irish and French retailing', *Irish Journal of Feminist Studies*, 1, 2, 83–102.

McGinnity, F., Russell, H., Williams, J. and Blackwell, S. (2005). *Time Use in Ireland 2005* (Dublin: Economic and Social Research Institute).

Manning, A. and Swaffield, J. (2005). 'The gender gap in early-career wage growth', *LSE Discussion Paper No 700*, (London: Centre for Economic Performance, London School of Economics).

NORDEN (2009). *Gender and Power in the Nordic Countries* (Oslo: Nordic Gender Institute).

O'Connor, P. (2010). 'Gender and organisational culture at senior management level: Limits and possibilities for change?' in J. Harford and C. Rush (eds), *Women and Higher Education in Ireland 1850–2010. Have Women made a Difference?* (Oxford: Peter Lang).

O'Connor, P. (2008a). 'The patriarchal state: Continuity and change', in M. Adshead, P. Kirby, M. Millar (eds), *Contesting the State* (Manchester: Manchester University Press).

O'Connor, P. (2008b). 'The elephant in the corner: Gender and policies related to higher education', *Administration*, 56, 1, 85–110.

O'Connor, P. (2007). 'Still changing places: Women's paid employment and gender roles', *The Irish Review*, 35, 64–78.

O'Connor, P. and Shortall, S. (1999). 'Does the Border make the difference?' in R. Breen, A. Heath and C.T. Whelan (eds), *Ireland: North and South: Social Science Perspectives* (Oxford: Oxford University Press).

O'Connor, P. (2000). 'Ireland: A man's world?' *The Economic and Social Review*, 31, 81–102.

O'Hagan, C. (2005). Family or economy friendly? Paper presented at Sociological Association Annual Conference, Nenagh.

O'Connell, P. and Russell, H. (2005). *Equality at Work?* (Dublin: Economic and Social Research Institute).

Perista, P. and Lopes, M. (coord) (1999). *A licença de parentalidade: Um direito novo para a promoção da igualdade* [*The parents' licence: a new right for the promotion of equality*] (Lisboa: DEPP-CIDES).

Perista, H. (coord) (1999). *Os usos do tempo e o valor do trabalho – Uma questão de género* [*The uses of time and the value of work- A gender question*] (Lisboa: DEPP-CIDES).

Perista, H. (2002). *Género e trabalho não pago: Os tempos das mulheres e os tempos dos homens* [*Gender and unpaid work: The women's time and men's time: a social analysis*]. *Análise Social*, 37, 163, 447–74.

Pordata (2010). http://www.pordata.pt/azap_runtime/ date accessed 16 June 2010.

Rake, K., Davies, H., Joshi, H. and Alami, R. (eds) (2000). *Women's Incomes over the Lifetime: A Report to the Women's Office* (London: Cabinet Office).

Riordan, S. (2007). Career psychology factors as antecedents of career success of women academics in South Africa, unpublished Doctoral Thesis, University of Cape Town.

SCB (2004). *Women and men in Sweden: Facts and Figures 2004* (Stockholm: Statistics Sweden).

Shackleton, L., Riordan, S. and Simonis, D. (2006). 'Gender and the transformation agenda in South African higher education', *Women's Studies International Forum*, 29, 6, 572–80.

South African Business Women's Association (SABWA) (2009). *South African Women in Leadership Census* www.bwasa.co.za , date accessed 29 May 2010.

Thornton, M. (2008). 'Where are the women? The swing from EEO to diversity in the academy', Working Paper No.22 (Canberra: Australian National University).

Universities Australia (UA) (2010). *Universities Australia Strategy for Women: 2011–2014* (Canberra: Universities Australia).

WEF (2009). *Global Gender Report.*

Whitehouse, G, Baird, M. Diamond, C and Hosking, A. (2006). 'The parental leave in Australia survey', November 2006 report, http://www.polsis.uq.edu.au/index.html?page=56021 accessed 3 May 2010.

Zacharias, N. (2006). 'Work-life balance: "Good weather" policies or agenda for social change: A cross-country comparison of parental leave provisions in Australia and Sweden', *International Employment Relations Review*, 12, 2, 32–47.

2
Gender Equality and the Shift from Collegiality to Managerialism

Anita Göransson

This chapter provides an overview of HE systems and then analyses the gendered character of academic staff in the eight countries in this study. It also explores the uneven shift from the traditional collegial to a new managerialist organisational form. There is no indication that either the collegial or the managerial system would be more conducive to gender equality. It is clear that the strength or absence of Equal Opportunity and Affirmative Action frameworks, as described in Chapter 1, has an impact on gender equality in universities.

2.1 Background

The first Western universities originated in the middle ages to provide the church and state with an educated priesthood and civil service, both of which were historically male monopolies. In the nineteenth century, HE expanded rapidly in industrialised countries as increasing numbers joined the emerging professions and required training. Towards the end of the century, universities were gradually opened to women in most Western countries. But for a long time it was mainly a small minority of more affluent families who could send their children to university. It was not until the 1960s, with the post-war baby boomers reaching adulthood and the expansion of welfare states resulting in increased demand for educated employees, that HE became more widespread in the broader strata of society.

This shift from elite to mass HE system (Scott 2000) forced the university to increasingly align with the democratic dynamics of society.

Today Western universities are similarly structured, even if it is still possible to discern traces of the various types in which they have traditionally been grouped (Rothblatt 1996). Three of these types are relevant for this study.[1] The *German* type of university also includes Scandinavia, the *French* type includes the Mediterranean countries, and the *Anglo Saxon* type has also served as a model for universities in countries that were colonised by Britain, such as South Africa, Australia and New Zealand in this study. These distinctions have now been blurred, and lingering differences mostly concern the state's role in establishing systems for financing and research or recruitment. Traditionally, European universities were considered as a public good and, in this sense, were much more closely connected with the state than American universities, which are usually dependent on private financing and tuition fees (Sundqvist 2010). Under new public management influence, European university systems have undergone structural changes oriented towards the market (Kogan et al. 2000; Reed 2002).

2.2 The shift from collegial to managerial systems

Western universities exist in a delicate balance between professional autonomy and political and economic forces. If the latter forces become too strong, the autonomy and quality of universities is questioned. On the other hand, democratic assemblies may be said to have a legitimate interest in auditing the use of the tax payers' money in publicly financed universities. It is also the intervention of politicians that has resulted in more women in leading positions, at least in Scandinavia. Now governments (and for Europe, in the last instance the European Union assemblies) are the driving force behind the introduction of new public management in universities, in an effort to enhance economic efficiency. The protests from within the system are concerned with the quality and autonomy of scientific work and teaching. It is claimed that universities are not like business enterprises.

In the *collegial* model launched by Wilhelm von Humboldt in the nineteenth century, the autonomy of researchers/teachers and the close connection between research and teaching are pivotal. This would ensure that research is not unduly influenced by non-scientific interests and that students benefit from the latest research in their training. To achieve this, the (full) professors (the highest position in the university) are next to irremovable. When new professors are recruited, evaluations from several peer experts are required. Quality standards in research and in teaching are upheld through collegial critical discourse at seminars and peer reviews (Sundqvist 2010). Authority is given from *the bottom up* by teachers/researchers who elect someone from among their ranks to become their academic leader (head of department, Dean, or Rector) – as *primus inter pares*. Important decisions are taken by collegial assemblies. The faculties led by Deans are by law responsible for upholding high quality in research and teaching.

Collegial leadership the traditional model in universities, has been described as governance by a community of scholars, as opposed to central managerial authority (Meek 2002, p. 254). In the collegial model the leader facilitates the process of decision making by consensus, and does not 'lead, direct, or manage anything' (Moore & Langknecht 1986, p. 1 quoted in Meek 2002, p. 254). Formal decision-making under the collegial model is through a collegial structure based on assemblies of academics which preserves their professional autonomy (Sundqvist 2010).

In the *managerial* model, decisions are made from the top down. Collegial elections are replaced by appointments by the top leader (primarily the Rector/Vice-Chancellor). Professors' power is reduced and their employment conditions are like those of any other employee. Collegial influence is abolished or reduced. The Rector/VC becomes a CEO, and the university is turned into a business enterprise. Accountability, evaluation and economic efficiency are key words.

The present study will show that, currently, senior managers in universities both across different countries and within the same country can be positioned at different points in this development (see Chapter 4).

In face of this increasing professionalisation of managers (Sundqvist 2010) in the transition from collegiality to managerialism a de-professionalisation of scholars occurs, as autonomy and control of their work decreases (Hasselberg 2009; Marginson & Considine 2000). Nevertheless other empirical results have also highlighted the way some academics have so far been able to maintain their power and autonomy (Bleiklie & Michelsen 2008; Carvalho & Santiago 2010a and 2010b). This trend is confirmed by respondents in this study, and it also implies an emerging new coexistence of two specialised careers, the scientific research and the managerial one (see also Bourdieu 1996).

Traditionally universities have been male-dominated organisations. But today in western countries, there are more women HE students than men, and in many countries as many women gain PhDs as men. The famous glass ceiling has moved upwards, but it is still there. Although universities have now been open to women for over a hundred years, there are still few women in leadership positions. In most countries, no more than 15–20 per cent of the professors are women, and their percentage is growing very slowly. In senior management positions the numbers are often even smaller.

2.3   Gender and HE institutions

The fact that organisations are gendered is generally acknowledged, but there are different ways of interpreting this. At least three approaches may be distinguished according to Halford, Savage & Witz (1997). The *contingent* approach suggests that the gendering of organisations is due to external factors, such as the different situation of men and women (for instance, their different responsibilities in the family) (Kanter 1977). The *essentialist* approach views organisations as inherently masculinist (Ferguson 1984 as cited by Halford, Savage & Witz). For example, bureaucracy is considered a specifically male way of organising. Ferguson (1984) argues that there is also a feminine way of organising, which is based on a special feminine capacity for friendship. She views these gendered ways of organising as a social process that results in gender-specific modes of behaviour and therefore organisation. Halford, Savage & Witz (1997) propose instead what they call an *embedded* approach, in which gendered organisations are seen in terms of socially situated practices. They are located in specific social, economic and cultural contexts and they always have both formal and informal gendered structures. The data in this book provides examples of these various interpretations that seem to vary between countries.

This study compares countries with more or less different *gender orders* (see Chapter 1). In the European context Thurén (2000) compared gender relations in northern and southern countries and noted similarities but also differences (the same can be expected for the other countries in this study). Gender-neutral areas have a wider scope in the north, while more areas are gendered in the south. For example, sanctions against women crossing into male areas (or vice versa) are harsher in Spain and not very noticeable in Sweden. This might explain why some Swedish respondents in this study had trouble understanding the question about differently gendered cultures and leadership styles. They recognise that women have difficulties reaching the top, but are reluctant to attribute this to male-coded leadership. Instead, they explain it by referring to the more or less unconscious exclusion of women by male networks, and by women needing to be pushed into applying for or accepting a position due to lack of confidence.

2.4   Gender equality in universities

Gender inequality in university positions is seen across all eight countries in this study, although the figures vary. Turkey has the

Table 2.1 Percentage of women in senior academic positions in the eight countries (and the EU)

Country	Rectors/ VC	Vice- Rectors/ DVCs	Pro- Rectors/ PVCs	Deans	Exec Dir	Full professors
EU-27	9	–	–	–	–	19
Australia	18	36	40	38	32	21
Ireland	0	14	18	25	–	10
New Zealand	0	17	17	17	35	15
Portugal	7	27	16	23	60	22
South Africa	22	30*	0**	28***	–	21
Sweden	41	35	55	30	48	18
Turkey	10	7	4	13	–	28
UK	8	6	21	20	–	18

Sources: Data for professors and Rectors (EU-27, Portugal, Turkey, Ireland, UK) WiS database (DG Research); Higher Education Authority for Irish data; *She Figures* 2009; Australia – UAEW, 2009; South Africa – collated from university websites; Portugal – collated from university web sites. Data for Sweden is compiled from Sweden's *State Calendar 2010*.
* includes Vice-Principals.
** Term only used in one university in South Africa.
*** includes Dean of Students.

highest percentage of women university professors in Europe – almost 30 per cent – but a considerably lower percentage of women university Rectors (only ten per cent) than, for instance, Sweden, which has the highest percentage. In Sweden, in contrast, the percentages are 18 per cent women professors and 41 per cent women Rectors (2010). Thus it is clear that more is required than a good academic background to achieve the goal of getting more women into leading positions. The interviews in this study confirm that being a professor is a necessary requirement, but not sufficient for a position in senior management.

In Table 2.1 data for EU-27 has been added as a comparison. There are few women Rectors in Europe, while women make up almost one-fifth of the professors. In general, women are under-represented as full professors, while senior management positions in Australia and Sweden include a larger share of women, although still a minority. An exception is Pro-Rectors in Sweden, where women are a majority. This is explained by the practice of appointing as Pro-Rector someone of the opposite gender to the Rector position, and therefore is an indicator of the male-dominance among Rectors. Sweden on the other hand has a lower proportion of female professors, but the highest proportion of women Rectors. This may be connected with the official gender equality goals that are more easily implemented in particularly visible positions in the public sector (Göransson 2007), while lower positions may still be male-dominated. Thus, gender equality is not necessarily a question of time.

2.5   Higher education and gender equity in this study

The chapter will now examine the development of HE in each country in this study. This will include a system perspective of the number and type of institutions, institutional governance and management and the factors influencing the transition from collegial to managerial regimes, and gender differences in academic staff.

2.5.1   Australia

HE in Australia has become increasingly important to the country's economy, and the international student sector is now the third largest export earner after coal and iron-ore. However, HE has recently witnessed a significant decline in students from Asia, as well as falling demand from China and countries like Vietnam. While the growth of domestic participation has exceeded expectations, each place is funded below cost, leaving universities reliant on an expanding international education sector (*CRW* 2010).

HE consists of 37 public and two private universities, three self-accrediting institutions, and non-self-accrediting providers accredited by State and Territory authorities. Decision-making, regulation and governance of HE are shared among the Commonwealth, State and Territory Governments and the institutions themselves. Universities receive most of their public funding from the Australian Government, through the *Higher Education Support Act 2003* and have a reasonably high level of autonomy to operate within the legislative requirements associated with this funding.

There are three main groupings of universities, formed to promote the mutual objectives of the member universities: the Group of Eight (Go8 – the 'sandstone' universities, marketed as the oldest and more prestigious), Australian Technology Network (ATN), and Innovative Research Universities Australia (IRU Australia).

In March 2008, the Commonwealth Government initiated a review of HE to examine the future direction of the sector, its fitness for purpose in meeting the needs of the Australian community and economy, and the options for ongoing reform. In response to its recommendations, the Government announced in 2009 that it would provide an additional $5.4 billion to support HE and research over the next four years in order to:

- support high-quality teaching and learning,
- improve access and outcomes for students from low socio-economic backgrounds,
- build new links between universities and disadvantaged schools,
- reward institutions for meeting agreed quality and equity outcomes,
- improve resourcing for research and invest in world-class tertiary education infrastructure.

(http://www.deewr.gov.au/HigherEducation/Pages/
TransformingAustraliasHESystem.aspx, accessed 4 August 2010)

Since the 1990s Australian HE has undergone dramatic change. Harman (2003, p. 109) notes that these changes include:

- substantial increases in total enrolments and international student enrolments;
- a more market-oriented and competitive regulatory environment, with less institutional dependence on government operating grants, with substantial increases in institutionally generated revenue, and with more dependence on student fees;
- major expansion in research and research training, with closer university–industry research links;
- new quality-assurance initiatives; and
- a more corporatist and entrepreneurial approach to institutional management and governance.

This transition to a mass HE system, with a stronger emphasis on market mechanisms (Harman 2003, p. 112), has impacted on collegiality.

According to Meek, in Australia, collegial governance has been subjected to government policy attacks and 'collegial decision making and the professional authority of the academic has given way to that of the university manager' (Meek 2002, p. 255; see also Marginson & Considine 2000, pp. 9–11). Vice-Chancellors have become Chief Executive Officers and increasingly their role has an external focus (O'Meara & Petzall 2005).

While the managerial model would appear to be clearly in the ascendancy in Australia, universities are not like public corporations or government departments. They are characterised by a complex set of interlocking relationships between managers and the academics they manage. There has been an ongoing discourse in Australia about the impact of managerialism on the autonomy of academic careers, and a good deal of resistance from the academy (Winter, Taylor & Sarros 2000; Meek 2002; Marginson & Considine 2000; Kekale 2003; Thornton 2008).

As managerialism permeates the University Executive, its trickle-down effect is often uneven within the organisation. Moodie argues that Deans 'are no longer primarily representatives of the disciplines but of senior management' (2002, p. 20). At the next level down Heads of Schools (HOS) or Departments are defined as middle management and, in the Australian context, would typically have responsibility for supervising 20 or more staff and managing sizeable budgets (Moodie 2002, pp. 20–1). As Moodie (2002, p. 21) observes, they are still, however, collegial appointments. Yet unlike middle management in other areas, they are part time and temporary appointments, with the incumbents expected to return to full time academia after their term as HOS. Moodie (2002, p. 21) notes that if the schools they manage do not perform, managerialism will impose change.

In Australia in 2008, 55.2 per cent of student enrolments were women, with 55.8 per cent commencing enrolments being female. But this gender composition was not reflected in representation of academic women who comprise 42 per cent of all academic staff (QUT, 2008) and 21 per cent of professors. Universities Australia (2010, p. 2) asserts that 'This picture raises questions about the role models that are being provided to students, especially those in the PhD cohorts who represent the future generation of university leaders'.

Gender is strongly on the agenda for Australian universities. As discussed in Chapter 1, the Australian university sector is a leader in parental leave provisions. Universities Australia – the peak lobbying organisation – *Strategy for Women: 2011–2014*, includes as one of its objectives to increase the proportion of women in senior leadership positions including Deans, Directors and Senior Managers and in a wider range of portfolios and discipline groupings. Nevertheless, as Bell (2009, p. 11) highlights the 'persistent vertical segregation in science and technology disciplines, in addition to continuing horizontal segregation, impact on women's capacity to participate, contribute and succeed in "non-traditional disciplines"'.

2.5.2   Ireland

Ireland has seven main publicly funded universities, and all but two date from before the foundation of the Irish state. In addition, there are several other institutions of HE that were established with a different focus (applied knowledge) and a different name (regional technical colleges). Universities saw these as possible 'feeder institutions', as a prelude to university graduation, but they are now considered as being in a University-like 'space' (and they provide a range of experiences up to PhD level).

With the introduction of mass HE, 60 per cent of the Irish cohort attend HE. In a context where, since the 1990s, students do not pay fees, the cost to the state is increasingly seen as prohibitive. Little attention has been paid by the state to universities for 40 years. The seven universities are by no means homogenous. Until the early 1970s, Catholics were not allowed to attend the oldest of them, Trinity College Dublin, without permission from their bishop, reflecting the fact that it was considered a bastion of Protestant thinking. Its structures and the titles of the positions are completely different to all other Irish universities.

The university system as a whole in Ireland is very much in a state of transition between collegiality and managerialism, with specific universities being differentially located on that continuum. The net effect of various forces is to place current economic needs at the heart of the university mission, a project that O'Carroll (2008, p. 54) argues is doomed to failure even in terms of those current needs.

Recent developments in Ireland have seen the emergence of new structures of control and regulation in HE. These have included

- the curricular and organisational consequences of the Bologna Agreement, with its requirement that universities 'compete in a global market place' (O'Sullivan 2005, pp. 178, 168);
- the proactive development of quality-assurance structures and processes;
- an increasing focus on restructuring and manageralism, as reflected in the increased use of appointment rather than nomination to senior management; and
- increasing stress on strategic plans and performance-indicators, as well as on performance-development reviews, as a mechanism for motivating faculty and staff, as opposed to relying on professionalism and collegial decision-making structures (Skillbeck 2001).

2.5.3   New Zealand

The New Zealand university system is based largely on the British one, although it is increasingly being influenced by practices from the United States. The origins have importance in terms of career structure. The Chief Executives of all universities are the Vice-Chancellors.

The standard academic staff hierarchy, as in the UK, is that of lecturer, senior lecturer, reader/associate professor, professor.

New Zealand has eight universities and a number of Polytechnics in its tertiary sector. The establishment of universities has been limited by statute, and there has only been one significant change of status in the last 40 years: in 2000 the Auckland Institute of Technology became the Auckland University of Technology. There is now a moratorium on the creation of new universities. Another component in the New Zealand tertiary system is the Wananga, or Maori institutions of learning, which are managed by the indigenous people and are almost entirely attended by Maori students. There are also a number of private providers of HE qualifications, but these tend to focus on very specific areas and are not part of the university system.

The beginning of the legislative move from a collegial to managerial model for universities was the *Education Amendment Act 1990*, which was an amendment to and extension of the Education Act 1989. This Act specifically refers to the heads of universities as chief executives. The Act provides that universities are to be governed by Councils made up of representatives and appointees, and that the Council's first statutory duty is to appoint the Chief Executive, who is the legal employer of all staff. Previously the Council, as the governing body, had been the employer of all staff. The Education Act specifies the role of the Chief Executive as managing the 'academic and administrative affairs of the institution'. In the *Review of New Zealand Tertiary Sector Governance* (Ministry of Education 2003) Professor Meredith Edwards indicated that the Chief Executive has an essential leadership, as well as management, role to play and should work with the Council to achieve the strategic leadership of the institution. The majority of the eight New Zealand universities are moving towards a more managerial model; in six of them the Vice-Chancellor acts as a CEO. While two of the six now have VCs who were recruited from outside the HE sector, the accepted ethos is that VCs will have a research record and understand the specific academic role of the university, rather than behaving as if the institution is just a business.

While women make up over 50 per cent of the students attending university in New Zealand, under 40 per cent of academic positions are filled by women, and the more senior the position, the less likely it is to be filled by a woman. Women comprise 15 per cent of professors, 23 per cent of associate professors, 39 per cent of senior lecturers and 51 per cent of lecturers. Women's representation in university senior management is consistently low, at 17 per cent for DVCs, PVCs and Deans, and currently with no women as VCs.

2.5.4   Portugal

Portugal has one of the oldest HE systems in Europe. Its first university was created in 1290. With the democratic revolution of 1974, a binary system was created, and new public universities and polytechnics emerged in Portuguese HE, opening pathways to a mass system. From the mid-1980s, it experienced a rapid expansion with a growing number of *numerus clausus* in public institutions and proliferation of private institutions (Amaral & Teixeira 2000). There are now 118 higher education institutions: 47 universities (14 public; 31 private and cooperative universities; one non-integrated university institution (the Catholic university); 65 polytechnics (15 public; 46 private and 4 non-integrated schools of polytechnic institutions) and 6 military and police HE institutions (4 military and police university institutions and 2 military and police polytechnic institutions) (MSTHE 2009).

The substantive increase of student enrolments includes high rates of female participation. The presence of the market and managerialism has been evident in Portuguese higher education since the 1990s (Amaral, Magalhães & Santiago 2003). Initially its presence was mitigated and mainly translated at a rhetorical level (Santiago & Carvalho 2004; Santiago et al. 2006). However, recent legal changes in the system (Law 62/2007) clearly indicate that it is now the main frame of reference driving HE policies and imposing narrow and coercive practices on increasingly corporate and entrepreneurial universities.

The new *Higher Education Act* (Law, 62/2007) reconfigures the traditional power of Portuguese HE, both at system and organisational levels. It imposes a new configuration on higher education governance and management structures and a new institutional power 'architecture' substantially different from that previously rooted in the collegial tradition. Among these changes are the choice for institutions to opt either for a public institute regime or for a public foundation (regulated by private law; only three public universities have adopted this); the creation of a general council (replacing the previous collegial bodies) with extended political and strategic power (even if the academic elected members remain the majority in this new governance body); the attribution of an executive dimension for university Rectors and polytechnic Presidents; the creation of a management council; and the reconfiguration of the 'academic-management' to line-management structures (Deans and Heads can be appointed for a fixed-term position, instead of election, depending on the model defined in each institution).

A woman took responsibility for an academic discipline in Portugal for the first time in 1911. However, women remained a huge minority in HE until the democratic revolution. By 2005 the total number of academics in public higher education in Portugal was 24,280. Of these, 14,063 (58 per cent) were men and 10,217 (42 per cent) were women. However, women's participation was higher in polytechnics (46.6 per cent) than in universities (38.9 per cent). Nevertheless, women's representation at professorial level is well below that of women as undergraduates (53.4 per cent).

There is both vertical and horizontal segregation in Portuguese academia. Women are concentrated in certain disciplines, such as education/teacher training (63 per cent) and humanities (54 per cent women) and are under-represented in engineering (77 per cent men) (Carvahlo & Santiago, 2010a and b). Vertical segregation is also pronounced: men have a higher representation in all academic ranks, but differences are more pronounced at the top – women comprise only 32 per cent and 22 per cent respectively of the total of the number of associate and full professors.

2.5.5 South Africa

South Africa is a country undergoing significant transformation, in an attempt to redress social, economic and legislative imbalances inherited from the apartheid era (Shackleton, Simonis & Riordan 2003 as cited in Riordan 2007). Universities in particular have been through a period of sweeping change since the first democratic election in 1994. In addition to the current pressures on universities internationally to become more market-driven and managerial in their approach, they underwent substantial structural and cultural changes.

Three inter-related factors have dominated HE in South Africa since 1994:

- Pressure on institutions to become more market-driven and managerial in their *modus operandi*;
- Restructuring of the HE landscape; and
- The need to address racial inequalities from the apartheid years (Shackleton, Simonis & Riordan 2003 as cited in Riordan 2007).

The traditional belief that universities were the primary repositories of knowledge in a society is currently under threat. Increasingly, publicly-funded universities all over the world are being required to justify their existence and in particular their expenditure. Terms such as 'corporate colonisation' and the 'new managerialism' are used somewhat disparagingly to describe the 'storming, capturing and occupation of the traditional hallowed corridors and ivory towers of academia by the unfettered forces of marketisation and corporatism' (Saunderson 2002, p. 380). South African universities are no different. Saunderson explained that the purported benefits of managerialism were enhanced levels of economy, efficiency, and effectiveness, but that the values underpinning this approach were fundamentally incongruent with the values of social justice with which HE was supposed to be concerned, and added that managerialism had effectively 'handcuffed equal opportunities in the academy' (Saunderson 2002, p. 381). Meanwhile, the assertion about managerialism limiting opportunities is particularly relevant in South Africa where, due to inherited inequities, universities are expected to both fulfil a redistributive social function and play an economic role in training the next generation of professionals.

Compared with universities in other parts of Africa such as Nigeria, South African universities operate with considerable autonomy (Prof A. Obejide personal communication, November 2003). Chancellors, Rectors and Vice-Chancellors are selected by the institution, not the state, but the state has required increasing accountability from the institutions (Shackleton, Simonis & Riordan 2003 as cited in Riordan 2007). This includes compiling and reporting against three-year rolling plans, and the revision of the state funding formula to ensure compliance with (racial) equity and quality requirements. Currently, state funding provides a portion of the operating funds of universities that can be as low as 40 per cent (Shackleton, Simonis & Riordan 2003 as cited in Riordan 2007). Additional income is derived from tuition fees, fund-raising and research income. Even those institutions that have traditionally claimed to be research-led have experienced a significant shift towards increasing their research outputs, due in part to the re-admittance of South Africa into the circle of international scholars after years of politically motivated isolation. A further incentive for universities to increase their research output has been the income derived from such activities (contract research, patents and state subsidies for published, and peer-reviewed research outputs). In short, research generates money, a distinctly corporate orientation.

Whichever side of the managerialism debate one adopts, the fact remains that in South Africa, significant changes within institutions have been imposed and have impacted on the content of work performed by academics and the context in which work is performed. Furthermore, a strong political need still exists to 'level the playing field' by eliminating the resource distinctions between institutions that were caused by differentiated funding by the apartheid government. This was pursued through state-instructed institutional mergers and the transformation of institutions.

Pre-1994 South Africa had 21 public universities and 15 technikons (similar to applied or technical universities in other parts of the world). Universities traditionally employed a research focus, whereas technikons enjoyed a strong teaching focus. Eleven universities and six technikons were specifically established to cater for the black[2] population, but resources were allocated unevenly. With the advent of democracy in South Africa, it was clear that the system required complete restructuring (Shackleton, Simonis & Riordan 2003 as cited in Riordan 2007). A new *Higher Education Act* was promulgated in 1997 and established the Council on Higher Education (CHE) to provide 'informed, considered, independent, and strategic advice' on HE issues to the Minister of Education (Council on Higher Education 2001, p. 77). It was also made responsible for quality-assurance through its sub-committee on HE Quality Control, and disseminated knowledge and information on HE (Shackleton, Simonis & Riordan as cited in Riordan 2007).

In June 2006 restructuring was finally completed. The total number of publicly funded institutions in South Africa was reduced from 36 to 23. This now includes: 11 traditional universities that offer theoretically-oriented university degrees, six universities of technology that offer practically-oriented diplomas and degrees in technical fields, and six comprehensive universities that offer a combination of both types of qualification (South African Higher Education 2006).

Traditional, research-focused universities continue to compete for research recognition as well as state and international funding. This is in contrast to universities of technology and comprehensive universities (as hybrid institutions) that historically had emphasised teaching over research. Consequently, many staff at these 'newer' universities have relatively poor research track records.

The merging of institutions and reallocation of resources in a more equitable fashion have had a major impact on the working lives of staff within the institutions. While much of this restructuring has engendered great resistance to change from some quarters, for others opportunities were perceived that previously did not exist. These changes become significant when considered in the light of opportunity structures for women academics. Many of these changes were rooted in the legislation aimed at redressing inequality throughout South African society.

Changing legislation, and merging previously separate institutions, may have been necessary conditions to begin to transform the higher education landscape, but they certainly would not be sufficient. After a number of unacceptable incidents at universities across the country, in 2008 the then Minister of Education, Naledi Pandor, MP, took a pro-active stand. She established a *Ministerial Committee on Progress Towards Transformation and Social Cohesion and the Elimination of Discrimination in Public Higher Education Institutions* to investigate and make recommendations to combat discrimination in public universities (*South African Government Gazette* 2008).

While analysis of their report is beyond the scope of this chapter, some recommendations are relevant, and indicate that, despite legislation and other specific state-initiated interventions, gender equity remains a challenge in South African universities. The most notable recommendations on gender equity are those suggesting that Vice-Chancellors be held directly accountable for achieving employment equity targets (that include gender equity), and that a transformation framework, including indicators and targets, should be the basis of their performance contract (South African Department of Education 2008).

Since the Report was released, the Department of Education has been restructured, and a new Minister of HE was appointed in 2009. As the statutory body responsible for advising the Minister of HE and Training, for assuring and promoting quality within the sector, and for supporting the development of HE, the Council on Higher Education (CHE) took the report seriously and issued a considered response (SA CHE 2009). Essentially the CHE undertook to include a number of the recommendations in future institutional audits. With specific reference to measures and indicators in Vice-Chancellor's performance contracts and the monitoring of such performance by statutory bodies, these developments send a clear message about where South African universities are located in respect of managerialism.

2.5.6   Sweden

Swedish universities are public authorities; their Rectors are appointed by the government (from a short list presented by universities, previously after collegial elections but now after hearing collegial assemblies), and they are therefore obliged to adhere to state gender-equality rules. Recruitment processes are transparent, and expert evaluations and peer reviews of candidates are public–measures that traditionally favour women.

Sweden has 14 publicly financed universities and 22 university colleges (www.regeringskansliet.se/utbildningsdepartementet 2010). There are also about ten private institutes for higher education including research (among them Chalmers Technical University, the foundation Jönköping School of Economics and Stockholm School of Economics). The first university was founded in 1477 in Uppsala, the second in 1666 in Lund. Towards the end of the nineteenth century, colleges were founded in the two biggest cities Stockholm and Göteborg and these became full universities in the 1960s. Today the big universities also include Umeå (from the 1960s) and Linköping (from the 1970s). Swedish universities were based on the Humboldtian idea of offering training on the basis of science and in close connection with research. The professor (chair) combined these tasks, and this position was appointed by the government for life in order to guarantee academic autonomy.

As in most other countries, Swedish HE expanded rapidly from the 1960s onwards, and the number of students has increased from 10,000 at that time to more than 300,000. Favourable study loans were made available for all students in the 1960s, independently of their economic situation, to attract students from all social strata. Today one third of the cost is provided as a grant, and two thirds are reimbursed at low interest. The great influx of students necessitated several changes. A new position was created, the lecturer with a PhD primarily to teach (Sundqvist 2010, p. 134) and an adjunct who was not required to have a PhD. The teaching positions are largely held by women, while professorships are dominated by men. This is consistent with the trend in Europe to mass higher education, with more women undertaking high teaching loads, while the mushrooming separate and well-financed research institutes are dominated by men. Thus, against Humboldtian principles, teaching and research are increasingly separated and at the same time differently gendered.

In the 1990s many new regional university colleges were established, some of which later reached the status of university. They primarily devote themselves to teaching (Sundqvist 2010). These two steps, new teaching positions and new colleges for teaching, were the first moves away from the Humboldtian model.

A 1977 reform resulted in most tertiary educational tracks being formally included in the university system. The number of women in the academy radically increased as colleges for nursing, teaching and fine arts were given academic status and provided with research facilities and a research education track.

More recently in Sweden, a systematic reconstruction has begun to introduce a managerial organisational model deemed more efficient in controlling costs and quality. This has been resisted by universities.

However, most of the changes will be law from 1 January 2011 and will radically shift the power over and within universities.

Practically all power will be vested in the Rector. At the same time, the power over universities will be decentralised. Only two types of positions will be regulated in future, the professor and the lecturer. When a full professor is recruited, there should still be at least one expert evaluation, according to the new law, and if there are several, gender equality is important among the evaluators. While faculties are now optional for the universities, the Rector may initiate other groups or individuals as decision-makers at various levels. Where there are groups, gender equality should be observed with the proviso that it is important only 'unless there are special reasons' not to consider it.

Therefore, only if the Rector supports equality will the line organisation support recruitment of women. Another group whose power will be increased substantially is the first line managers: the heads of department (prefects). Mass education and new tasks such as self-evaluations have increased their work, and it becomes more difficult to combine this position with research and/or teaching. In recent years, more and more women seem to be recruited to these positions.

Swedish universities were first opened to women in 1873, when a woman entered Uppsala University. The first woman professor in Sweden was employed in the then private Stockholm university college, in 1884, and was the first woman professor in mathematics in the world. But the first woman professor in a public university, Nanna Svarts in medicine, was not appointed until 1937 (Göransson 2007b, pp. 108, 171).

For the last 40 years gender politics in Sweden has emerged as an important political and administrative field, beginning with so-called state feminists and other politicians reacting to the women's movement (for instance Hernes 1987; SOU 1983, p. 4; Göransson 2010). There is a strong reformist tradition of the state embracing social movements, supporting but at the same time disarming and adapting them to mainstream politics. For equality policies, it was probably imperative that many civil servants were women who understood and supported the women's movement. In universities, grass-roots organisations for gender research and for the promotion of women researchers were formed from 1978 onwards, so that in the mid-1980s all universities and several university colleges had their 'Forum for Women's Studies and for Women Researchers'. These units soon received support from the state, in order to secure their continued existence. They are now included in universities as centres or institutes for gender studies. Equality policies are an integral part of the agenda of political parties, and are included in legislation and acts governing higher education, as well as in public agencies and university teachers' organisations. The Government Agency for Higher Education, the Universities and College Universities Association, and the Swedish Associations of University Teachers are all engaged in and committed to gender equality in the academy.

Gender equality reforms were introduced later in universities than in the labour market. The equality legislation of 1980 required universities to work against gender discrimination and to support gender equality. Ten years later a paragraph was added about sexual harassment. Today employers with more than 24 employees are required to develop equality plans every three years. There is also a yearly conference for equality managers and gender researchers at universities and college universities. Recently all previous authorities responsible for eliminating discrimination were merged into one, the Discrimination Ombudsman (2008). There have been several official investigations of gender relations and equality measures in universities, and about 20 dissertations have been written on various aspects of gender in the Swedish academy. Dahlerup (2010) argued that, while it is easy to demonstrate salary differences, it is more difficult to make visible the subtle processes that give rise to inclusion and exclusion in various academic contexts.

Under current Swedish legislation, recruitment to public positions should always be gender equal, and at least 40 per cent of positions should be occupied by the under-represented sex. Short lists should also always include candidates of both sexes. In the universities, this relates, for instance, to faculty Deans and other elections. However, the prerequisite for senior management is usually the rank of (full) professor and this is the real bottle neck for women, as less than one fifth of professors are women.

Therefore, in 1995 the Minister of Education Carl Tham, introduced 30 professorships (Tham professorships) that were ear-marked for women. This was a controversial measure, but it increased the number of women professors. A more general measure, introduced in the 1990s, was for lecturers to be allowed to apply for a promotion to full professors on the basis of their performance. Previously they needed to wait until a professor retired and the position was advertised. This made the attainment of the rank of professor a matter of competence not competition. But this measure did not increase the number of female professors, since more men applied than women. However, no new resources were provided for these new professors; they received no increased time allowance for research or higher salary. This measure could be seen as a transition from the German model of the professor's role (chair) to the Anglo Saxon one.

The government, the Universities and Colleges Universities Association, and the University Teachers' Association all strongly advocate gender equality policies. Initiatives have been taken from above but also from below, for instance the creation of networks for women professors. In 1999, a group of women in the Universities and University Colleges Association observed that the number of women Rectors had decreased. They formed a national network of women in senior management, and in 2000 developed a five-year national policy project to improve the recruitment of women leaders and women's leadership. The project, Identification, Development, Advancement and Support (IDAS), was an umbrella network organisation comprising many local- and national-level equality studies and measures (2003–7). It has initiated several other projects to support and promote women senior managers (see IDAS Reports 2005, 2007).

To sum up, significant improvement in gender equality in universities has occurred in the last decade but has been uneven. But it may be a Swedish or Nordic phenomenon that due to the strong equality discourse, more women are recruited to conspicuous leading positions than to lower less visible ones (SOU 2007, p. 108). This improvement in gender equality does not necessarily translate to a strong recruitment base of women at lower levels. Therefore, gender equality in senior management may not be a question of time, after all.

2.5.7   Turkey

The foundation of Turkish universities was provided by reforms introduced by Ataturk in 1923. The constitution of the new republic gave women equal rights and opportunities with men, including in education. In 1937, Turkey became a secular state, leading to further relaxation of laws and social norms which had constrained women's full participation in the public life (Bilge 1995). The Convention of Elimination of all Forms of Discrimination against Women was signed by Turkey in 1985.

New HE legislation in 1981 established the Council of Higher Education, a fully autonomous supreme corporate public body responsible for the planning, coordination, governance and supervision of HE. It made provision for non-profit foundations to establish HE institutions. In 1981, there were 19 universities; by 2010 the number had increased to 139 (94 state universities and 45 institutions of HE established by Foundations, that is, private universities). State universities do not enjoy financial and administrative autonomy.

Women's participation in the Turkish universities has been increasing, especially since the 1940s (Özkanlı 2007). The number of female professors increased by 75 per cent in the last decade of the 20th century, and now 28 per cent of full professors and 31 per cent of associate professors are women (Özkanlı & White 2008). Currently, 39 per cent of all academic personnel in the universities are women. Interestingly, Turkey, which has no national gender equality framework, has the highest representation of women in the professoriate of the countries in this study.

Özkanlı and Korkmaz (2000) found that the low representation of women in senior management in Turkey, as indicated in Table 2.1, was mostly due to cultural factors. Some academic women pointed to gender discrimination while others said they were not willing to take on administrative responsibilities because they accepted and internalised traditional social roles of women, and prioritised wife and mother roles (see also Acar 1986, pp. 307–24; Köker 1988, p. 339). Moreover, women avoided business trips and extra work load for fear of not fulfilling their traditional roles (Ersöz 1988).

2.5.8   United Kingdom

UK universities have generally been instituted by Royal Charter, Act of Parliament or an instrument of government under the Education Reform Act 1988; in any case generally with the approval of the Privy Council. Only such recognised bodies can award degrees of any kind. Most universities in the country may be classified into six main categories:

- Ancient universities: seven universities founded between the twelfth and sixteenth centuries;
- The University of London, The University of Wales, Lampeter and Durham universities, which were chartered in the nineteenth century;
- 'Red Brick' universities: six large civic universities chartered at the turn of the twentieth century before World War I;
- 'New' universities chartered in the 1960s;
- The Open University, Britain's 'open to all' distance-learning University, established in 1968; and
- Post-1992 Universities, formed from polytechnics or colleges of HE.

There are 165 HE institutions in the UK (including England, Scotland, Wales and Northern Ireland) and 115 institutions that use the title 'university'

Table 2.2   Number of UK institutions (August 2010)

Country	Universities	Higher education institutions
England	89	131
Scotland	14	19
Wales	10	11
Northern Ireland	2	4
United Kingdom	115	165

Source: Universities UK website www.universitiesUK.ac.uk.

(see Table 2.2 above). Federal institutions such as the University of Wales and the University of London are counted as one University. The term HE institutions includes universities, university colleges, specialist higher education institutions and other higher education colleges. In addition, there are also a significant number of further education colleges at which HE students study.

The UK HE sector is now very diverse in terms of the institutions that offer HE and research opportunities. While all universities undertake research and teaching, the mission focus and balance of activities varies. Some institutions, such as the post-1992 universities, concentrate primarily on teaching, while others are more research intensive.

The vast majority of UK universities are government financed, with only one private university where the government does not subsidise the tuition fees. As the universities are generally public institutions, there is less corporate influence. UK universities receive much smaller financial endowments, in comparison to many larger universities in the US. Similarly, while certain universities retain ancient traditions, none are directly funded by religious organisations.

British undergraduate students, and students from other EU countries who qualify as home students, have to pay university tuition fees. A government-provided loan is available which may only be used towards tuition fee costs, and many universities provide bursaries to students with low financial capabilities.

The UK HE sector has changed significantly over the past few decades, for both staff and students. Expansion, changes in funding, widening participation, internationalisation, new technology, a greater engagement with the wider world, increased customer focus, and mangerialism are a few of the many policy developments that make the sector more complex and more differentiated. And these developments have led to increased focus on issues of inclusion and equality of opportunity in these institutions, both as learning providers and workplaces. But despite a strong commitment to equality of opportunity and diversity by the previous New Labour Government and the Funding Councils, which supported legislation and a range of equality initiatives over the past decade or so, various inequalities are still clearly evident at both institutional and sector levels. These range from differences in student participation rates and graduate outcomes, to the segregated nature of many jobs and pay differentials.

The history of women in universities in the UK is one of total exclusion until the end of the nineteenth century. Women had to fight a hard and bitter battle to enter universities. Women were not admitted to full membership at Oxford University until 1921 and at Cambridge until 1948. Even then, both universities set quotas, of 25 per cent and 10 per cent respectively, on the proportion of women students. Even as late as 1970, women made up only 11 per cent of students at Cambridge.

Women now form more than 50 per cent of the student body. However, women academics have not enjoyed the same success. Their position has moved from one of exclusion, to the maintenance of relatively stable horizontal segregation, especially by discipline, and vertical segregation by grade. While the first woman was appointed as an academic in 1893 and the first woman as a professor in 1894, since then there has been very slow progress. Even by the 1970s, the proportion of women academics was virtually the same as in the 1920s, and the proportion holding senior posts virtually the same as in the 1930s.

Women constituted only 12 per cent of academics in the late 1970s, and were disproportionately concentrated in the worst paid, lowest status and least secure positions. By the academic year 1991–2, they had increased to 22 per cent, but there was little change in the predominance of men at senior level. Women held only five per cent of professorships.

Analysis of the most recent HE staff statistics shows that 18 per cent of professors are female. The proportion of female academic staff in all grades is 42.6 per cent. However, 42.4 per cent of female academics work part-time, compared with 23.1 per cent of male academics. The continuing low representation of women in senior management in UK universities reflects a low recruitment pool in the professoriate; there are almost six full-time male professors for every female professor.

There are significant differences between the post-1992 and the 'old' (pre-1992) universities, with a few post-1992 universities setting good examples in terms of recruitment of women into senior management. This success is attributed to more open recruitment processes, whereas many of the older universities operate a rotating basis where an academic is elected to do three or four years in a position of management.

2.6 Discussion and conclusion

This chapter has shown that there are differences in the organisation of research and HE between, on one hand, the UK and its former colonies, where the managerial model seems to have settled in more strongly, and, on the other hand, the countries in continental Europe where remnants of the collegial system are still lingering.

But there is no self-evident connection between either the collegial or the managerial system and the recruitment of women to leading positions. So far, there are more women in senior management in the Anglo Saxon and Swedish universities than in the Mediterranean ones (Turkey and Portugal). On the other hand, there are more women professors in Turkey than in most of the other countries. But generally, the proportion of women professors is roughly the same in all investigated countries.

A recruitment base of many women professors seems to be a necessary but not sufficient criterion for achieving more women in leading positions in the universities.

It seems that the general discourse and equality laws on gender are more important than the university's organisational model, for women's access to power positions. It is evident from the Swedish example that gender equality reforms may be controversial, but are not impossible to accept, as long as they are formulated in a way that is acceptable to the academic field and its self-conception (Törnqvist 2006).

In the debate about gender equality in universities, two theses are often put forward (Dahlerup 2010). One is the so-called *time lag thesis*, according to which it is only a question of time before women and men are found equally often in top positions. The other thesis holds that the gender order will always be reproduced and that there will be a *glass ceiling* for women (see Ryan & Haslam 2004). Another metaphor is that of *the leaking pipeline* where women are seen to be seeping out on their way to the top (see Allan & Castleman 2001). The results of the empirical research are more nuanced; on one hand, men still become professors to a much greater extent than women, on the other hand there are many more women now than before as professors and in leading positions.

Male dominance comes in many forms and varieties. In the collegial system, male informal networks and homosociability may exclude women from leading positions, as discussed in Chapters 7 and 8. Under the managerial system, gender equality will depend on the views of central management, and experience from business management in enterprises is not promising. Also local governance has a history of being more negative to female competitors than, for instance, national governments (Göransson 1988; SOU 2007, p. 108).

It is probably safe to conclude that the future of women leaders will depend on the pressure from public opinion and political forces which may induce colleagues as well as top management to take action to include women in decision-making positions. The general conclusion of all previous international research is that women's chances of advancement are always better when recruitment processes are open and transparent. This will improve meritocratic promotion, while closed processes, whether in male networks or in the Rector's/VC's/President's chambers, will not enhance the recruitment of women.

Notes

1. The higher education systems in Europe were influenced by different ideas. One of the most influential thinkers was the German Wilhelm von Humboldt who defended the coexistence of research and teaching as the dominant role of academics. To assure these roles, universities had to simultaneously be part of state administration and guarantee institutional autonomy. Newman influenced the British model, which was based on the idea that higher education should be mainly concerned with students' development. In this model universities were private non-profit institutions governed by elected board members. Finally, the Napoleonic model was developed in France, and was closer to public bureaucracies since universities were conceptualised as an integral part of state administration.
2. Peculiar to South African reporting conventions is the use of capital letters when reference is made to race. Black = persons of black African descent whereas black = all other race groups except White, that is, black = Black + Indian + Coloured (mixed race) persons.

References

Acar, F. (1986). 'Working women in a changing society: The case of Jordanian academics', *METU Studies in Development*. 10, 307–24.

Allan, M. and Castleman. T. (2001). 'Fighting the pipeline fallacy', in A. Brooks and A. Mackinnon (eds), *Gender and the Restructured University* (Buckingham: Society for Research into Higher Education and Open University), 151–65.

Amaral, A., Magalhaes, A. and Santiago, R. (2003). 'The rise of academic managerialism in Portugal', in A. Amaral, L. Meek and I. Larsen (eds), *The Higher Education Managerial Revolution?* (Dordrecht: Kluwer Academic Publishers), 131–53.

Amaral. A. and Teixeira, P. (2000). 'The rise and fall of the private sector in Portuguese higher education?', *Higher Education Policy*, 13, 3, 245–66.

Bell, S. (2009). *Women in Science in Australia: Maximising Productivity, Diversity and Innovation* (Canberra: FASTS).

Bleiklie, I. and Michelsen, S. (2008). 'The university as enterprise and academic co-determination', in A. Amaral, I. Bleiklie and C. Musselin (eds), *From Governance to Identity, a Festschrift for Mary Henkel* (London: Springer), 57–80.

Bilge, N. (1995). *Laiklik ve Islamda Ortunme Sorunu*, Cumhuriyet (31 January).

Bourdieu, P. (1996). *Homo Academicus* (Stockholm/Stehag: Brutus Östlings Bokförlag/Symposion).

Campus Review Weekly (CRW) (2010). 'Political spin overwhelms the revolution: Marginson', 12 July.

Carvalho, T. and Santiago, R. (2010a). 'NPM and middle-management: How do deans influence institutional policies?', in L. Meek, L. Goedegebuure, R. Santiago and T. Carvalho (eds), *Changing Deans. Higher Education Middle Management in International Comparative Perspectives* (Amsterdam: Springer).

Carvalho, T. and Santiago, R. (2010b). 'Still academics after all', *Higher Education Policy*, 23, 397–411.

Dahlerup, D. (2010). 'Jämställdhet i akademin – en forskningsöversikt' ['Gender equality in Academia: a research overview'], *Rapport 2010*, 1 (Stockholm: Delegationen för jämställdhet i högskolan).

Ersöz, A. G. (1988). '*Kamu Yönetiminde Yönetici Olarak Çalışan Kadınların Geleneksel ve Çalışan Kadın Rollerine İlişkin Beklentileri*' ['Traditional and women's roles of women managers in Turkish public sector'], in O. Çitci (ed.), *Yüzyılın Sonunda Kadınlar ve Gelecek* [*Women and Future in the End of 20th Century*] (Ankara: TODAİE Publication), 255–64.

Göransson, A. (1988). *Från familj till fabrik. Teknik, arbetsdelning och skiktning i svenska fabriker 1830–1877* [*From Family to Factory: Technology, Division of Labour and Stratification in Swedish Factories, 1830–77*] (Diss. Lund: Arkiv förlag).

Göransson, A. (ed.) (2007a) *Maktens kön. Kvinnor och män i den svenska makteliten på 2000-talet.* [*The Gender of Power: Women and Men in the Swedish Power Elite in the 21st Century*] (Nora: Nya Doxa Bokförlag).

Göransson, A. (2007b). '*Vetenskap och högre utbildning*' ['Science and higher education'] in *Kön, makt och statistik* (Stockholm: Regeringskansliet/Fritzes).

Göransson, A. (2010) '*Att bygga ett vetenskapligt fält. Förutsättningar och utvecklingslinjer*' ['Building a new scientific field: Pre-conditions and developments'], in K. Niskanen and C. Florin (eds), *Föregångarna. Kvinnliga professorer om liv, makt och vetenskap.* [*The Pioneers: Women Professors about Life, Power and Science*], (Stockholm: SNS Förlag).

Halford, S., Savage, M. and Witz, A. (1997). *Gender, Careers and Organisations. Current Developments in Banking, Nursing and Local Government* (Basingstoke: Macmillan).

Harman, G. (2003). 'Australian academics and prospective academics: Adjustment to a more commercial environment', *Higher Education Management and Policy*, 15, 3, 105–22.

Hasselberg, Y. (2009). *Vem vill leva i kunskapssamhället? Essäer om universitetet och samtiden* [*Who Wants to Live in the Knowledge Society? Essays About the University and Our Times*] (Hedemora: Gidlunds förlag).

Hernes, H. (1987). *Welfare State and Woman Power: Essays in State Feminism* (Oslo: Norwegian University Press Cop).

IDAS (2005). *Rektor på 20 sätt. Personliga reflektioner om hur det är att leda universitet och högskolor.* En intervjubok från IDAS-projektet. [*Rector in 20 Ways: Personal Reflections on What it is Like to Lead Universities and University Colleges. A Book of Interviews from the IDAS Project*].

IDAS (2007). *Ett urval av insatser på nationell och lokal nivå.* Ett ledarförsörjningsprojekt för universitet och högskolor. [*A Selection of Projects at a National and Local Level: A Leadership-Providing Project for Universities and University Colleges*] An anthology from the IDAS project (Växjö: Grafiska Punkten).

Kekale, J. (2003). 'Academic leaders as thermostats', *Tertiary Education and Management*, 9, 4, 281–98.

Kogan, M., Bauer, M., Bleiklie, I. and Henkel, M. (2000). *Transforming Higher Education: A Comparative Study* (London: Jessica Kingsley).

Köker. E. (1988). *'Türkiye'de Kadın, Eğitim ve Siyaset: Yüksek Öğrenim Kurumlarında Kadının Durumu Üzerine Bir İnceleme'* [Woman, Education and Politics in Turkey: The Situation of Women in Higher Education], unpublished PhD Thesis, Ankara University.

Marginson, S. and Considine, M. (2000). *The Enterprise University: Power, Governance and Reinvention in Australia* (Cambridge: Cambridge University Press).

Meek, L. (2002). 'On the road to mediocrity? Governance and management of Australian higher education in the market place', in A. Amaral, G. Jones and B. Karseth (eds), *Governing Higher Education: National Perspectives on Institutional Governance*, (Amsterdam: Kluwer), 253–78.

Ministry of Education (2003). *Review of New Zealand Tertiary Sector Governance.* (Wellington: Ministry of Education).

Moodie, G. (2002). 'Fish or fowl? Collegial processes in managerialist institutions', *Australian Universities Review*, 45, 2, 18–22.

Ministry of Science, Technology and Higher Education (2009). *Tertiary Education in Portugal. Background Report.* (Lisbon: MSTHE).

O'Carroll, J. P. (2008). 'Higher education policy: Banishing a vital power?' in M. P. Corcoran and P. Share (eds), *Belongings: Shaping Identity in Modern Ireland* (Dublin: IPA), 43–54.

O'Meara, B. and Petzall, S. (2005). 'Vice chancellors for the 21st century? A study of contemporary recruitment and selection practices in Australian universities', *Management and Research News*, 28, 6, 18–35.

O'Sullivan, D. (2005). *Cultural Politics and Irish Education since the 1950s: Policy, Paradigms and Power* (Dublin: IPA).

Özkanlı, Ö. (2007). 'The situation of academic women in Turkey', *TED Education and Science Journal*, 3, 144, 59–70.

Özkanlı, Ö. and White, W. (2008). 'Leadership and strategic choices: female professors in Australia and Turkey', *Journal of Higher Education Policy and Management*, 30, 1. 53–63.

Özkanli, Ö. and Korkmaz. K. (2000). 'Academic women in Turkey: The structure of attitudes towards role conflict', *The Global Awareness Society International Ninth Annual International Conference Proceedings* (New York: Bloomsburg University Publications), 314–22.

Queensland University of Technology (2008). *Selected Inter-Institutional Gender Equity Statistics.* (Brisbane: Queensland University of Technology).

Reed, M. (2002). 'New managerialism, professional power and organisational governance in UK universities: A review and assessment', in A. Amaral,

G. Jones and B. Karseth (eds), *Governing higher education: National perspectives on institutional governance* (Dordrecht: Kluwer Academic Publishers), 163–85.

Riordan, S. (2007). Career psychology factors as antecedents of career success of women academics in South Africa, unpublished PhD Thesis, University of Cape Town.

Rothblatt, S. (1996). Akademiska traditioner – Amerika och Europa [Academic traditions – America and Europe]. Speech at the History Days in Uppsala in 1995, in Om universitetet, gymnasieskolan och kvinnan [About the University, the Secondary School and Women]. Aktuellt om historia, 1996 (Stockholm: AB Grafisk Press), 2–3.

Ryan, M. and Haslam, A. (2004). Obstacles beyond the glass ceiling: the glass cliff and the precariousness of Women's Leadership Positions, presentation to ATN WEXDEV conference, Sydney.

Santiago, R. and Carvalho, T. (2004). 'Effects of managerialism on the perceptions of higher education in Portugal', *Higher Education Policy*, 17, 4, 427–44.

Santiago, R., Carvalho, T., Amaral, A. and Meek, L. (2006). 'Changing patterns in the middle management of higher education: The case of Portugal', *Higher Education*, 52, 215–50.

Saunderson, W. (2002). 'Women, academia and identity: Constructions of equal opportunities in the "new managerialism" – A case of lipstick on the gorilla?' *Higher Education Quarterly*, 56, 4, 376–406.

Scott, P. (2000). 'Globalisation and higher education: Challenges for the 21st Century', *Journal of Studies in International Education*, 4, 3–10.

Skillbeck, M. (2001). *The University Challenged: A Review of International Trends and Issues with Particular Reference to Ireland* (Dublin: The Higher Education Authority).

South African Government Gazette (2008). Notice 441, *Government Gazette* No. 30967, 28 March.

South African Higher Education (2006). 'South African Universities Vice-Chancellors Association'. From http://web.archive.org/web/20050301015907/http:/www.sauvca.org.za/highered/, accessed 13 September 2006.

South African Council on Higher Education (SA CHE) (2009). *The Response of the Council on Higher Education to the Report of the Ministerial Committee on Transformation and Social Cohesion and the Elimination of Discrimination in Public Higher Education Institutions*, from http://www.che.ac.za/documents/d000202/CHE_response_to_Ministerial_Committee_Report_Dec2009.pdf, accessed July 2010.

South African Department of Education (2008). *Report of the Ministerial Committee on Transformation and Social Cohesion and the Elimination of Discrimination in Public Higher Education Institutions*, from www.pmg.org.za/files/docs/090514racismreport.pdf, accessed 5 July 2010.

SOU (1983). *Om hälften vore kvinnor [If One Half were Women]* (Stockholm: Regeringskansliet/ Fritzes).

SOU (2007). *Kön, makt och statistik [Gender, Power and Statistics]* Betänkande av utredningen "Kvinnor och män på maktpositioner i det svenska samhället" (Stockholm: Regeringskansliet/Fritzes).

Sundqvist, B. (2010). *Svenska universitet – lärdomsborgar eller politiska instrument? [Swedish Universities – Fortresses of Learning or Political Tools?]* (Hedemora: Gidlunds förlag).

Thornton, M. (2008). 'Where are the women? The swing from EEO to diversity in the academy', Working Paper No.22 (Canberra: Australian National University).

Thurén, B. (2000). On force, scope, hierarchy: Concepts and questions for a cross-cultural theorization of gender. Paper presented at the European Feminist Conference in Bologna (Short version published in Swedish as '*Om styrka, räckvidd och hierarki samt andra genusteoretiska begrepp*', in *Kvinnovetenskaplig tidskrift* (1996), 3–4.

Törnqvist, M. (2006). *Könspolitik på gränsen: debatterna om Varannan damernas och Tham-professurerna*. [*The Borders of Gender Politics: Swedish Debates on Gender Quotas in Politics and Positive Action in the Academy*]. (Diss. Lund: Arkiv förlag).

Universities Australia (2010). *Universities Australia Strategy for Women: 2011–2014*. (Canberra: Universities Australia).

Winter, R., Taylor, T. and Sarros, J. (2000). 'Trouble at mill: quality of academic worklife issues within a comprehensive Australian university', *Studies in Higher Education*, 25, 3, 299–4.

www.deewr.gov.au, accessed 11 July 2010.

http://www.yok.gov.tr, accessed 23 June 2010.

www.sulf.se/universitetslararen, accessed 7 August 2010.

www.regeringskansliet.se/utbildningsdepartementet, accessed 15 August 2010.

www.ec.europa.eu/research/science-society/document_library/pdf_06/she_figures_2009_en.pdf, accessed 30 July 2010.

www.universitiesUK.ac.uk accessed 15 August 2010.

3
Research Design

Jenny Neale and Özlem Özkanlı

3.1 Introduction

The research reported here is the first multi-country study to examine the dynamics of men and women working together in higher education senior management teams. It provides a comparative analysis of gender, power and university management across eight countries: Australia (AUS), Ireland (IRE), New Zealand (NZ), Portugal (PT), South Africa (SA), Sweden (SWE), Turkey (TR), and the United Kingdom (UK).

This chapter outlines the research design and critically explores and analyses the approach taken. The three phases of the research were:

- quantitatively analysing the representation of women in HE senior management in each country;
- undertaking qualitative research with senior managers, including current and former Rectors/Vice-Chancellors/Presidents, that focussed on getting into and getting on in senior management, doing senior management, and perceptions of broader management culture; and
- development of interventions for women who are interested in applying for senior management positions.

In the first stage of the research, investigators in each country analysed the representation of women in senior management, using publicly available data from university websites and government sources such as Ministries and Departments of Education. Trends in the representation of women in university management were then analysed. This confirmed that the continuing under-representation of women in the professoriate, which acts as the recruitment pool for senior management (as discussed in Chapter 2), meant that universities could argue there are insufficient eligible women available to undertake such positions. Further, those in physical sciences, engineering and technology (SET) are more likely to reach the top because of the focus on international collaboration, the predominant tradition of working in research teams with assistants to carry out the day-to-day research, and the large sums of research money they are able to attract. Therefore, discipline area becomes important, and the majority of senior management in most of the countries under study came from a SET background (Machado, Özkanlı and White 2007).

Having established the broader context for this study in relation to senior management, in the second stage of the research the aim was to explore the career experiences of women and men in senior management positions. A qualitative approach was deemed appropriate to capture this information. In qualitative research, the challenge is to assess the fit between the purpose and method (Maxwell 2005; Richards & Morse 2007; Patton 2002; Abrahamson 1983; Berg 2001), and in this case the research questions could only be answered by qualitative data. The chosen method was individual semi-structured interviews. 'Qualitative interviewing begins with the assumption that the perspective of others is meaningful, knowable, and able to be made explicit' (Patton 2002, p. 341).

3.2 Interviewing senior managers

There is a general tendency for researchers to study down rather than up but, particularly in the current study, this was not such an issue, as senior managers, as an elite group, were considered likely to share with the researchers the academic value ascribed to research (Lee 1993). Senior managers in universities can be considered an elite group in that they have established barriers that set them apart from rest of society (Hertz & Imber 1993). Access to elite groups for the purposes of research is often considered to be difficult, though difficulties may be exaggerated. Access can sometimes be easier for those who already have links with prospective participants (Duke 2002; Ostrander 1993). While two of the researchers were members of senior management at their universities, the other researchers were not part of this elite group. However, most had links that enabled them to access the appropriate people to interview. Half of the researchers interviewed at least one senior manager from their own university.

Hertz and Imber (1993) point out that elites have an expectation that interviewers will have done their 'homework' and know something about the situation they are researching. As academics themselves, the Network researchers had a good knowledge of the sector they were researching, and the interviewees thus felt they could share meanings of concepts without the need for extra explanation. On the one hand, the researchers could be regarded as having 'insider' status because of this. Herod (1999) indicates that often being positioned as an 'insider' is considered preferable and a more authoritative place to be than that of an 'outsider'. Outsiders see things but only understand some things (Acker 2009 personal communication). In the present research insider-blindness was minimised because of the multi-country perspective and co-operation with team members across countries.

On the other hand, we were not all members of senior management and were thus 'outsiders' in this respect. As Naples (1996) points out, discussion of outside/insider locates the possible positions of the researcher as being polar opposites, which does not acknowledge the inherent fluidity of the position, which may change. All researchers start with different positions at different times and with different people, and this is important to bear in mind. When the researcher assumes the role of 'informed outsider' (Welch, Marsechan-Piekkari, and Tahvanainen 2002, p. 625), the research experience becomes a continual balancing act in reconciling the roles of 'insider' and 'outsider'. The distance between the interviewer and interviewee cannot be eliminated, but it can at times be turned to advantage, for example, when asking for clarification around answers.

Access, power, openness and feedback have all been identified as issues when interviewing elites. Respondents may take control of the interview (Ostrander 1993; Duke 2002; Welch, Marsechan-Piekkari, and Tahvanainen 2002), as they are accustomed to having others interested in and listening to what they have to say. Thus, the exchange between interviewer and interviewee has implications for reliability and validity. Further, Ostrander (1993) notes that there can be difficulty around 'exposing' the real concerns and viewpoints of the interviewees. There is a balance to be struck between being appreciative of subjects' willingness to participate and being deferential; and interviewers must avoid the assumption that interviewees will answer questions as fully and directly as they can.

3.3   Feminist research

As discussed in the introduction, this research adopts a feminist stand-point, which foregrounds women's experiences in university senior management. Stanley and Wise (1993) suggest that one of the tenets of feminist research is that the personal is political, and although women may not agree on analyses about oppression, they share the experience of its consequences. Thus, analysis of individual stories and experiences join to create patterns where the personal is political. A further development of feminist consciousness is that in which women see 'the same reality differently' (Stanley & Wise 1993, p. 64). Women come to appreciate diversity, difference and the contradictions inherent in everyday life. What distinguishes feminist research from other forms of research is the 'question we have asked, the way we locate ourselves within our questions and the purpose of our work' (Maynard & Purvis 1994, p. 14).

Several researchers have emphasised the importance of lived experience and the significance of everyday life and knowledge as women, as a basis for feminist research (for example, Stanley & Wise 1983, 1991; Weiler 1988; Mies 1983). To paraphrase Cummerton (1986), our research is undertaken from a feminist perspective where women's experiences, ideas and needs are valued in their own right, and where women are at the centre of the study providing a unique perspective from their own lived experience.

3.4 Women interviewers

Flores-Macias and Lawson (2008) suggest that the gender of the interviewer does need to be considered. They posit two competing explanations for the differences found when respondents are interviewed by same or opposite gender interviewers. Differences are either due to the effects of respondents wanting to please certain interviewers or alternatively the gender of the interviewer makes the questions more salient to considerations that respondents already hold.

All the Network researchers are women and, except for in the UK, Sweden and Australia, the majority of those being interviewed were men. In terms of the power differential between the interviewer and the interviewee, and the display of typical masculine traits, women interviewing men raises some of the same issues as does the interviewing of elites. Like elites, men often attempt to control the interview when being interviewed by women, thereby challenging the power of the interviewer (McKee & O'Brien 1983 in Lee 1997). Oakley (1981) and Finch (1984) discuss the opposite situation, which arises when women interview women, and stress the way the commonality of gender creates a rapport and a non-hierarchical situation; but they also caution that the perception of similarity may lead to a greater level of disclosure, with which interviewees may subsequently feel uncomfortable. However, in the current research, the difference in status between the women being interviewed and the women doing the interviewing was in most cases likely to be a mitigating factor.

Respondents may assume different shared experiences based on the gender of the interviewer, thus making the interview itself another gendered experience. As Williams and Heikes (1993) found with in-depth interviews, male interviewees took the gender of the interviewer into account by developing responses within a gendered context, endeavouring not to offend the interviewer.

Female interviewers elicit different considerations on gender-linked topics compared to male interviewers (Huddy et al. 1997). Of particular relevance to the current research is the contention that males answer differently to women interviewers on more commonly debated topics like work-place gender inequity. Kane and Macaulay (1993) found that both male and female interviewees express more egalitarian gender-related attitudes or are more critical of existing gender inequalities when responding to female interviewers. Further, men offer different responses to questions dealing with female employment inequality, while women's responses concentrate more on gender-related collective action, policy, and group interests. Kane and Macaulay (1993) suggest that this may be a reflection of the gender constraints that apply generally in female/male interactions. Thus, because the interviewers were all women, the responses elicited during the current research may be more of a critical appraisal than may have occurred if there were both female and male interviewers.

3.5   Interview schedule

The researchers constructed the interview schedule, taking into account themes that arose from the initial analysis from stage one, as well as those identified from relevant literature. The schedule included three sections: getting into and on in senior management; doing senior management, including the dynamics of men and women working in senior management teams, and gendered leadership styles; and a final section, which focussed on the structure and broader management culture in the Universities. This final section, included the typical career path into senior management, the typical appointment processes for Rector/VC/President, and influential bodies in these processes, and the gender profile of senior management. There were additional questions for Rectors/VCs/Presidents (see Appendix 2 for the interview schedule).

3.6   Ethics

The researchers from Australia, Ireland, New Zealand, and the UK applied for ethics approval through their respective universities. Detailed information on the process is provided on each of the university web sites (see the reference list at the end of this chapter for details of the relevant web sites). The South African researcher obtained verbal consent from each participant and, where requested, a summary was emailed to participants after the interview for their approval and before the information was included in the data set. Ethics approval is not required for research in Turkey, Sweden and Portugal. However, in these countries there is tacit agreement that the identity of interviewees will be kept confidential. In Turkey, an official letter from Ankara University was presented to each participant. An interview summary was emailed to each participant for comment before the data was finalised.

3.7   Sample selection

A sample of male and female senior managers, including current and former Rectors/Vice-Chancellors/Presidents was interviewed. 'Senior Management' was defined in this study as those academic managers at Dean level or above with university wide responsibilities, who were currently or who had been in senior management in the past five years.

The process for the appointment of senior managers differs in the participating countries. In Ireland, Presidents are appointed by a Selection Board in the majority of universities. The appointment is for a fixed term, and typically they do not return to academia at the end of their contract. Rectors in Portugal, Sweden and Turkey are elected for a fixed term and then often return to academia. VCs in Australia, New Zealand, South Africa and the UK are appointed by the University Council or Senate and are unlikely to return to academia at the end of their contract (the only exceptions are VCs who are appointed from smaller to larger universities).

The interview sample (see Table 3.1) in the study is purposive rather than representative. In selecting the sample, the researchers mostly started at the top and worked their way down. The majority of Rectors/Vice-Chancellors/Presidents are male, with women in support roles. The composition of the sample therefore reflects the reality of the situation in senior management. In some countries, all universities were covered and in others the sample was drawn from a selection of universities, reflecting the larger size of the sector. In New Zealand,

Table 3.1   Interviews by country and gender

Country	Female	Male	Total
Australia	14	7	21
Ireland	9	14	23
New Zealand	13	13	26
Portugal	9	14	23
South Africa	8	9	17
Sweden	7	2	9
Turkey	8	16	24
United Kingdom	18	–	18
Total	**86**	**75**	**161**

there are only eight public universities and the sample included senior managers from them all. In Australia, Ireland, Portugal, South Africa and the UK participants were selected only from the publicly funded universities. In Turkey and Sweden, the sample was selected from public and foundation (private) universities.

3.8   The interview process

The interviews in each country were conducted by the Network researcher(s) in that country over the two-year period 2008–10. It is acknowledged that significant changes in HE systems occurred in some countries (for example Portugal) either during or after data collection. Interviews varied in length from 30 minutes to two hours, with the majority of them being over an hour. Even though confidentiality was assured, on occasions where the interview was being recorded, participants requested the researcher to turn off the tape while sensitive information was being discussed. This information was not included in the interview summaries.

The Australian participants were identified from the Universities Australia list of senior managers in the 38 publicly funded universities, and were then contacted by email. Once they agreed to participate, the plain language statement, interview schedule and consent form were forwarded to their executive assistants. All interviewees were required to complete the consent form before the interview commenced. Australian interviews varied in length from 45 minutes to two hours. All but six of the Australian interviews were tape-recorded and took place face-to-face. The remaining six were by telephone due to the challenge of distance. The researcher took notes during telephone interviews with these six.

In Ireland, the participant interviewees were contacted initially by email, with follow up contact being made at the secretarial level. Because of their level, and to ensure an adequate response rate, all interviews were conducted by the Irish investigator, who signed the introductory letter formally as Dean. It was clear from several of the interviews that this enhanced the credibility of the exercise. Interviews varied in length from 40 minutes to 90 minutes, with the majority of them being over an hour. All of the interviews were face-to-face and tape-recorded, with detailed verbatim notes being made during the interview. Following the interviews, the tapes were replayed and any additional material was inserted in these verbatim notes.

In New Zealand, initial contact was by email, with a follow-up phone call. Because of the relatively small size of the university sector, identifying senior managers was straightforward, and only two of those approached to participate were unable to do so, both due to time constraints. A formal letter, consent form and interview schedule were sent to each of the participants once they had agreed to be interviewed. Twenty-four interviews took place in the office of the interviewee and the other two were by phone. Interviews generally lasted about one hour, varying between 30 and 90 minutes. Extensive notes were taken and subsequently the transcripts transferred to computer.

In Portugal, prospective participants were approached by the researchers after initial contact was made by a former Rector; and president of National Council of Portuguese Rectors (CRUP). All the interviews except one were tape-recorded.

In South Africa, all participants were initially approached by email. They were invited to participate in the study, provided with a copy of the interview schedule and assured of confidentiality. A total of 20 interviews, each over an hour in length, were conducted, of which 17 met the sample criteria of academic managers. All interviews were conducted face-to-face and tape-recorded and, when requested, summaries were posted to participants prior to data analysis.

In Sweden, all participants were initially approached by email and invited to participate in the study. They were informed about the study, its aim and questions and assured of confidentiality. A total of nine interviews were carried out, taking between 60 and 90 minutes. Eight interviews were conducted face-to-face and tape-recorded and there was one phone interview.

The majority of interviews in Turkey were face-to-face and ranged from 60 to 90 minutes in length. There was one phone interview during which the researcher took notes. All the other interviews were tape-recorded, with detailed verbatim notes being made during the interview. Following the interviews, the tapes were replayed and summaries were made.

In the UK, initial contact was made with participants through their secretaries, and 18 interviews were conducted, which lasted from one to two hours. Detailed notes were taken at the time of the interview, and read through directly afterwards to ensure accuracy. Eleven interviews were undertaken by telephone and seven were face-to-face. Interviewees were interviewed by telephone when they had stated that due to the demands of their job they could not take the time to arrange a formal interview.

Completed interviews in the eight countries were then summarised and analysed for dominant themes in relation to the career paths of senior managers, the power of VCs, the characteristics and qualities valued in senior managers, and the contribution of the VC to the organisation and, especially, to the gender balance of management teams. The higher proportion of men interviewed in some countries, like Ireland, Portugal, and Turkey is offset by other countries, such as Australia, Sweden and the UK, where women were the majority of those interviewed. Discussion of the differences in the sample between the eight countries is important and will be elaborated on later.

3.9 Data analysis

De-identified summaries of the completed interviews were circulated to and analysed by the whole research Network. The Portuguese, Swedish and Turkish interview summaries were translated by the respective researchers and provided to the Network in English. In this research, we selected major themes emerging from the data for analysis (Miles & Huberman 1994). This approach increases the effectiveness and efficiency of such learning (Lewins & Silver 2006). The analysis initially focussed on the three key areas: getting into and on in senior management; doing senior management; and the structure of and broader management culture in universities. Further thematic analysis was undertaken in the light of themes emerging from the data in conjunction with those from the literature. One strong theme to emerge that was not the focus of the interview schedule was the tension between collegiality and new managerialism in universities and the impact it had on management style.

Each set of country interviews was numbered sequentially. The data reported identifies the country of the interviewee, their gender and the number of the interview; for example, AUS woman 13, and PT man 15. It was agreed among the researchers that the role of the interviewee

Table 3.2   Numbers interviewed by position

Position	Female	Male
Rector/Vice-Chancellor/President	14	38
Vice-Rector/Deputy Vice-Chancellor/Vice-President	24	23
Pro Vice-Chancellor	24	2
Dean	14	5
Other*	10	7
Total	**86**	**75**

* Former Vice-Rectors, assistant VC, Deputy PVC, Acting PVCs, Bursar.

would not be reported – for example Rector/VC, Vice-Rector/PVC – to ensure anonymity, particularly in those countries where there were a small number of universities and few women in management roles (see Table 3.2 for summary statistics on the roles of the participants).

While each chapter in the book takes a thematic approach and includes data from each of the eight participating countries, it is important to remember that the interviews were carried out by the investigator in each country, who then summarised them. The advantage of this approach is that each interviewer has a broad understanding of the HE system and major policy debates in their particular country and of legislative change that impacts on the operations of the university sector. Thus, when the chapters were in draft form, errors of interpretation could be addressed.

This study, as a collaborative piece of research, has the methodological advantage of exploring in some depth a topic on which it is difficult to obtain robust statistics, but one that is of common interest to all the countries involved. The use of an agreed interview schedule and sampling procedure enables comparisons to be made across the participating countries as like is compared to like. The diversity of backgrounds of the researchers provided further rigour, especially at the data analysis stage, as they were able to draw on both common and disparate sources of earlier research aligned to their disciplinary background. The uniting factor was the belief in gender equity and the importance of 'voice'.

References

Abrahamson, M. (1983). *Social Research Methods* (New Jersey: Prentice Hall).
Berg, B. L. (2001). *Qualitative Research Methods for the Social Sciences* (London: Ally Bacon).

Collet, B. A. (2008). 'Confronting the insider-outsider polemic in conducting research with diasporic communities: towards a community-based approach', *Refuge* 25, 1, 77–83.

Cummerton, J. (1986). 'A feminist perspective on research: what does it help us see?', in N. Van Der Bergh and L. B. Cooper (eds), *Feminist Visions for Social Work* (USA: National Association of Social Workers Inc), 80–100.

Deem, R., Hilliard, S. and Reed, M. (2008). *Knowledge, Higher Education and the New Managerialism* (Oxford: Oxford University Press).

Duke, K. (2002). 'Getting beyond the "Official Line": Reflections on dilemmas of access, knowledge and power in researching policy networks', *Journal of Social Policy*, 31, 1, 39–50.

Ethics web pages

Monash University, Australia: http://www.monash.edu.au/
Loughborough University,
UK: http://www.lboro.ac.uk/admin/committees/ethical/index.html
Victoria University of Wellington, New Zealand:
vuw.ac.nz/Amphora!~~policy.vuw.ac.nz~POLICY~000000000744.pdf
University of Limerick, Ireland:
http://www.artsoc.ul.ie/Userfiles/fahssrecguidelines.pdf?PHPSESSID=4dbd97e
de416204a40c0fa2c8d302390 and www.ul.ie/researchethics

Finch, J. (1984). '"It's great to have someone to talk to": The ethics and politics of interviewing women', in C. Bell and H. Roberts (eds), *Social Researching: Politics, Problems, Practice* (London: RKP), 70–87.

Flores-Macias, F. and Lawson, C. (2008). 'Effects of interviewer gender on survey responses: findings from a household sample in Mexico', *International Journal of Public Opinion Research*, 20, 1, 100–10.

Herod, A. (1999). 'Reflections on interviewing foreign elites: praxis, positionality, validity, and the cult of the insider', *Geoforum*; 30, 4, 313–27.

Hertz, R. and Imber, J. (1993). 'Fieldwork in elite settings: Introduction', *Journal of Contemporary Ethnography*, 7, 22, 3–6.

Huddy, L., Billig, J., Bracciodieta, J., Hoeffler, I., Moynihan, P. and Pugliani, P. (1997). 'The effect of interviewer gender on the survey response', *Political Behaviour*, 19, 3, 197–220.

Kane, E. W. and Macaulay, L. J. (1993). 'Interviewer gender and gender attitudes', *American Association for Public Opinion Research*, 57, 1–28.

Lee, D. (1997). 'Interviewing men: vulnerabilities and dilemmas', *Women's Studies International Forum*, 20, 4, 553–564.

Lee, M. L. (1993). *Doing Research on Sensitive Topic* (London: Sage Publications).

Lewins, A. and Silver, C. (2006). *Using Software in Qualitative Research, a Step-by-Step Guide* (Thousand Oaks: Sage Publications).

Machado, M., Özkanlı, Ö. and White, K. (2007). Tracking the barriers to women achieving seniority in Universities, paper presented to EAIR Forum, Innsbruck.

Maxwell, A. (2005). *Qualitative Research Design* (Thousand Oaks: Sage Publications).

Maynard, M. and Purvis, J. (eds) (1994). *Researching Women's Lives from a Feminist Perspective* (London: Taylor and Francis).

Mies, M. (1991). 'Women's research or feminist research? The debate surrounding feminist science and methodology', in M. M. Fonow and J. A. Cook (eds). *Beyond Methodology* (Bloomington: Indiana University), 60–84.

Mies, M. (1983). 'Towards a methodology for feminist research', in G. Bowles and R. Duelli Klein (eds), *Theories of Women's Studies* (London: Routledge & Kegan Paul), 117–39.

Miles, M. and Huberman, A. (1994). *Qualitative Data Analysis: An Expanded Source Book* (London: Sage Publications).

Naples, N. (1996). 'A feminist revisiting of the Insider/Outsider debate: the "Outsider Phenomenon" in rural Iowa', *Qualitative Sociology*, 19, 1, 83–106.

Oakley, A. (1981). 'Interviewing women: A contradiction in terms', in H. Roberts (ed.), *Doing Feminist Research* (London: Routledge), 30–61.

Ostrander, S. (1993). '"Surely you're not in this just to be helpful": access, rapport and interviews in three studies of elites', *Journal of Contemporary Ethnography*, 22, 7, 7–27.

Patton, M. (2002). *Qualitative Evaluation and Research Methods* (Thousand Oaks: Sage Publications).

Richards, L. and Morse, J. (2007). *Read Me First for a User Guide for Qualitative Research Design* (Thousand Oaks: Sage Publications).

Stanley, L. and Wise, S. (1983). '"Back into the personal" or: our attempt to construct "feminist research"', in G. Bowles and R. Duelli Klein (eds), *Theories of Women's Studies* (London: Routledge and Kegan Paul), 192–209.

Stanley, L. and Wise, S. (1991). 'Feminist research, feminist consciousness and experiences of sexism', in M. M. Fonow and J. A. Cook (eds), *Beyond Methodology* (Bloomington: Indiana University Press).

Stanley, L. and Wise, S. (1993). *Breaking Out Again: Feminist Ontology and Epistemology* (London: Routledge).

Weiler, K. (1988). *Women Teaching for Change: Gender, Class and Power* (New York: Bergin & Garvey Publishers).

Welch, C., Marsechan-Piekkari, P. H. and Tahvanainen, M. (2002). 'Corporate elites as informants in qualitative international research', *Institutional Business Review*, 11, 611–28.

Williams, C. L. and Heikes, E. J. (1993). 'The importance of researcher's gender in the in-depth interview', *Gender & Society*, 7, 2, 280–91.

4
Senior Management in Higher Education

Teresa Carvalho and Maria de Lourdes Machado

4.1 Introduction

Management has always been associated with men, and an implicit and universal correlation has been drawn between men, power and authority. Even the first scientific studies on management neglected the gender variable. Although women have been progressively entering the labour market and increasing their qualifications worldwide, as discussed in Chapter 2, they are still under-represented in organisational top positions.

Universities, which are supposed to be based on merit and universal principles, should be an exception to this trend. However, they reproduce the same horizontal and vertical segregation phenomena as the other social, political and economic institutions and organisations in society.

Nevertheless, universities have historical, cultural, symbolic and organisational specificities, particularly in relation to university governance and management models, which have undergone radical changes in the last decades. Universities are increasingly moving from collegial and democratic models of governance, rooted in the Humboldtian tradition (discussed below) to more business and industrial models, with a strong concentration of power at the top. Is it possible that the discourses concerning gender relations are also changing in this context? Do women's and men's discourses reveal the same reasons for gender segregation inside universities? Or is it possible that new dynamics emerge in this new context?

The purpose of this chapter is twofold. First, based on a phenomenological approach, it will provide an analysis of the discourses of women and men in senior management and analyse the key changes in university leadership roles. Second, it will confront these discourses with the dominant theoretical frameworks concerning women's position in academia to determine if there are any dominant perspectives across the countries.

4.2   The global context: Gender, management and higher education

The comparative study developed in this book includes countries with distinct characteristics at the macro level of higher education (HE) resulting from their distinct original influences (including Humboldtian, Newmanian and Napoleonic influences discussed in Chapter 2) (Clark 1983). In spite of these differences, it is possible to detect some similarities between them. All have institutionalised common beliefs and shared norms concerning the important role of HE in society. These similarities are associated with the explicit or implicit mission of universities of the disinterested pursuit of knowledge, the implementation of the interconnectedness between research and teaching, and the involvement in students' personal development. These social expectations were founded on the ideas of academic autonomy and freedom to create and diffuse knowledge and were mainly assured by state financial support (Barnett 2004; Clark & Newman 1997; Santiago & Carvalho 2010a).

In order to accomplish these aims, universities are organised in a particular way. One of the most notable features of this organisational setting is the responsibility given to professionals, to develop administrative and management tasks. To the traditional rules and norms of organisational bureaucracy, as defined by the Weberian ideal-type,[1] Weber added a dual academic and administrative organisational structure (Weber 1995). Mintzberg (1989) described this configuration (similar to that of hospitals) as a professional bureaucracy. Within the professional bureaucracy, two types of bureaucracy co-exist: one of a democratic nature, for the professionals (academics); the other of a mechanical nature (support staff).

Traditionally, institutional governing bodies were mainly constituted by academics who, based on principles of representative democracy, were in charge of all relevant decisions. This collegial way of decision-making led Cohen and March (1974) and Cohen, March and Olsen (1992) to characterise universities as 'organised, anarchies', meaning that generally they do not have consistent organisational objectives, and that decision making does not follow a global rational logic. Power is invested in diverse conflicting academic actors (groups), consensus is always problematic, and co-ordination is better explained as a sponta-neous phenomenon.

Another important feature of the traditional HE organisational model was that it was a loosely coupled system – meaning that different organisational parts wished to maintain their own individual identity and separation. As Weick (1976, p. 3) explained, 'coupled events are responsible, *but* each event also preserves its own identity and some evidence of its physical or logical separatedeness'.

Within this organisational environment, leadership was of particular importance to universities (Neave 1992; van Vught 1989). The major institutional figure should be someone who can align the interests not only of the different bureaucracies but also of the distinct identities co-existing inside the professionals' democratic field. In this context, the academic leader was elected by the academic community and was recognised as *primus inter pares* (first among equals). Even if the HE system and institutions were socially recognised as based on merito-cratic and neutral principles, to have a woman as the 'first', even among 'equals' was, and still is today, an exception worldwide.

Usually, achieving appointment to a senior university management position has been the culmination of an academic career. Traditionally, full professors (internally recruited) assumed a senior position after being submitted to an election or selection process involving the aca-demic community. After the election or selection, they assumed univer-sity posts for a set number of years and then relinquished them after their term of office.

Even if these tendencies were broadly similar across participating countries, job titles differ in some cases. The most senior individual leading a university is known as the Vice-Chancellor (VC), Rector (Rec) or President (Pres). He or she is supported by a senior management team that consists of a leader from each clearly defined unit or divi-sion in the university. Titles vary among countries but may include Pro-Vice-Chancellors (PVC), Deputy Vice-Chancellors (DVC), Provosts, Vice-Presidents (VP), Vice-Rectors (VR), Pro-Rectors (P-Rec) Associate Vice-Presidents, General Secretary, Registrar, Bursar, Deans, Associate or Assistant Deans, and Executive Directors (ED).

A core top management group usually includes up to ten individuals who consult regularly with a broader group of about 20–30 senior man-agers. A summary is provided in Table 4.1 of the usual composition of senior managers in different countries.

At present, the recruitment to senior positions is not similar across the countries under study. In Australia and the UK, VC positions are

Table 4.1 Senior management titles

Country	VC	DVC	PVC	Pres	VP	Rec	VR	PRec	GS	Reg	Bursar	Dean	ED
Australia	✓*	✓	✓									✓	✓
Ireland				✓	✓							✓	✓
New Zealand	✓	✓	✓									✓	✓
Portugal						✓	✓	✓				✓	
South Africa	✓	✓								✓		✓	✓
Sweden						✓	✓	✓				✓	
Turkey						✓	✓		✓			✓	✓
United Kingdom	✓	✓	✓								✓	✓	✓

*Australian VCs also generally have the title VC and President.

advertised nationally and internationally by the University Council. The Chancellor normally chairs the selection panel and has an active role in the recruitment of the new VC (O'Meara & Petzall 2007, p. 27). VCs are still largely drawn from academia rather than private industry, but the HE profile is changing towards them becoming the Chief Executive Officer (CEO) of a complex organisation in an increasingly competitive environment. Recruitment firms are widely used in the search for university senior managers. It has been argued that this practice does not assist women to be appointed to these positions (Bagilhole & White 2008).

In most but not all Irish Universities, the position of President (called Provost in one University) is advertised, with external search consultants used. Nevertheless, it is very common for an internal candidate to be appointed President. In most universities, the members of the highest decision-making body in the University are all appointed by the President.

In New Zealand, VC positions are advertised, usually using a commercial recruitment company. The advertising is done both nationally and internationally. The recruitment company tends to do the shortlisting along with representatives from the university governing body (called either the University Council or University Senate). There is some variation in whether the final process is a public or private one. In some universities, a committee does the final interviews and the candidates meet with various groups of staff as well as give a public seminar. In others, the process is confidential and there is no university-wide knowledge of who is on the shortlist and no public seminar.

Traditionally, in Portugal the Rector was elected from among the internal full professors, in a general assembly of the university, including all academic staff with a PhD and representatives of students and administrative staff. With the new Higher Education Act (Law 62/2007), Rectors are now elected by a general council composed of representatives of academics, students and external stakeholders. The position is advertised nationally and internationally. In most cases, the candidates present a seminar to the general council outlining their strategic vision for the university. The mandate is four years and a Rector can have two terms of office.

In accordance with the Turkish Higher Education Law (1981), Rectors in state universities in Turkey are appointed by the President of the Republic from candidates holding the academic title of professor, and selected by the teaching staff of the university. The term of office is four years, at the end of which a Rector may be re-appointed, following the same process, for a maximum of two terms of office. The Council of Higher Education proposes to the President of the Republic three candidates, whom it selects from among the six candidates receiving the highest number of votes in the aforementioned balloting process. In private universities, the selection of candidates and appointment of the Rector are carried out by the board of trustees. The Rector may select up to three of the university's salaried professors to act as Vice-Rectors. However, in universities responsible for centralised distance education, a Rector may select five Vice-Rectors, when deemed necessary.

In South Africa, recruitment firms are seldom used to appoint Vice-Chancellors. Rather, a typical process would require the university Council to constitute an internal selection committee, which would then initiate the process. All Vice-Chancellor positions are advertised nationally and internationally, with the Selection Committee preparing a shortlist. The shortlisted candidates are presented to the broader university community of staff and students by the Chair of Council (usually via a presentation from each candidate). The selection committee makes a final recommendation to the Senate, with a validation of the process coming from the Institutional forum. The Council finally approves the appointment, which is for a (renewable) period of five years.

In Sweden, as universities are state authorities, the government appoints the Rector. The proposals for Rector are sent to the government by the board of the university, which has 14 members (including the Rector). There are three representatives of the teaching staff (who are elected) and also three representatives of the students. The board members are appointed for three years. The Rector is employed through the decision of the government for six years at most, as recommended by the university board. His/her employment may be prolonged, but only twice, each time for a period of no more than three years. In proposing a Rector, the board shall as far as possible present both women and men candidates and account for how gender equality has been taken into consideration. The Pro-Rector is the Rector's deputy and is appointed by the university board for no more than six years. In order to be a legitimate candidate for Rector or Pro-Rector a person must meet the demands of employment as a professor or lecturer.

Due to processes of Europeanisation, globalisation and internationalisation all of these systems are being subjected to the same international pressures. Under the influence of managerialism, universities have been influenced by the notions of the market, competition, individual choice, responsibility and efficiency.

The influence of managerialism/NPM is experienced at macro and micro levels (Deem, Hillyard & Reed 2007). In the former, political strategies have been implemented to reorganise the systems, with the state steering HE from a distance. In the latter, changes are evident at the institutional level of university governance and management, but also in the institutional culture and behaviour of individual professionals (Slaughter & Leslie 1997; Musselin 2008; Bleiklie & Michelsen 2008; Carvalho & Santiago 2010b; Deem, Hillyard & Reed 2007).

Universities are increasingly adopting business and industrial management structures and decision-making processes (Middlehurst 2004). In this context, universities as communities of scholars (Deem, Hillyard & Reed 2007) or as 'academic communities' have been replaced by 'managed organisations' (Harley, Muller-Camen & Collin 2003). Internally, the loosely coupled systems are compelled to adapt to a vision of an integrated, unitary (Carvalho & Santiago 2010a) or complete organisation (Enders, De Boer & Leisyte 2008), meaning that they are compelled to act as a single body and not as loosely coupled systems.

Within this context, the traditional mission of universities is being reconfigured. Higher education is now seen as an economic resource, to be deployed to support the restructuring of the traditional industrial tissue, and to promote a new 'sustainable' social and economic development through the mentoring of the knowledge economy and society (Olsson & Peters 2005). Knowledge is increasingly based on applied research, especially in SET fields (Slaughter & Leslie 1997; Slaughter & Rhoades 2004), and learning is ever more reconfigured with instrumental and vocational purposes, in order to enhance the employability of students, who are seen as consumers. To accomplish these missions, more diversified sources of financial support are applied (Clark & Newman 1997; Santiago & Carvalho 2004).

This new HE framework puts pressure on the traditional bureau-professional model in the sense that it changes internal management structures, decision-making arrangements and leadership roles (Middlehurst 2004). The restructuring of the governance structure of universities results in strategic and political power being concentrated at the top and in the attempt to replace collegial structures with line-management from the top to the institutional 'shopfloor'.

In this context, rather than *primus inter pares*, Rectors/VCs/Presidents are increasingly signified as CEOs. Senior HE leadership and management positions are advertised and recruited externally, and tend to be appointed by a board of trustees. Top university positions may be on a permanent or fixed-term contract, and an important requirement is to be able to obtain financial support or raise funds from the external environment, including the corporate sector.

It appears that in this new leadership and management role women are, as is usual in business and industrial management, marginalised. According to Middlehurst (2004), further diversity in senior management roles remains a proposition for the future.

Looking at leadership in two ideal-types, schematically one can represent them in two inter-related axis. On the one hand a leader's roles can be defined along the continuum between the symbolic – as the representative of academia and the administrative executive. On the other hand, the orientation of their performance can also be situated somewhere along a continuum, between the concentration on internal and external organisational sets. Even if is true that senior managers were always interpreted as the external representatives of the institution, the nature of their role has been changing, and external orientation increasingly means that they must develop a role as fund raiser for the institution. Senior managers are increasingly expected to relate with the outside world in order to gain more financial resources for their institutions.

Data analysis from interviews in all countries was used to situate the dominant leader's role in each country. The analysis of interviewees' discourses revealed that there was a general tendency for senior managers to attempt to classify themselves and their roles in relation to either a collegial or a CEO ideal-type. The configuration of *primus inter pares* was mainly dominant in the Southern European countries – Portugal and Turkey – but vestiges of this model remained in some other countries as well. Universities are represented as specific and different from business and industrial institutions and requiring as a result, according to this discourse logic, a different model of management centred on traditional collegial decision-making:

> University academic staff are very clever and academic management is different than classical management. Consensus in the university is very important. Academic senior managers must create a consensus atmosphere.
>
> (TR man 8)

> I think this is a serious misconception that exists in Portugal because Rectors are not managers; Rectors govern universities, which is different. Managers are professionals who know about management and they seek to follow the general guidelines of the university's governance. I have always drawn Rectors attention, in the Rector's Council, to avoid this artifice.
>
> (PT man 14)

In this model, senior managers are expected to develop a role more oriented to the internal environment of universities. Interviewees assumed a position of internal representatives of the institution and of a 'builder of institutional consensus':

> It is great to be able to identify agendas, ways of achieving them and to enable and facilitate other's achievements.
>
> (UK woman 2)

Along with this position in the internal academic network, a sort of hybrid role emerged at times resulting from the influence of managerialism. Some discourses, while still emphasizing the collegial model and democratic decision-making, also introduced other values (such as efficiency), traditionally associated more with business and industrial management:

> I would have been just as happy continuing teaching and research but I had a holistic understanding of how the University works and firmly believe that academics should play a role in management and administration of the University as far as that is consistent with efficiency.
>
> (IRL man 8)

Others went even further in describing in a clear way the integration of the two leadership models, but keeping the academic trajectory as the main frame of reference to acquire power legitimacy:

> Managerialism versus collegiality is a false dichotomy. Universities need good managers who are collegial and seek consensus and commitment. In a university like ours it is hard to command credibility without an academic track record.
>
> (AUS man 21)

Yet other discourses clearly approached the CEO ideal-type, particularly when they emphasised efficiency and effectiveness as one of their main concerns and defined the main orientation of their action as external:

> The key contribution of the President is strategy and fund raising.
>
> (IRL man 3)

> The VC's key contributions are to be able to represent the university to the outside world, decisiveness, efficiency, effectiveness, strength.
>
> (UK woman 13)

> The university has a well articulated strategy driven by compact based funding. It is critical to establish its distinctiveness and serve labour force needs. As Australia is linked to global education, positioning is critical. VCs have a lot more of an external role, but if they neglect their internal one then there would be a problem.
>
> (AUS woman 18)

Some references were common to the two ideal-types, namely the role conflict resulting from the assumption of a dual academic and management career. However, one can expect this conflict to be stronger in the CEO model since it seems to emphasise more the managerial values:

> the move into senior management has brought what had always been two parallel careers into one single career.
>
> (NZ man 5)

Confirming this conflict were some discourses emphasising the difficulties of reconciling two different cultures, translated as looking for consensus between academic and managerial staff.

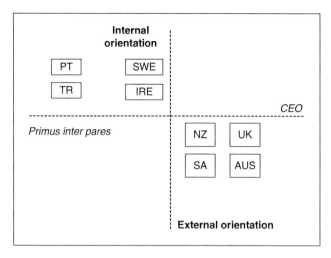

Figure 4.1 Country position according to leadership roles

> It's difficult sometimes to get staff to co-operate with the require-
> ments of those at the top.
>
> (UK woman 15)

While the discourses within each country were not homogeneous, with
senior managers assuming different (and sometimes even opposite positions), it was possible to identify a general tendency in the different
countries along the continuum of the ideal-types in leadership roles
discussed previously, as indicated in Figure 4.1.

Portugal and Turkey seemed to be countries where the described
roles of senior managers were closer to a collegial model of governance
and management in universities. They look at themselves as the representatives of academia and as 'builder[s] of internal consensus'. The
discourses of senior managers in Ireland were also more closely suited
to a collegial definition of their roles – as *primus inter pares*. And even
if some emphasised more the importance of the external role (as fund
raisers), the majority still highlighted the internal symbolic power
they have in the institutional landscape. In Sweden, senior managers
described their roles as mainly internal representatives of the academic
community, and they were internally recruited. The other countries –
UK, NZ, AUS and SA – were on the opposite side of the axis, indicating
a general tendency increasingly to define senior managers as CEOs.

From this analysis, it is possible to make the assumption that there is a tendency for leadership roles to be more in line with the CEO perspective in those countries based on the British model. This may be explained by the fact that UK was one of the first countries to implement managerial practices (Deem, Hillyard & Reed 2007). As a consequence, those systems historically more influenced by British HE are also those closer to these tendencies. Even if in the other European countries maintenance of a collegial model of the senior management role is more evident, the discourses also reveal some influences of the CEO perspective, supporting the hypothesis that it is rapidly spreading to other HE systems.

Finally, despite having different governance and management models inside universities, most described the typical senior manager as a man with a high academic reputation.

The following description of a VC in the UK was typical:

> Scientist or engineer. Male, well-known, good reputation, bags of experience.
>
> (UK woman 15)

4.3   Attempts to explain segregation in Higher Education

In order to conceptualise the different theoretical perspectives developed to explain the exclusion from, or limited entry to, the centres of masculine power, Le Feuvre (1999) identifies four interpretative frameworks: the patriarchy approach, 'feminitude' (femininity), 'virilitude' (surrogate maleness) and 'de-gendering' (gender erosion).

The patriarchy approach includes research on women entering men's dominant fields, asserting that 'the entry of women into male bastions reflects the almost unlimited capacity of masculine domination to reappear under new guises' (Le Feuvre 2003, p. 11). This category includes those who support the argument that either women gain access to a profession when it is no longer attractive to men (Reskin & Roos 1990), or that when women do gain entry, they are kept in the lower grades (Bourdieu 1998). In this context, 'both dimensions of the sex/gender system continue to operate unchanged and men maintain their monopoly over the macro-level economic and symbolic power structures' (Le Feuvre 2003, p. 12). With this perspective, the increasing presence of women in the labour market does not change anything in practice. There is a structural stability that is maintained under the illusion of change. This category can include those studies in

HE that emphasise the low representation of women in top positions (Bagilhole & White 2008; Husu 2001; O'Connor 2009; Özkanli & White 2008) and those revealing mechanisms that associate merit, promotion and recognition with masculine values (van den Brink 2007; Carvalho & Santiago 2008). The theoretical framework of this ideal-type is based in materialist feminism and neo-structuralist sociology (Bourdieu 1998; Delphy 1998, 2001).

The 'feminitude' perspective includes those who defend women's ability to get to jobs or particular positions because of their different attributes. In this perspective authors highlight the different dimension of the sex/gender system and argue that women take advantage of their 'different attributes' to affirm themselves in particular jobs or positions. The theoretical basis of this perspective is supported in French feminism (Irigaray & Whitford 1991) with insights from socio-psychology or psychoanalysis.

The 'Virilitude' ideal-type includes those who attribute the success of women in male bastions of power to their having been socialised in a masculine way (Bagilhole 2009). Sometimes these 'surrogate men' are not easily accepted by their subordinates due to their autocratic behaviour or lack of femininity. Several studies that have analysed women pioneers in male bastions of power in HE (Cacouault 1984; Crompton & Harris 1998; Bagilhole 2000) are also included in this category.

The 'De-gendering' perspective is based on a constructive framework (Butler 2004; Connell 2002; Lorber 2000; West & Zimmerman 1987) which interprets the entrance of women into the male domain as the consequence of changes in the macro-level gender contract. 'Late modernity offers the opportunity to transgress both dimensions of the sex/gender system by production of the social conditions for a progressive in-differentiation of male and female behaviour and the loss of legitimacy of all forms of biological essentialism and inequality' (Le Feuvre 2003, p. 13).

These ideal-typical models are particularly useful in analysing the experience of women in senior management in HE in a cross-national perspective. The interviews with senior managers refer interchangeably to all these four ideal-types. Nevertheless, the patriarchy approach is most frequently identified. References to the importance of patriarchy start with the dominant gender regime in society (Connell 1987). Interviewees refer to institutionalised broader gender relations in society to justify the scarcity of women at the top:

> In my opinion, this isn't only related with a sexist attitude. It has to do with the fact that women have a professional and family life

and they usually worry more with this than men do. I don't think there are internal barriers. If any, they aren't institutional, but rather social and cultural. I don't think this happens due to a lack of opportunities, but because people are focussed on several things, not only on their career. And I think that's good, it means that one can look at the career through different perspectives.

(PT Man 16)

In doing so, these interviewees are also assuming that universities are gender neutral. However, there are other discourses that highlight the patriarchal influence inside their universities. Several assert that gender differences in top positions are structural. In contrast to Kanter's (1977) perspective, interviewees argue that even when teams were mixed the leadership style and role continued to be masculine:

(...) when you change institutions you realise some things are different but some stay the same. Says something about the type of leader they are, independent of gender ... In the previous institution there was a strong feeling that even though there were senior women on the team they were not quite as important as the men. But the women were aware that we were treated a little differently.

(AUS woman 1)

At the same time, the traditional stereotypes in leadership styles between female and male leaders were still present, with women perceived as having a transformational leadership style and men associated with a transactional one:

Women have different management styles. They have effective communication skills. They are more soft.

(TR man 19)

Men put aggression out there and then move on.

(NZ woman 4)

Women create a warmer and more open space to work together whereas men tend to create cold spaces with little humanity.

(SA woman 16)

It could be expected that transformational leadership would be more associated with the collegial perspective – *primus inter pares* – and in this sense could create a more 'women friendly' environment. As one interviewee explained, 'Women are more co-operative and collegial' (UK woman 2).

Nevertheless, in a more consensual decision-making process, reflecting the collegial model, women identify difficulties related to the obstacles arising from negotiation processes that again emphasises the patriarchy approach. These include the influence of processes of the 'old boys' network':

Hard macho skills, powerful decision makers, but also wheelers and dealers, bringing in favours. You scratch my back and I'll scratch yours.

(UK woman 17)

It seems that the managerial environment creates some obstacles. A common theme in all the discourses was the specific nature of managerial work, referred to as demanding and time consuming. These descriptions were more consistent with the dominant notions of masculinity and were, in this sense, presented as an obstacle for women due to juggling with their other prevailing roles in the private domain. As a New Zealand respondent emphasised, it included a huge evening work load, and was 'not the kind of job you can turn off from' (NZ woman 1).

Others described how:

It has definitely affected my work life experience. It is very demanding on a day-to-day level. I am used to working all week and on Sundays. The issue in management is that you have much less flexibility in organising your time.

(AUS woman 3)

In this job ... you are supposed to represent the university, you have to be here and there, and it is evenings and it is weekends, so there is quite a lot that way.

(SWE woman 2)

Thus, even if this patriarchal perspective is dominant, other perspectives cannot be neglected. In fact, patriarchy cannot be interpreted in a single direction. Rather, emphasis on leadership stereotypes can also be interpreted as a way for women to use their stereotypes to affirm them, reflecting a feminitude (femininity) perspective.

In this perspective women are presented as central to top management teams because they have unique leadership traits:

> Having women in the senior management team does make a difference. In the context of a regional university, the life experience of senior women is different to that in metropolitan universities. There are positives then if we have their input in management. Connectivity women have with the sense of community is important. To have their depth and breadth is important and makes a difference.
>
> (AUS man 2)

> Women are seen as representing the 'softer' side but they acknowledge they need this.
>
> (UK woman 6)

These traditional stereotypes of leadership styles are actually used strategically by women to affirm themselves in a masculine environment, even if the majority argue against the existence of gender differences in academia. This contradiction demonstrates that most of these women are not gender conscious. They are actually 'doing gender' in their daily interrelations but do not recognise it:

> As we are now, men don't value us because we think we have to be like them. No, our value lies in our difference. And so, let's be women and not try to be men. In this way, we will achieve much more rather than using force, masculinity, leadership. No. We should be women in all aspects.
>
> (PT Woman 10)

Even the low number of women in senior management positions can be interpreted as an advantage, because being under-represented allows them to gather the support of other women in some instances:

> Most women in the Faculty are very supportive; I think they are pleased to see a woman in this position; very unusual. The Women Professor's group is a good sounding board for me.
>
> (UK woman 15)

But assuming traditional stereotypes in leadership styles demands extra effort. These women need to be simultaneously feminine enough to demonstrate their different traits and masculine enough to fit into the senior management culture (Wajcman 1998):

> [women] have to be careful not to mimic male style even if it appears to be successful for them as it will backfire, and be seen as inappropriate behaviour for women and labelling.
>
> (UK woman 2)

This may be one reason for the residual presence of the virilitude (surrogate maleness) perspective. Only in exceptional circumstances do women acknowledge their masculine style:

> Male colleagues think I'm a 'cold fish' I think. I'm very work oriented and not very feminine in the traditional sense of the word.
>
> (UK woman 17)

Therefore, gender symbolic transgression is not assumed by many interviewees, even if most acknowledge that they have been socialised in the role by men, who are often mentors.

> I did have a mentor in the university sector. This is key to everyone in management, you need to have people who would push you and position you ... He provided career support, role modelling, social support and even he continued to be a support when I took over from him as Head of School and even when I applied for the Vice-President's post.
>
> (IRE woman 5)

However, it is possible to identify some examples of the de-gendered approach in the discourses of these interviewees. Women and men were not presented as dual and opposite (with women being the Other), but as interchangeable actors both in the professional and domestic spheres. In the professional sphere, men could take up a traditional feminine leadership role. This was largely possible due to the institutionalised notion that management should be 'softer' and leadership should include emotional intelligence (Alimo-Metcalfe & Alban-Metcalfe 2005):

> A leading SA academic described me as having fire in my heart and ice in my head. I like that description of how I conducted myself in leadership roles. I am constantly open to the ideas of others and think about them critically. I am thinking all the time about what is appropriate for my institution at a point in time. It is critical to remain open to seeing things around you and being disappointed by

things that cannot be tolerated. I feel shame if things are wrong and even if angry I must intervene intellectually. I believe I lead with consensus and give people autonomy to resolve issues appropriately. This requires leadership when you do not assume you know everything.

(SA man 2)

In the domestic sphere, men were described as developing domestic tasks and similar work–family conflict to women:

I reached what I reached regardless of being woman or man. My family, and in this case my family is my husband, always did the same amount of housework. I can't say he does the same tasks because they aren't the same, but he always had the same level of intervention at home. And during those times I had more pressure, his involvement was greater than mine.

(PT Woman 1)

We therefore identified changes in the way leadership roles are developing in universities in all the different countries. However, it is not clear how this affects gender relation dynamics. Using the dominant interpretative framework for women in the academy developed by Le Feuvre (1999) it is possible to identify that the traditional stereotypes still dominate in leadership roles and behaviour. However, this does not translate into 'feminine subordination'. Instead, traditional stereotypes are also used as a strategy to make the 'feminine' more visible and unsubordinated. There are also changes in the dominant gender notions with women and men demonstrating more interchangeable roles at work and at home.

4.4 Conclusion

It can be concluded that there are no homogeneous or linear realities when one refers to the identity of senior managers or reflects upon the experiences of women and men in these positions. Using a postmodern approach, one can say that these conclusions were expected since reality as we comprehend it is fragmented, paradoxical and inconsistent (Bauman 1995).

In analysing recent changes in senior management roles, it was possible to identify an increasing tendency for leadership to reflect a CEO perspective and to become simultaneously more oriented to the university's external environment. However, the way this may impact on gender relations inside academia is far from clear.

Using Le Feuvre's (1999) typology one can say that, in making sense of their managerial experiences, the senior managers interviewed in all countries did not make use of any single theoretical gender perspective. Experiences are, in this sense, constructed – based on the paradoxical nature of gender notions. On the one hand, traditional stereotypes were reinforced with a variety of consequences for women. In fact, if stereotypes revealed the persistence of patriarchal cultures constraining women's progress, they were also presented as an opportunity to enhance women's positions. On the other hand, in making sense of their working experience, women and men revealed the institutionalisation of new gender relations, presenting men and women as interchangeable, which was not consistent with the persistent under-representation of women in top positions. In this sense, senior managers' discourses reveal the coexistence of a myriad of complex reasons that constrain women's progress in universities, exposed in the dialectic confrontation between traditional and new visions of gender relations in HE.

Note

1. To Max Weber (1995) bureaucracy was the most rational and efficient form of organisation. The main characteristics were a hierarchical division of labour based on explicit and formal rules impersonally applied by full-time professionals who depended on the income from their job.

References

Alimo-Metcalfe, B. and Alban-Metcalfe, J. (2005). 'Leadership. Time for a new direction?', *Leadership*, 1, 1, 57–71.

Bagilhole, B. (2000). 'Too little too late? An assessment of national initiatives for women academics in the British university system', *Higher Education in Europe*, 23, 2, 139–45.

Bagilhole, B. (2009). *Understanding Equal Opportunities and Diversity: The Social Differentiations and Intersections of Inequality*. (Bristol: The Policy Press).

Bagilhole, B. and White, K. (2008). 'Towards a gendered skills analysis of senior management positions in UK and Australian Universities', *Tertiary Education and Management*, 14, 1, 1–12.

Barnett, R. (2004). 'The purposes of higher education and the changing face of academia', *London Review of Education*, 2, 1, 61–77.

Bauman, Z. (1995). *Life in Fragments. Essays on Postmodern Morality* (Oxford: Blackwell).

Bleiklie, I. and Michelsen, S. (2008). 'The university as enterprise and academic co-determination', in A. Amaral, I. Bleiklie and C. Musselin (eds), *From Governance to Identity, a Festschrift for Mary Henkel* (London: Springer), 57–80.

Bourdieu, P. (1998). *La Domination Masculine* (Paris: Seuil).

Butler, J. (2004). *Undoing Gender* (New York: Routledge).

Cacouault, M. (1984). 'Diplôme et celibate. *Les femmes professeurs de lucée entre les deux guerres'*, [Degree and celibate. Women professors in colleges between the two world wars] in A. Farge and C. Klapisch-Zuber (eds), *Madame ou mademoiselle. Itinéraires de la solitude feminine XVIIIéme siècle* [Miss and Mrs. Itineraries of Female Loneliness in the 18th century] (Paris: Editions Montalba), 177–203.

Carvalho, T. and Santiago, R. (2010a). 'New public management and "middle-management': How do deans influence institutional policies?' In L. Meek, L. Goedegebuure, R. Santiago and T. Carvalho (eds) *The Changing Dynamics of Higher Education Middle Management*, 1st edn, Higher Education Dynamics, (Dordrecht: Springer), 165–96.

Carvalho, T. and Santiago, R. (2010b). 'Still academics after all', *Higher Education Policy*, 23, 397–411.

Carvalho, T. and Santiago, R. (2008). 'Gender differences on research: Perceptions and use of academic time', *Tertiary Education and Management*, 14, 4, 317–30.

Clark, B. (1983). *The Higher Education System. Academic Organization in Cross-National Perspective* (London: University of California Press).

Clarke, J. and Newman, J. (1997). *The Managerial State.* (London: Sage).

Cohen, M., March, J. and Olsen, J. (1992). 'A garbage can model of organizational choice', *Administrative Science Quarterly*, 17, 1, 1–25.

Cohen, M. and March, J. (1974). *Leadership and Ambiguity, the American College President* (New York: McGraw-Hill).

Connell, R. W. (2002). *Gender* (Cambridge: Polity Press).

Connell, R. W. (1987). *Gender & Power: Society, the Person and Sexual Politics* (London: Polity Press).

Crompton, R. and Harris, F. (1998). 'Gender relations and employment: The impact of occupation', *Work, Employment & Society*, 12, 2, 297–315.

Delphy, C. (2001). *L'énnemi principal: penser le genre* (Paris: Syllepse).

Delphy, C. (1998). *L'ennemi principal: èconomie politique du patriarcat* (Paris: Syllepse).

Deem, R., Hillyard, S. and Reed, M. (2007). *Knowledge, Higher Education, and the New Managerialism. The Changing Management of UK Universities* (Oxford: Oxford University Press).

Enders, J., de Boer, H. and Leisyte, L. (2008). 'On striking the right notes: Shifts in governance and organisational transformations of universities', in A. Amaral, I. Bleiklie and C. Musselin (eds), *From Governance to Identity. A Festschrift for Mary Henkel* (London: Springer), 113–30.

Harley, S., Muller-Camen, M. and Collin, A. (2003). 'From academic communities to managed organisations: The implications for academic careers in UK and German universities', *Journal of Vocational Behaviour*, 64, 2, 329–45.

Husu, L. (2001). 'On metaphors on the position of women in academia and science', *NORA – Nordic Journal of Feminist and Gender Research*, 9, 3, 172–81.

Irigaray, L. and Whitford, M. (1991). *The Irigaray reader* (Oxford: Blackwell).

Kanter, R. (1977). *Men and Women of the Corporation* (New York: Basic Books).

Le Feuvre, N. (2009). 'Exploring women's academic careers in cross-national perspective. Lessons for equal opportunity policies', *Equal Opportunities International*, 28, 1, 9–23.

Le Feuvre, N. (1999). 'Gender occupational feminisation and flexibility', in R. Crompton (ed.), *Restructuring Gender Relations and Employment. The Decline of Male Breadwinner* (Oxford: Oxford University Press), 150–78.

Lorber, J. (2000). 'Using gender to undo gender', *Feminist Theory*, 1, 1, 79–95.

Middlehurst, R. (2004). 'Changing internal governance: A discussion of leadership roles and management structures in UK universities', *Higher Education Quarterly*, 58, 4, 258–79.

Mintzberg, H. (1989). *Mintzberg on Management: Inside Our Strange World of Organizations*. (New York: Free Press).

Musselin, C. (2008). 'Towards a sociology of academic work', in A. Amaral, I. Bleiklie and C. Musselin (eds), *From Governance to Identity, a Festschrift for Mary Henkel* (London: Springer), 47–56.

Neave, G. (1992). Managing higher education international cooperation, *Referent Document, UNESCO* (unpublished).

O'Connor, P. (2009). Are universities really male dominated? Limits and possibilities for change, paper presented at International Women's Day Conference at the University of Limerick, 3 March 2009.

Olsson, M. and Peters, M. A. (2005). 'Neoliberalism, higher education and the knowledge economy: from the free market to knowledge capitalism', *Journal of Educational Policy*, 20, 3, 313–45.

O'Meara, M. and Petzall, S. (2007). 'How important is the role of the chancellor in the appointment of Australian vice-chancellors and university governance?', *International Journal of Educational Management*, 21, 3, 213–31.

Özkanli, Ö. and White, K. (2008). 'Leadership and strategic choices: Female professors in Australia and Turkey', *Journal of Higher Education Policy and Management*, 30, 1, 53–63.

Reskin, B. and Roos, P. (1990). *Job Queues, Gender Queues. Explaining Women's In-Roads into Male Occupations* (Philadelphia, PA: Temple University Press).

Santiago, R. and Carvalho, T. (2004). 'Effects of managerialism on the perceptions of higher education in Portugal', *Higher Education Policy*, 17, 4, 427–44.

Slaughter, S. and Leslie, L. (1997). *Academic Capitalism: Politics, Policies and the Entrepreneurial University* (Baltimore: John Hopkins Press).

Slaughter, S. and Rhoades, G. (2004). *Academic Capitalism and the New Economy: Markets, State and the New Economy* (Baltimore: Johns Hopkins University Press).

Van den Brink, M. (2007). In search for the best: Professorial recruitment and gatekeeping practices in Dutch academia, paper presented to the 5th Gender Equality in Higher Education Conference, Berlin.

Vught, F. van (ed.) (1989). *Governmental Strategies and Innovation in Higher Education*. (London: Jessica Kingsley).

Wajcman, J. (1998). *Managing Like a Man: Women and Men in Corporate Management*. (Cambridge: Polity Press and Blackwell Publishers).

Weick, K. (1976). 'Educational organizations as loosely coupled systems', *Administrative Science Quarterly*, 21, 1, 1–19.

Weber, M. (1995). *Économie et Société/1. Les catégories de la sociologie* [Economy and Society: Categories from sociology] (Paris: Plon/Pocket).

West, C. and Zimmerman, D. (1987). 'Doing Gender', *Gender & Society*, 1, 2, 125–51.

5
Paths to Success in Senior Management

Sarah Riordan

5.1 Introduction

This chapter will investigate the career trajectories of women and men who have risen to lead and manage universities in Europe, Africa and Oceania. It will address questions such as: What was their career path? Did they plan to become university leaders when they started their careers? Who helped them succeed? What are the benefits and challenges of senior university management? The chapter includes data from the eight participating countries in the WHEM research project, focussing on how one becomes a senior manager and exploring typical career paths into senior management. As a starting point, career stages are discussed, because the participants in this study represent a particular cohort of individuals whose careers are located within classic career stage theory. Then the career paths of participants are described with a view to establishing if a 'typical career path' existed. This is followed by an examination of the factors or people that were most supportive in achieving seniority in the sector and how being in senior management affected work/life experience. Finally, the competencies considered essential for individuals aspiring to senior management roles are discussed.

5.2 Career stage development

Career theorists typically examine stages in career development as they connect to life stages, recognising that career development is an element of a complex set of life spheres. Thus, traditional linear models of career development have been linked to chronological age (Schreuder & Theron 1997). By linking career stages with life stages, an implicit assumption is made that careers do not develop in isolation. Rather they are a function of the context in which the individual is located. These contexts may involve changes in respect of biological, psychological, social, spiritual, economic, cultural and historical factors (Schreuder & Theron 1997). Traditional career theory divides the lifespan into distinct phases where career challenges are firmly located within a set of life challenges and tasks that require resolution.

5.2.1   Early career stage

As far back as 1978, Schein postulated that a young adult is expected to adjust to multiple new roles relating to work, family and community life, often simultaneously. He suggested that psychological well-being is informed by individual coping responses to multi-role adjustment (Schein 1978).

The early career period consists of a number of new career tasks to be confronted by the individual. These include dealing with reality shock, adjusting to work routines, becoming effective quickly, achieving acceptance at work, accepting responsibility, developing special skills, balancing individual needs with organisational demands and deciding whether or not to stay in the organisation (Feldman 1976; Schein 1978; Wanous 1980). More recent research does not dispute these challenges. In fact Evans and Heinz (1995, p. 3) argue that 'the transitions of early adulthood and early careers are becoming increasingly disorderly and less predictable than in the past'.

In addition to adjusting to the demands of full-time employment, early-career woman usually try to balance family and career needs, leading to the 'superwoman' notion, which requires that they hold down full-time employment outside of the home and work inside the home with minimal assistance from their spouse or partner (Gordon & Whelan-Berry 2004; Hyman & Summers 2004; Newell 1996; Rana et al. 1998). In their study of early-, mid- and late-career individuals, Gordon and Whelan-Berry (2004) define early-career women as those under the age of 35 years. They note that the key responsibilities for women in this period include establishing their career goals and reputation, developing structures for childcare and managing their households, and establishing a life structure to facilitate the resolution of life and career issues. They also argue that the current generation of early career women are more likely to earn comparable salaries to those of their partners/ husbands than earlier generations of women in this career period. This is relevant to the current study, where the participants passed the early career stage many years ago. It suggests that the career paths of the men and women in the current study may have had very different, and gendered, early-career experiences, by virtue of the prevailing social norms when they were starting out in the sector.

It is clear from the literature that the primary career challenges of the early-career period involve establishing a career and then providing evidence of achievement or success. Individuals who display talent in the early-career period, called 'potentials' (Dolezalek 2007), are difficult to identify and the perception of them differs between organisations. However, across industries three types of drivers (individual and organisational) lead to the advancement of this group of employees. These include individual ability to leverage relationships, genuine commitment from the organisation to staff advancement, and access for individuals to structured job challenges (Dolezalek 2007).

5.2.2   From early- to mid-career

The timing of the transition from early adulthood to midlife is not exact. In the Western experience, middle adulthood is broadly accepted as encompassing the adult years from age 40 to 60 (Louw, van Ede & Louw 1998). However, caution should be exercised around the rigid use of these age limits, as individual experience requires the adoption of flexible boundaries. Exactly when midlife occurs depends largely on who is asked, when they are asked, and where and in which historical era they are asked. Obviously, the concept of midlife is inextricably linked to life expectancy.

During the twentieth century, life expectancy increased dramatically in western countries. In 1900 men and women were expected to live until about 50 years of age, yet by 1980, women were likely to live to age 78 and men to approximately age 70 (Hunter & Sundel 1989). In the twenty-first century a woman in America who reaches age 50 without cancer or heart disease, can expect to see her ninety-second birthday, and men will typically live to age 81 (Sheehy 1995). However, in third world countries the scenario is distinctly different. Officially life expectancy in South Africa was age 50 in 2003 and without HIV/AIDS interventions, this was predicted to decrease to age 41 by 2010 (South African Institute of Race Relations 2003). However, these average figures do not reflect the vast differences that exist across different socio-economic groups within the total South African population. These statistics suggest that the traditional label of midlife in some contexts may in fact be old age in others. Beyond the purely quantitative understanding of midlife, is the subjective view of when midlife is experienced.

According to Lachman and James (1997), younger adults report midlife commencing at 35 years of age, while older adults suggest it starts later, at 40 or even 50 years of age. They propose that this difference of opinion is grounded in varying time perspectives across adulthood with younger adults looking ahead, older adults turning their attention to the past and midlife containing a perspective that includes the past, the present and the future. Furthermore, Hunter and Sundel (1989) note that social class, physical health and cultural issues are likely to influence perceptions of the timing of midlife. Tamir (1989) found distinct differences in the perception of when midlife occurred between blue- and white-collar workers with the former reporting midlife commencing at age 40 and the latter much later.

Merriam (1999) emphasises the importance of time as an integrative factor when studying adult development. She believes that time has three connotations in this context, and she identified chronological age, historical time (period in history) and social time (a culturally dependent timetable that outlines appropriate behaviour in the life-cycle), as critical to understanding development. The concept of social time is illustrated by Sheehy's (1995) research. One of her most consistent findings, since her earlier research in the 1970s, is the dramatic disparity that people in midlife report between their chronological age and how old they feel. This suggests that 'appropriate midlife behaviour' in the 1970s is not necessarily applicable to current cohorts of midlife individuals.

Most theorists agree that midlife is a time for re-evaluation of life choices and an opportunity to make changes if necessary (Erikson 1963; Levinson 1978; Schein 1978; Sheehy 1976). As mentioned earlier, Levinson postulated that during early adulthood, individuals formulate 'the dream' and it is this that is re-evaluated during middle adulthood. However, according to Kittrell (1998) the critical difference between men and women is the nature of the dream and the timing of its formulation. Men typically conceptualise their dream in occupational terms and achieve this during their twenties. Women, even career women, have vague notions of a dream in their twenties that combines marriage, children and work with the first two receiving precedence. Long-term career goals among women appear to be formulated much later (Kittrell 1998). This finding has significant implications for the nature of re-evaluation that reportedly takes place during midlife.

The concept of reflection and reappraisal is regarded by Bejian and Salomone (1995) as an independent stage in career-development models, not a task within a specific stage. According to them, this stage of reflection occurs between the early- and mid-career stages. Furthermore, they suggest that this distinct stage has its own tasks, including self-appraisal, reorganising personal and career goals, and reorienting to present and future planning. They suggest that renewal may be a confluence of Erikson's (1963) 'life stage of generativity versus stagnation', Levinson's (1978) 'midlife transition', and Super's 'midlife transition period', as reported by Sharf (2002).

5.2.3   Mid-career stage

If, as traditional career theory suggests, career development is a linear process, then the mid-career stage would be a time of reappraisal of the past and an appraisal of long-term career plans: an assessment of real progress measured against ambitions (Shreuder & Theron 1997).

Erikson (1963) identifies the primary life task during middle adulthood to be resolution of the generativity versus stagnation crisis. Peck (1968) argues that midlife crises need to be articulated in order to highlight physical, psychological and social changes during adulthood that required successful adjustment. Schein (1978), Levinson (1978, 1986) and Gould (1978) all note a period of questioning that arises during midlife and results in a conscious process of re-evaluation by the individual.

Erikson (1963) argues that generativity manifests itself in caring for others and is a crucial midlife activity. However, Sheehy (1976) makes the point that midlife for women is not about shifting priority towards caring for others, as most women had been primarily caregivers up to this point. Rather, the midlife challenge for women is to extend their generativity beyond the family into community issues. As Gordon and Whelan-Berry (2004, p. 262) observe, 'women at midlife often seek new challenges at work and in personal interests'. This suggests that career-development theories developed by and for men may require revision when applied to women's experiences.

Theorists such as Shein (1978) identify specific work-related tasks to be completed during middle adulthood, one of which he actually labels 'the midlife crisis', making the questionable assumption that it applies to everyone. Super (1990 as cited in Sharf 2002) also lists developmental tasks for individuals during midlife. Those tasks in his maintenance phase (age 45–65) include finding strategies to hold onto current positions, updating knowledge and innovating within the profession. Williams and Savickas (1990) added three more tasks to Super's model that they consider are relevant to current work life realities: preparing for retirement, questioning future direction and goals, and continuing education, which they argued is as much a coping mechanism in a world of rapid technological change as it is a development task. Certainly, this last point is relevant in the context of the current study where, in a university, the ongoing pursuit of knowledge is a core job element.

In terms of career development, the generativity versus stagnation crisis could be aligned to the concept of career advancement. In traditional career theory, advancement is evaluated by the number and rate of upward moves in a career (Schreuder & Coetzee 2006). Individuals who have been promoted are regarded as successful (Kirchmeyer 2002; Nabi 1999; Turban & Doherty 1994).

Those who are not promoted are considered to have reached a career 'plateau' when there is no further opportunity for advancement (Leibowitz, Kaye & Farren 1990). Plateauing is identified as either structural or content in nature (Bardwick, 1986 as cited in Leibowitz, Kaye & Farren 1990). Structural plateauing results from blockage caused by organisational hierarchies or the classic pyramid shaped organisational structures where one manager oversees the efforts of a number of employees. Content plateauing occurs when the job itself offers little further challenge (Bardwick as cited in Leibowitz, Kaye, B. L. & Farren). Other researchers (Mathur-Helm 2006; Large & Saunders 1995; Ryan & Haslam 2006; Thomas, Bierema & Landau 2004) refer to the well-documented 'glass ceiling' when they discuss the careers of women that appear to have plateaued. Simpson (2000) specifically notes that the glass ceiling does not affect younger women as much it affects mid-career women because, according to her, the ceiling has moved up the organisational hierarchy in recent years. Morison, Erickson and Dychtwald (2006, p. 78) refer to 'middlescence' when describing mid-career individuals who are 'burned out, bottlenecked or bored'. They believe that current cohorts of individuals in this situation are worse off than their predecessors because of increased longevity, delayed (and multiple) marriages and two-career families that juggle the care-giving of children and parents with demanding jobs.

Nachbagauer and Riedl (2002) investigated the effect of career plateauing on performance, commitment and satisfaction of university staff. They found that

- structural plateauing is less important than task stagnation (job content plateauing);
- staff who are work-content plateaued work fewer hours than their colleagues;
- both structural and content plateauing causes task dissatisfaction; and
- content plateauing has a negative effect on affective commitment but a positive effect on continuance commitment.

This last finding is explained by the fact that, because of structural plateauing, university staff did not expect promotion. Instead, they sought interesting and varied jobs. Consequently, expectations of promotion were moderated by an assessment of opportunities, which appear to be few. This finding is interesting given the current study, as it suggests that career advancement to a senior position within the university sector is not necessarily viewed as the only indicator of success. This is discussed later in the chapter.

5.2.4 Late-career stage

As with earlier career stages the late stage is characterised by specific challenges. These range from accepting physical changes, to adjusting to changes concerning one's partner, to actually retiring or disengaging from an organisation. However, a number of positive adjustments in work perspective appear to occur for those in the late-career stage. These include the ability to integrate the efforts of others, adopting a broader perspective of the organisation, and being able to select and mentor the next generation. Differential disengagement is a conscious adjustment strategy employed by individuals who retire from only certain aspects of work and continue with others (Schreuder & Coetzee 2006).

In the present study, participants were not asked their age, nor were they asked to identify their career stage. However, it would be reasonable to state that all participants were at least in their mid-career stage with many in the latter stages of their careers. This is a function of internationally accepted promotion criteria that require many years to achieve. Furthermore, within the sample, historical, social, economic and cultural contexts informed the opportunity structures presented to individuals, thus shaping the individual career paths of participants. Achieving appointment to a senior university management position is often the culmination of a career that has evolved over years of accumulated experiences, but it is interesting to investigate whether a typical career pattern exists.

5.3 Career patterns and paths

According to Schreuder and Coetzee (2006), a career includes the significant learning and experiences that identify an individual's professional life, direction, competencies, and accomplishments through positions, jobs, roles and assignments. It is an accumulation of experiences and responsibilities as the individual navigates the corridors of academia. A career pattern is the shape and direction of an individual's career over time. According to Brousseau (1990), career patterns differ in terms of three dimensions: the stability of an individual's occupational field; the direction of movement in a career; and the duration of time spent in a particular field. He identifies four career patterns that account for most individual's experiences including:

- the *linear* career, characterised by upward mobility to positions of higher authority within a particular field;
- the *steady* state, characterised by minimal movement within a particular field, but the individual may become an *expert* within the field;
- the spiral pattern, characterised by major (often lateral) changes to different fields every five to ten years; and
- the transitory pattern characterised by frequent (often lateral) changes every two to four years into entirely different fields.

Central to this theory of career patterns are the underlying values that Brousseau (1990) identifies that motivate individuals to pursue one or other path. His research reveals that those with a linear pattern value power and achievement; those with a steady state (expert) pattern value expertise and security; those with a spiral pattern value personal growth, creativity and the opportunity to develop others; and those with a transitory pattern value variety and independence. Inherent in this theory is the notion that individuals consciously shape their career patterns according to their internal value systems and have a measure of control over their career choices.

More recent research, by Clarke (2009) in Australia, suggests that not all individuals are proactive in their career management. She too identifies four career patterns that explain individual experience. However, she describes career patterns as a combination of self-management (conscious planning), career mobility (stable or varied), career orientation (present or future) and self-perceived employability. Thus, individuals are described as:

- *Plodders* who have traditional careers with job security as long as they work hard and remain loyal to the company, engage in little/no career planning and have a short-term focus with respect to their skills development;
- *Pragmatists* who enjoy traditional careers within one organisation that offers security and stability as well as variety and professional development. Career decisions are made in the light of opportunities within the organisation, which allow for both horizontal and vertical career moves;

- *Visionaries* whose careers are carefully and deliberately planned, from an early stage, then executed with conscious career choices that build a long-term career trajectory. They are willing to change jobs within or across organisations and to physically relocate to take up a new and challenging career opportunity; and
- *Opportunists* who display a protean approach to their careers by frequently seeking and taking up 'opportunity' and 'change'. They pursue varied career paths within a range of jobs and organisations, seeing each move as a chance to learn new things and gain different experiences.

Lindholm (2004) interviewed academics to find out what attracted them to academic life, how their career interests developed and what paths their careers had taken. She found that for both men and women the fundamental attractions to academic life are the same. These include the need for autonomy, independence and individual expression and the perception that an academic environment would provide challenge, excitement and freedom. In a study conducted among academic women in South Africa, Riordan (2007) discovered that autonomy (defined as the desire to work independently and control the flow and content of work) is the only one of eight possible career anchors that positively correlate to career success (defined as achieving at least the rank of Associate Professor). It could be argued that the twin attractions of freedom and autonomy that appear to encourage, retain and accelerate the success of academics may well be the very elements undermined by managerialism, with its implied interference agenda, as discussed in Chapter 4.

In the present study, across all countries, a strong theme emerged that advancement to senior management positions was not planned initially. With only a few exceptions, men and women report arriving at the senior level 'accidentally' (AUS woman 14) or 'serendipitously' (SA man 3). As three explain 'it just happened' (IRE man 10), 'it sprang out of the blue' (UK woman 1) and, in Sweden 'No. No. I never have (planned it) – The start was that I was offered. I was offered different types of academic leadership' (SWE man 3). Time and again, participants in all countries state that their careers, at least initially, were 'not planned at all' (TR man 10). In terms of Clarke's (2009) classification, the participants could be described either as pragmatists or opportunists.

The pragmatists report taking opportunities as they present themselves within their institutions and their careers took on a linear pattern (Brousseau 1990), 'a series of opportunities led to me ending up as deputy head of school and then I was encouraged to apply externally.'

(UK woman 4); 'happened through a series of co-incidences and being in the right place at the right time' (NZ woman 2); 'I took advantage of these opportunities' (AUS man 2) and 'an unplanned opportunity presented itself' (IRE woman 2). In contrast, the opportunists pro-actively weave in and out of universities and external bodies, taking up new challenges that shape a spiral career pattern (Brousseau 1990):

> I started as a junior lecturer, moved universities, worked up to associate professor, then left that university to join (a national research body) then came back to another university as DVC, then left to assume a position as head of (another national HE body). I always got involved.
>
> (SA woman 14)

Others reported moving between universities and unions or governing bodies and, in South Africa, political parties, assuming new and challenging roles that interested them. 'I have always seen myself as an activist: a student activist, an academic activist, an advisory activist, now I am a VC activist' (SA man 2). As one reflected, 'I decided to take the non-academic career route, despite having a PhD, as that's where women have more opportunities in universities' (UK woman 17).

A second consistent finding was that participants from the UK, New Zealand, Australia, Portugal, Sweden and South Africa almost all reported that the traditional career path to senior management was that of an academic. When asked to describe a typical career path to senior management, the responses were consistent: 'Academic route through the hierarchy' (UK woman 10); 'very much through the hierarchical, incremental steps: course coordinator, HOD, HOS etc' (AUS man 5); 'you have to be a professor first' (SWE man 3); 'the academic path combined with getting experience by serving on committees across the university' (SA woman 1). Although typical, it was not always regarded as ideal:

> A person begins as a teacher and as a researcher later. It is a typical path in Portugal, there's no other. Whether I consider this typical course the best, well ... I've doubts about it. I don't think it's absolutely necessary to be a full professor to perform well the duties of a Rector, but this is undoubtedly a typical course.
>
> (PT woman 23)

In Turkey, despite the legal requirement that an individual has to achieve the rank of professor before they can be appointed as Dean, many participants claimed that a typical career path did not exist. Participants from Ireland were divided, with some reporting that the traditional linear academic route was not always followed, especially if individuals showed talent for roles, then they were 'plucked' out and advanced (IRE man 9).

A typical academic career path evolves from the position of junior lecturer, through lecturer and senior lecturer to reader or associate professor and finally, professor. Promotion is largely based on research output. A general model of academic work is offered by Poole and Bornholt (1998) who researched the career development of academics in eight countries – Australia, Germany, Hong Kong, Israel, Sweden, Mexico, Great Britain and the USA. They characterise an academic by three main activities (research, teaching and consulting) and by the rewards of the occupation (high income and involvement in policy-making). They acknowledge that within this model variations may exist among countries but, in general, men are more likely than women to assume the role of researcher, and consequently more likely to enjoy the rewards of high income and involvement in policy-making. Women are more likely to be involved in teaching and other student-related activities. Specifically, they note that 'the orientation to teaching or research by gender impacts directly on academic work in terms of income, hours spent in research, and access to resources and support' (Poole & Bornholt 1998, p. 117), thus having an impact on involvement in policy-making, a traditional linear indicator of a more developed career. In her research on the vocational behaviour of academics, Schaupp (1995) identifies academic tasks to include research, teaching and service. Women in academic institutions in a number of countries often carry higher teaching, administrative and pastoral care loads than men (West & Lyon 1995; Neale & White 2004) and service to the university and the community are found to be less likely to assist career development than research activities (Bagilhole 1993).

In their study of factors that contribute to the success of women academics in Malaysia, Ismail, Rasdi and Wahat (2004, p. 121) label women who achieve professorial status by the age of 48, as 'high-flyers'. This accommodates time within the career timeline to bear and raise children, and suggests that the challenge for women's advancement within academia initially is to reach the position of professor. Thereafter it may be easier to achieve a senior position. As participants in our study revealed:

> No it was not difficult to become a senior manager but I think it is tough for women to get Chairs, which is essential for senior academic management positions.
>
> (UK woman 17)

only that I was quite old when I got it (senior position), younger women with family responsibilities are not considered as serious.

(UK woman 12)

Yes, [I did experience difficulties in achieving a senior position] at the beginning.

(TR woman 4)

If the majority of senior managers are drawn from the pool of professors in the sector, then the women managers are likely to be in the late career stage. This is consistent with the finding of our study where most of the participants anticipate that in five years time they would be retired or 'doing some professor-type things such as serving on Boards' (NZ man 25) or 'having a very pleasant time being involved in academic matters at the European level' (IRE woman 6).

5.4 Factors facilitating success

The participants in our study are all senior managers who, by definition, have achieved career success, which is defined as 'the positive psychological or work-related outcomes or achievements one has accumulated as a result of one's work experiences' (Judge et al. 1995, p. 486). Career success has been described as having both objective and subjective components (Callanan 2003). Objective success is typically measured by observable career accomplishments such as salary, number of promotions achieved and position in an organisation (Kirchmeyer 2002; Nabi 1999; Turban & Doherty 1994), whereas subjective success is less easy to measure because it is a personal appraisal of how successful an individual feels. It is a function of the individual's perception of job satisfaction and career progress (Callanan 2003). It is worth exploring how our participants achieved such success.

Prior research into career success provides two classes of influencing variables. First, individual factors including demographic variables (Judge et al. 1995), personality factors (Lau & Shaffer 1999; Simonetti 1999) and career enhancing behaviours (Nabi 1999; Simonetti 1999; Turban & Dougherty 1994). Second, structural factors that may limit or facilitate career success, such as opportunities to engage in career enhancing behaviour, the availability of mentors (Burke & McKeen 1994), social capital (Seibert, Kraimer & Liden 2001) and organisational culture (Callanan 2003). In Australia, academic career success criteria are identified as research output (producing original work and attracting large research grants), hard work and productivity. Advancement within the system apparently depends on having an institutional perspective, developing a good political sense and spending many hours at work (Harris, Thiele & Currie 1998). In addition to early childhood experiences, women academics in Malaysia attribute their academic career success to having very high work centrality, as evidenced by their hard work and self-motivation (Ismail, Rasdi & Wahat 2004).

In the present study a combination of individual and structural factors are reported to have contributed to achieving senior management positions. At the individual level, career-enhancing behaviours were evident throughout the sample. Many participants ascribed their success to working very hard, 'no-one (supported me) but I am a very hard working man' (TR man 17), 'I have always been a workaholic' (AUS man 15). Others believed that they had ambition and focus: 'I was single minded in doing my research and publications' (UK woman 8). Most reported that they kept abreast of current events: 'my knowledge concerning laws and regulations helped' (TR male 10), 'they (men) listen to me, in many cases I would be the one to identify something in the document that is not supposed to be there' (SA woman 17). Actively volunteering for committee work contributes to the career success of participants: 'I was involved in all sorts of committees' (NZ woman 19), as do specific qualifications: 'having a PhD from [a prestigious university] has immense career capital' (SA man 3), 'I must confess my academic specialisation, management, was definitely an asset' (TR man 10). These factors are consistent with the leadership roles played by senior managers (see discussion in the introduction and Chapters 6 and 7). However, far more than individual factors, participants ascribe their success to receiving the support of others.

Almost every participant reports being invited or encouraged to apply for senior positions, which suggests that they are fairly well known in the sector and that they enjoy high social capital. In popular parlance, 'it's not what you know but who you know'. If recruitment is conducted in an informal manner, without rigorous attention paid to transparent processes, then opportunities for women's advancement within the sector may be compromised. 'The old boys club' is discussed more fully in Chapter 7. However, according to Leden et al. (2007, p. 986), gate keeping also produces 'a pervasive culture of negative bias – whether conscious or unconscious – against women in academia, resulting in a lack of professional support and networking'. Furthermore, Benschop (2009, pp. 222–3) demonstrates that 'intertwined processes of networking and gendering are micro-political processes: they reproduce and constitute power in action in everyday organisational life'.

According to Siebert, Kramer and Liden (2001), high social capital in the form of a strong network structure (measured as the number of developmental contacts at the same and higher organisation levels as participants), impacts positively on career success via access to information, access to resources and career sponsorship. In his study about the career success of academics in the UK, Nabi (1999) noted a positive correlation between networking and subjective career success. He found that in an academic community peer support is a more powerful predictor of men's subjective success, whereas personal support is a more powerful predictor for women's subjective success. In the present study, support from others is clearly evident in three distinct categories: from senior or external individuals, from peers and from personal relationships.

Social capital and high visibility among superiors are achieved via a number of interactions both internal and external to the university. As two Irish participants explain: 'I made a lot of international contacts in the private sector before and after entering the university' (IRE man 20) and 'my research success attracted a lot of money to the university and high calibre people' (IRE man 9). Further evidence of the power of networking came from other participants, when they were asked about the process of advancing: 'I was shoulder-tapped at a Christmas party' (NZ man 18); 'I served on a number of university and national research committees' (SA woman 14); 'most of the time people approached me and asked if I was interested in applying' (SA woman 11); 'my rector invited me' (TR men 12,13,14); 'in a country such as Turkey, relations are more influential and important than so called merit, my personal links at the governmental level ... were the really important factors' (TR man 10); 'by the time I was a senior manager I was networking a lot externally at various functions' (AUS man 5); 'my Dean was very supportive' (UK women 13, 14, 15); and 'I have had a lot of support, primarily from women' (SWE woman 7). The role of social engagement prior to senior appointment is viewed as a natural part of the process:

> The former female VC was very supportive ... but it was also a couple of men in the senior management group who contacted me, took me out to dinner, all that usual grooming and preliminary discussions.
>
> (AUS woman 9)

Some participants are able to cite examples of deliberate career sabotage from individual colleagues. However, most report receiving positive support from men and women peers and subordinates in the sector: 'encouragement from peers and from future peers in the new post' (UK woman 6).

I am supported by peers and some of the people that report to me. Across the university my peers, other PVCs, are supportive. Best support comes from a couple of other female PVCs.

(AUS woman 1)

As two others explain:

I got great support from faculty and school

(IRE woman 4)

and

If people invite one to do something then there is a greater consensus that you will be accepted.

(SA man 4)

Some participants credit their partners and other family members with providing support for their career advancement. But these are notably all woman participants (with one exception from Turkey). The following comment is an example:

My partner was good ... to talk through organisational dynamics. My mother [was] very significant ... encouraged me to go as far as I can. ... She cooked meals for the family time and time again.

(AUS woman 13)

The role of developmental relationships on career success was investigated by Burke and McKeen (1994) who believe that the availability of mentors and sponsors is more useful to career success than training or development programmes. However, they went on to note that women have more difficulty obtaining this support than men. Mentoring is cited as a career enhancing strategy by some participants in our study although access to mentors is inconsistent and not always ascribable to gender: 'I was often singled out and mentored, and this is a crucial practice that should be encouraged' (NZ man 6). 'I had very supportive HoD who mentored me early, showed me how to publish, told me the rules of the game ... that really encouraged me. His career took off and I followed his path' (SA woman 17). Similarly in Portugal: 'I've worked with the Rector ... I've learned a lot from him, because in what concerns human relations he is the best person I know' (PT woman 1). In contrast: 'it wasn't mentoring; basically, I have never had a mentor' (AUS woman 7).

Despite these examples of support for career advancement, it should be noted that in at least two countries, significant structural barriers are present that negatively affect participants earlier in their careers. However, these examples also show how political decisions can and do change the status quo. In South Africa the *apartheid* regime significantly limited access to educational and occupational opportunities for black individuals pre-1994:

> political exigencies shaped my career. Academic development was not originally my field but early in my career, because I am black, my previous university assigned me to helping every struggling black student in the department.
>
> (SA woman 1)

But the experience was not all negative: 'we did not allow apartheid to influence our careers negatively, we were strengthened by it' (SA man 7). In Ireland the marriage bar was in existence until 1973 (O'Connor 2009) which impacted on women's careers 'you were keeping a job from a man' (IRE women 5). These structural impediments directly shaped the careers of individuals who did not conform to the dominant demographic profile of academics in participating countries during the twentieth century, namely white males. However this is no longer the case in South Africa: 'Being a white male in the 1980's was hugely advantageous but now is a decided disadvantage' (SA man 3), and 'the senior white staff at the time (post 1994) appointed me (to a senior position) because they needed a black face to deal with 'them' [black students]' (SA man 8).

Returning to the issue of hard work and dedication being responsible for career success in academia, leads to exploration of how being appointed to a senior position impacts on work/life balance.

5.5   Balancing roles

Numerous articles have been written about the obstacles women face within the academy, the challenge of juggling family and work commitments and the hostile organisational climate experienced (Bagilhole 1993; Caplan 1995; Lindholm 2004; Lu 2005; Morley 2000, 2001; Saunderson 2002; Schaupp 1995; West & Lyon 1995). Wilson (2003) reported that women academics who choose to have children experience high levels of stress and are more likely to derail their careers. On occasion this is regarded as deliberate or the accepted status quo. One of the participants in this present study notes that many women in his university who are in their mid-30s have children, and this is a factor 'holding them back from being able to do a bit more in teaching and research because they are still seen as mothers' (NZ man 3). Another notes that 'this has to do with the dual role of women: family and professional, and this family role limits their availability to advance in their career as fast as men' (PT man 21). In Turkey, some men use family responsibility to explain women's lack of success, suggesting that women preferred the family role.

A contrary finding in a recent international study about women's decisions for work was published on International Women's Day (ITUC Report 2010). The results were particularly interesting for two reasons: first, the countries included (Argentina, Brazil, India, Mexico, South Africa, Netherlands and the UK) all enjoy national regulations that provide maternity protections at work, tackle discrimination, formally ensure equal pay for work and comply with the standards outlined by the International Labour Organisation. Second, the study was internet based thus biasing the participant profile towards a 'younger and more highly educated workforce than is the case for the whole population, because this group is generally more likely to have access to and use the internet' (2010, p. 7). Despite the expected findings, that most household and childcare responsibilities are taken up by women, they have a worse opinion about their career prospects than men due to restricted opportunities. More women than men indicate that they are overqualified for the job they do, but report having the same career aspirations as men. Specifically, the most important career drivers are a decent salary and reward opportunities, among both men and women, with and without children. The present study suggests that women and men share similar aspirations and that both would like work/life balance; however both reported that work/life balance had 'gone out of the window' (AUS man 5).

Without exception, the overriding experience of senior managers in academia, from all participating countries, is that of a high workload that demands a deep level of time commitment: 'it is not the kind of job you can turn off from' (NZ woman 1) as it takes up 'a lot of actual time and a lot of thought time' (NZ man 13).

> If you are talking about work life balance it has been almost entirely negative. This is probably one of my greatest failures, is finding that appropriate balance particularly at key times ... It becomes all consuming.
>
> (IRE man 12)

His experience is echoed across the countries in this study:

> in terms of personal life, obviously this created a huge transforma-
> tion, because it is a much more demanding position, which obliges
> me to spend a greater amount of time in the institution. I start my
> work at 8 am and leave after 8 pm. It also demands that you travel
> almost uninterruptedly.
>
> (PT man 12)

One single mother of four children admitted:

> The job does pinch quite a bit of family time [due to the long hours
> and frequent absences demanded by the job] you need a very
> strong and stable family base to convince your family that you are
> still there even if not physically there ... it is quite a challenge.
>
> (SA woman 10)

A number of participants in South Africa, Portugal and the UK maintain
two living spaces and commute weekly (often thousands of kilometres)
between the two in order to meet work demands and not 'uproot the
children' (UK woman 10).

Drew and Murtagh (2005) describe the greatest obstacle to achieving work/life balance as the 'long hours' culture demanded in some
sectors. The Centre for Work-Life Policy in New York (Hewlett &
Luce 2006) identifies 'extreme jobs' as those that include long hours
(70-hour weeks) plus performance pressures. The study claimed that
such jobs carried high risks for individuals' health and personal relationships and are particularly difficult for mothers. The present study
provides support for these findings among some of the participants.
Repeatedly, time and role-conflict are reported as stresses, with more
than one individual citing loneliness as a consequence of their senior
role. Others spoke of marriages failing:

> I have many colleagues that got divorced because they didn't have
> time to be with their families, and the fact that they are in such
> positions caused several divorces.
>
> (PT woman 10)

Other notable regrets expressed by senior managers include sacrific-
ing research time for management responsibilities: 'the disadvantage
is of course that you come away from actual research and something

that I have always thought is a lot of fun, tutoring PhD students' (SWE woman 5). Others regretted having increased blood pressure for the first time, a loss of social life and far less opportunity for reflection. A loss of privacy and freedom is experienced at the highest levels of university leadership:

> being President changes your life entirely, you lose your private space and lose status as a private individual and become a public figure, you have no freedom at all ... you are committed every minute, your life is not your own, utterly and completely.
>
> (IRE man 19)

> That you are such a public person is also a disadvantage, I think. Some might think it is an advantage, but I think it is a disadvantage. You are like a politician who is discussed in the daily press and is recognised everywhere.
>
> (SWE man 3)

> I cannot assume I am just me and walk on the beach as an individual without knowing I represent the university ... you are always the VC of a university so you lose your identity to some extent.
>
> (SA woman 10)

Work centrality as a career construct may help to explain the time commitment of academic senior managers. Work centrality is a concept that is concerned with the relative importance of work in an individual's life at a particular point in time (Meaning of Work (MOW) 1987). Work centrality contains two main theoretical components: a value component about working as a life role and a decision component about preferred life spheres for one's activities.

The value component of work centrality concerns identification with work and involvement with work. Identification with work as central to one's self-image is a consequence of a cognitive comparison of work activities and self-perception. Work involvement then becomes the affective response to this cognitive evaluation, and it is observed as time spent on work-related activities. The decision component of work centrality concerns the life spheres of an individual and the extent to which the individual chooses the behaviours associated with a particular life sphere, one of which may be work (MOW 1987). Thus, the two components are similar in that they both address a person's identification with working in general. But the value component relates work to self and the decision component relates work to other possible life spheres such as family or leisure.

As mentioned earlier, in their study exploring factors that contributed to the success of women academics in Malaysia, Ismail, Rasdi & Wahat (2004) identify career centrality (regarded as equivalent to work centrality for the purposes of this discussion) as a critical success factor. They define career centrality as 'the extent to which an individual sees involvement in a career as central to their adult life' (Ismail, Rasdi & Wahat 2004, p. 126). Nabi (1999) found a positive relationship between work centrality and subjective career success among academics in Britain.

Work as a central life interest is thoroughly explored by Dubin (1992) who reports that work is a central life interest for most professionals (unlike industrial workers and managers for whom it holds considerably less interest). Dubin (1992) further states that for work to be a central life interest, three conditions must be present: the work must be creative; it must involve personal responsibility for outcomes; and it should entail a measure of risk. He argues that, collectively, these three conditions create a highly autonomous working environment that is attractive to professionals (Dubin 1992). However, it should be noted that his research does not focus specifically on academics.

Despite all the apparent negatives, almost all participants in the present study identify role benefits that more than compensate for the heavy workloads they bear. The advantages of holding a senior management university position are perceived as numerous and desirable. Over and again participants from all countries report that they work in interesting environments with stimulating colleagues and enjoy opportunities to effect positive change. The power to influence the shape and direction of universities is consistently valued: '[I experience an] amazing range of opportunities, considerable chance to influence/shape the institution' (UK woman 4); 'being able to harness the potential of the university to deliver to the regional community [is satisfying]' (AUS man 2); 'a real opportunity to drive the way the institution goes' (AUS woman 6); 'having a position to drive and force the institution in the way of your vision' (TR man 3); you can affect things, that you have power and can get things done ... you get to do interesting things (SWE man 3); and, finally, 'the major advantage of being in a senior position is that you have power to get the job done, not power over people but access to resources' (SA man 3). Passion was evident in the responses of participants who spoke of dreams and visions for universities and of leading the academic project as 'the highest stake in our country' (SA man 6).

One New Zealand participant describes the positives as 'privileges' when he speaks of 'huge opportunities to make a difference' (NZ man 6). Similarly, an Irish participant believes that 'as an academic I am essentially paid to perform my hobby' (IRE man 11). The notion of work being fun is also articulated by participants in the UK and South Africa. One goes as far as to remark wryly that as he is married to an academic, 'our idea of fun is writing research papers over the weekend!' (SA man 3). Harris, Thiele & Currie (1998, p. 139) report from their Australian study that successful academics are seen as 'single-minded writing machines' or 'single-mindedly career-oriented people'. This suggests that work is a central life interest for successful academics.

A further distinct advantage of a senior management role is the expanded international network that is developed. It is best explained as follows:

> this position allows you to establish contacts that otherwise I wouldn't get. It allows me to have access to information that otherwise wouldn't be possible. From this point of view, it's a great enrichment in the noblest sense of the word, because it means personal recognition, gaining experience.
>
> (PT man 14)

This sentiment clearly reflected a sense of subjective career success.

The positive sentiments expressed by participants in the present study support a more recent literature trend that (in contrast to the traditional view that work and family commitments conflict) suggests that many individuals are balancing home and work demands successfully. Terms such as 'positive spillover', 'facilitation' and 'resource enrichment' are used by researchers who report positive interactions (via resources or skills) between the role requirements of work and family for both men and women (Grzywacz & Bass 2003; Kirchmeyer 1992, 1993; Ruderman et al. 2002, Greenhaus & Powell 2006). Once again, the notion of identity being informed by work or engagement in a meaningful purpose is raised. The psychological benefits and feelings of self-worth derived from purpose-driven activities may discount the stresses of balancing multiple roles.

It could be argued then that notions of appropriate work/life balance are subjective. If an individual with high work centrality and deep passion and commitment towards the academic project, is 'having fun' at work, then the 'long hours' culture of university senior management may prove, if not attractive, at least worthwhile. Nevertheless, the role appears to be more difficult for women. In addition, both women and men express clear ideas of what competencies the role requires.

5.6 Competencies

Definitions of competencies vary across the literature but the term is commonly understood to encompass the knowledge, skills, and abilities required to perform a job effectively. Combined with other personal characteristics, such as values, initiative, and motivation, these qualities contribute to successful individual and organisational performance. Competencies are not only about what the individual knows, but how they apply it. In the present study participants were asked what qualities they believed are required to be effective university leaders. The results are fascinating, in that they strongly reflect organisational culture and the broader societal context within which the university operates. Only one competency is non-negotiable across every country in this study, and that is to be taken seriously as a university leader. Individuals need to have a strong academic orientation because it is 'hard to command credibility without an academic track record' (AUS man 21) and 'in the academic world, you lead from the front' (SA man 5). Beyond this common knowledge base, clear distinctions are discernable between countries but also between universities within countries. Different competencies are valued depending on where the university is positioned along the collegial/managerial continuum. Furthermore, the focus of university management, as reflected in their perceived primary role, informs preferred competencies.

In Figure 4.1 in Chapter 4, a general distinction is made regarding where countries in the present study are located both on the collegial/managerial axis and on the internal/external axis. This positioning has a direct bearing on the competencies for success in each country.

Participants from those countries with a strong collegial orientation emphasise the importance of interpersonal skills and personality. In Turkey two participants mention the need for being 'a good academician' (TR man 23, TR woman 24) but every participant cites interpersonal skills ranging from 'social relations' (TR woman 2), 'warm personality' (TR man 3), 'team spirited' (TR man 5, TR man 15) to 'democratic and participatory management' (TR man 21). Emphasising the internal focus in Turkey one participant goes so far as to say that 'there are no specific personal qualities valued in senior management, being a Dean who is elected by faculty members is enough' (TR man 6). The noteworthy point about these responses is that this is the full extent of competencies cited, confirming the strong collegial culture prevailing in the sector. Once again, it is social capital that is valued, and if access to networks is limited, it follows that so is the advancement of women's careers. In Portugal, the emphasis is also on having a strong academic track record, but external links are mentioned too:

> the most important [quality] is being a person with an academic and scientific life ... an academic, a professor, a researcher, he/she must be someone with a broad knowledge of the Portuguese (national) and international, academic and scientific life.
>
> (PT man 18)

A shift is observable in the responses from Irish participants where a culture of hard work, quick decision-making and getting the job done appears to be valued: 'a person who can get an issue off my desk is valued' (IRE man 7). However, having said that speed, action and taking responsibility are valued, there is a simultaneous emphasis on placing the university's best interests at the forefront of decision-making. Strong leadership skills are described as including listening skills, strategic thinking and creative thinking' (IRE man 9). In addition, a number of participants believe that collegiality, in the form of conformity, helps one get ahead: 'outspoken is probably not a good idea' (IRE woman 4); 'there is a collegiality here, very good arguments are kept internal ... people are generally supportive of each other, you are not going to see people going to the courts all the time' (IRE man 20); 'a lack of confrontation and loyalty are valued' (IRE woman 1); and 'being reasonably agreeable with colleagues' (IRE woman 23). The external focus of Presidents in Ireland is clear in the number who speak of fund-raising efforts, and is well-articulated by one who says he has 'a curious mixture between involvement in what is going on and a slight separation from it'. He claims to be very visible when he 'launches receptions, functions, less visible in other circumstances' (IRE man 8).

Like Ireland, participants from the UK cite 'decisiveness' (UK woman 1, 7, 8, 13) and 'tough decision-making skills' (UK woman 11) as critical to success. However, the UK participants add 'hard macho skills' (UK woman 1, 14, 17) and 'an aggressive/assertive style that scorns collaboration' (UK woman 16) to give an image of harsh and uncompromising leadership. Specific skills include the ability to manage finances and to implement policies and procedures with the emphasis on control by 'laying down the law from on high' (UK woman 12). The focus is leaning away from the collegial model.

In both New Zealand and South Africa, participants speak of leaders who have vision and a willingness to engage with others and listen to various points of view, in a transparent and consultative manner. Strong people skills are valued in both countries. Some New Zealand leaders are very clear about the managerial responsibility, and use corporate language when discussing being responsible for the 'business side of the university such as deficit management' (NZ man 24), or when talking about 'setting standards, policies and the overall direction and tone of the university' (NZ woman 26). As one explains:

> an understanding of the challenges of the open market are important, an incoming VC has to understand the reality that universities are huge companies and have to run as a business.
>
> (NZ man 25)

In contrast, in South Africa there is less consensus on the collegial/ managerial divide, with older traditional research universities favouring the former and newer universities of technology leaning towards the latter. However all university leaders believe that political savvy 'to see the hidden agendas' (SA man 9) and being able to 'read the landscape' is critical. In this way one is able to 'see the traps ahead of you and be ahead of the game' (SA man 6) in order to 'read situations sensitively' (SA woman 16). As one woman explains: 'it is useful to be politically savvy but women are not socialised to do this' (SA woman 11), and she admits to struggling to form networks. One participant has a clearly gendered view of women's competencies at work. He believes that women should be employed as DVC Operations because:

> I think that is exactly the job where ... a woman would do exceptionally well because operations are all about order and women are less likely to be concerned with benefiting themselves through contracts.
>
> (SA man 6)

In addition to being on the lookout for political traps both inside and outside the university, the external focus requires particular competencies, including strategic visioning, dealing with research agencies and fundraising because 'you must be able to find the money, look after it and plug the leaks' (SA woman 10).

Australian participants value many of the competencies already mentioned, such as 'strategic vision' (AUS woman 7), a high research reputation (AUS woman 3, man 5) a high commitment to the university (AUS woman 6) and an alignment of values with the university (AUS woman 14). They demand an ability to set strategic direction and then achieve it through collaboration with people. The ability to delegate is seen as important because 'control freaks are not a good idea' (AUS man 8). Leaders are expected to work across all levels of the university. One participant offers the view that the internal or external focus is gendered, with males being more externally focused and women being 'a bit more hands on and directive than males' (AUS woman 7). She considers that the required skills depend on where the university is in its development. Certainly, the Australian participants have a strong managerial orientation:

> Universities are multi-million dollar corporations and are all working internationally ... A VC these days needs to be someone who can run a multi- national corporation.
>
> (AUS man 5)

To gain a sense of just how different the skills sets required are, depending on the country context, compare this last view with its antithesis from an Irish participant: 'there would be a very strong reaction here against managerialism, the corporatisation of the University; the language that goes with that such as referring to students as clients does not go down well here' (IRE man 9).

5.7   Conclusion

This chapter explored the career stories of participants by examining what challenges typically faced those in the mid to late career stage while acknowledging that the early career experiences of participants in this study would have been located in a different socio-politico-cultural context from the present day.

This study sought to understand the career paths and patterns of senior university leaders at an individual level, with a view to identifying if a typical career path exists. Starting as a lecturer and working through the ranks, with promotion largely dependent on research output, is the path most commonly followed by those who eventually lead universities. Although most participants did not initially plan to attain a senior leadership position, they were responsive to opportunities to advance. Most had supportive colleagues or superiors, who actively encouraged or invited them to apply for more senior positions. Clearly, hard work, mentors and a strong professional network facilitate career advancement in academic circles. This social capital was easier to acquire for men than for women, given the obvious gate-keeping that took place in certain circles. In some countries, such as the UK, Ireland and Turkey, where recruitment practices were opaque, significant reliance appeared to be made on social capital as a route to advancement.

Once in the role, significant sacrifices are made in terms of relinquishing individual research interests, personal freedom and family or leisure time. Long hours are a given at these career levels, as is frequent travel. Again, the gendered nature of care-giving responsibility in all the countries included in this study makes achieving a senior position that much more difficult for women. Different competencies are valued in different university- and country-specific cultures. The competencies that are valued are directly informed by the position assumed by each country in relation to the matrix offered in Chapter 4. The only universal competency is a strong academic research record, which is likely to be achieved later by women than men, because of women's additional care-giving responsibilities. However, once in the position, the rewards are significant too. Opportunities to interact with stimulating people across sectors, and the power to effect positive change with lasting impact for future generations, are highly valued by the leaders of academia. Having achieved objective career success, as defined by their rank, most appear also to have achieved subjective career success.

References

Bagilhole, B. (1993). 'Survivors in a male preserve: A study of British women academics' experiences and perceptions of discrimination in a UK University', *Higher Education*, 26, 4, 431–77.

Bejian, D. V. and Salomone, P. R. (1995). 'Understanding midlife career renewal: Implications for counselling', *Career Development Quarterly*, 44, 1, 52–64.

Benschop, Y. (2009). 'The micro-politics of gendering in networking', *Gender, Work and Organisation*, 16, 2, 217–37.

Brousseau, K. R. (1990). 'Career dynamics in the baby boom and baby bust era', *Journal of Organisational Change Management*, 3, 3, 46–58.

Burke, R. J. and McKeen, C. A. (1994). 'Training and development activities and career success of managerial and professional women', *Journal of Management Development*, 13, 5, 53–63.

Callanan, G. A. (2003). 'What price career success?' *Career Development International*, 8, 3, 126–33.

Caplan, P. (1995). *Lifting a Ton of Feathers: A Woman's Guide for Surviving in the Academic World* (Toronto: University of Toronto Press).

Clarke, M. (2009). 'Plodders, pragmatists, visionaries and opportunists: career patterns and employability', *Career Development International*, 14, 1, 8–28.

Dolezalek, H. (2007).'Got high potentials?' *Training*, 44, 1, 18–22.

Drew, E. and Murtagh, E.M. (2005). 'Work/life balance: senior management champions or laggards?', *Women in Management Review*, 20, 4, 262–78.

Dubin, R. (1992). *Central Life Interests: Creative Individualism in a Complex World.* (New Brunswick: Transaction).

Erikson, E. H. (1963). *Identity: Youth and Crisis* (London: Faber & Faber).

Evans, K. and Heinz, W. (1995). 'Flexibility, learning and risk: Work, training and early careers in England and Germany', *Education + Training*, 37, 5, 3–11.

Feldman, D. C. (1976). 'A contingency theory of socialisation', *Administrative Science Quarterly* 21, 433–51.

Gordon, J. R. and Whelan-Berry, K. S. (2004). 'It takes two to tango: An empirical study of perceived spousal/partner support for working women', *Women in Management Review*, 19, 5, 260–73.

Gould, R. L. (1978). *Transformations: Growth and Change in Adult Life.* (New York: Simon & Schuster).

Greenhaus, J. H. and Powell, G. N. (2006). 'When work and family are allies: A theory of work-family enrichment', *Academy of Management Review*, 31, 1, 72–92.

Grzywacz, J. G. and Bass, B. L. (2003). 'Work, family and mental health: Testing different models of work-family fit', *Journal of Marriage and Family*, 65, 1, 248–61.

Harris, P., Thiele, B. and Currie, J. (1998). 'Success, gender and academic voices. Consuming passion or selling the soul?', *Gender & Education*, 10, 2, 133–49.

Hewlett, S.A. and Luce, C. B. (2006). 'Extreme jobs: The dangerous allure of the 70-hour workweek', *Harvard Business Review*, 84, 12, 49–59.

Hunter, S. and Sundel, M. (1989). 'Introduction: An examination of key issues concerning midlife', in S. Hunter and M. Sundel (eds), *Midlife Myths: Issues, Findings and Practical Implications* (California: Sage), 8–28.

Hyman, J. and Summers, J. (2004). 'Lacking balance? Work-life employment practices in the modern economy', *Personnel review*, 33, 4, 418–29.

Ismail, M., Rasdi, R. M. and Wahat, N. W. (2004). 'High-flyer women academicians: factors contributing to success', *Women in Management Review*, 20, 2, 117–32.

International Trade Union Confederation (ITUC) Report (2010). *Decisions for Work: An Examination of the Factors Influencing Women's Decisions for Work.* www.incomesdata.co.uk

Judge, T. A., Cable, D. M., Boudreau, J. W. and Bretz, R. D. (1995). 'An empirical investigation of the predictors of executive career success', *Personnel Psychology*, 48, 3, 485–519.

Kirchmeyer, C. (1992). 'Perceptions of nonwork-to-work spillover: Challenging the common view of conflict-ridden domain relationships', *Basic and Applied Social Psychology*, 13, 2, 231–49.

Kirchmeyer, C. (1993). 'Nonwork-to-work spillover: A more balanced view of the experiences and coping of professional women and men', *Sex Roles*, 28, 9/10, 531–52.

Kirchmeyer, C. (2002). 'Gender differences in managerial careers: Yesterday, today and tomorrow', *Journal of Business Ethics*, 37, 1, 5–24.

Kittrell, D. (1998). 'A comparison of the evolution of men's and women's dreams in Daniel Levinson's theory of adult development', *Journal of Adult Development*, 5, 2, 105–16.

Lachman, M. E. and James, J. B. (1997). 'Charting the course of midlife development: an overview', in M. E. Lachman and J. B. James (eds), *Multiple Paths of Midlife Development* (Chicago: University of Chicago Press), 1–17.

Large, M. and Saunders, N. K. (1995). 'A decision-making model for analyzing how the glass ceiling is maintained: unblocking equal promotion opportunities', *International Journal of Career Management*, 7, 2, 21–8.

Lau, V. P. and Shaffer, M. A. (1999). 'Career success: The effects of personality', *Career Development International*, 4, 4, 225–31.

Leden, A., Bornmann, L., Gannon, F. and Wallon, G. (2007). 'A persistent problem: traditional gender roles hold back female scientists', *EMBO Reports*, 8, 11, 982–7.

Leibowitz, Z. B., Kaye, B. L. and Farren, C. (1990). 'What to do about career gridlock?', *Training & Development Journal*, 44, 4, 28–34.

Levinson, D. J. (1978). *The Seasons of a Man's Life* (New York: Knopf).

Levinson, D. J. (1986). 'A conception of adult development', *American Psychologist*, 41, 3–13.

Lindholm, J. A. (2004). 'Pathways to the professoriate: the role of self, others, and environment in shaping academic career aspirations', *The Journal of Higher Education*, 75, 6, 603–35.

Louw, D. A., van Ede, D. M. and Louw, A. E. (1998). *Human Development* (2nd edn) (Cape Town: Kasigo Tertiary).

Lu, Y. (2005). 'Sibship size, family organization and children's education in South Africa: Black-white variations', *International Sociological Association Research Committee on Social Stratification and Mobility* (RC28), Los Angeles, August 2005.

Mathur-Helm, B. (2006). 'Women and the glass ceiling in South African banks: an illusion or reality?', *Women in Management Review*, 21, 4, 311–26.

Meaning of Work (MOW) (1987). *The Meaning of Work* (London: Academic Press).

Merriam, S. B. (1999). 'Time as the integrative factor', *New Directions for Adult and Continuing Education*, 84, 67–78.

Morison, R., Erickson, T. and Dychtwald, K. (2006). 'Managing middlescence', *Harvard Business Review*, 84, 3, 78–86.

Morley, L. (2000). 'The micropolitics of gender in the learning society', *Higher Education in Europe*, 25, 2, 229–36.

Morley, L. (2001). 'Subjected to review: Engendering quality and power in higher education', *Journal of Education Policy*, 16, 5, 465–78.

Nabi, G. R. (1999). 'An investigation into the differential profile of predictors of objective and subjective career success', *Career Development International*, 4, 4, 212–25.

Nachbagauer, A. G. M. and Riedl, G. (2002). Effects of concepts of career plateaus on performance, work satisfaction and commitment', *International Journal of Manpower*, 23, 8, 716–33.

Neale, J. and White, K. (2004). 'Almost there: a comparative case study of senior academic women in Australia and New Zealand', *Proceedings of NAWE Pay and Employment Equity for Women conference*, Wellington. http://www.nacow.govt.nz/conference2004/papers.html

Newell, S. (1996). 'The superwoman syndrome: a comparison of the "heroine" in Denmark and the UK', *Women in Management Review*, 11, 5, 36–41.

O'Connor, P. (1998, reprinted 1999). *Emerging Voices: Women in Contemporary Irish Society* (Dublin: Institute of Public Administration).

Peck, R. C. (1968). 'Psychological developments in the second half of life', in B. L. Neugarten (ed.), *Middle Age and Ageing* (Chicago: University of Chicago Press), 88–92.

Poole, M. and Bornholt, L. (1998). 'Career development of academics: Cross-cultural and lifespan factors', *International Journal of Behavioral Development*, 22, 1, 103–26.

Rana, A. K., Kagan, C., Lewis, S. and Rout, U. (1998). 'British south Asian women managers and professionals: Experiences of work and family', *Women in Management Review*, 13, 6, 221–32.

Riordan, S. (2007). Career psychology factors as antecedents of career success of women academics in South Africa. Unpublished Doctoral Thesis, University of Cape Town.

Ruderman, M. N., Ohlott, P. J., Panzer, K. and King, S. N. (2002). 'Benefits of multiple roles for managerial women', *Academy of Management Journal*, 45, 2, 369–86.

Ryan, M. and Haslam, A. (2006). 'What lies beyond the glass ceiling?', *Human Resource Management International Digest*, 14, 3, 3–5.

Saunderson, W. (2002). 'Women, academia and identity: Constructions of equal opportunities in the "new managerialism" – A case of lipstick on the gorilla?', *Higher Education Quarterly*, 56, 4, 376–406.

Schaupp, D. (1995). A sociological model of career choice and vocational behavior, paper presented at the 103rd Annual Convention of the American Psychological Association, New York.

Schein, E. H. (1978). *Career Dynamics: Matching Individual and Organizational Needs* (Philippines: Addison-Wesley).

Schreuder, M. G. and Theron, A. L. (1997). *Careers: An Organisational Perspective* (South Africa: Juta & Co. Ltd.).

Schreuder, M. G. and Coetzee, M. (2006). *Careers: An Organisational Perspective* (3rd edn) (South Africa: Juta & Co. Ltd.).

Seibert, S. E., Kraimer, M. L. and Liden, R. C. (2001). 'A social capital theory of career success', *Academy of Management Journal*, 44, 2, 219–38.

Sharf, R. S. (2002). *Applying Career Development Theory to Counseling* (3rd edn) (California: Brooks/Cole Thomson Learning).

Sheehy, G. (1976). *Passages: Predictable Crises of Adult Life* (New York: Bantam Books Inc.).

Sheehy, G. (1995). *New Passages: Mapping your life across time* (New York: Ballantine Books).

Simonetti, J. L. (1999). 'The key pieces of the career survival and success puzzle', *Career Development International*, 4, 6, 312–17.

Simpson, R. (2000). 'The time bonded glass ceiling and young women managers: Career progress and career success – evidence from the UK', *Journal of European Industrial Training*, 24, 2/3/4, 190–8.

South African Institute of Race Relations (2003). *South African Survey: 2002/2003*. (Johannesburg: J. Henderson).

Tamir, L. M. (1989). 'Modern myths about men at midlife: an assessment', in S. Hunter and M. Sundel (eds), *Midlife Myths: Issues, Findings and Practical Implications* (California: Sage), 157–79.

Thomas, K. M., Bierema, L. and Landau, H. (2004). 'Advancing women's leadership in academe: New directions for research and HRD practice', *Equal Opportunities International*, 23, 7/8, 62–77.

Turban, B. and Doherty, T. W. (1994). 'Role of protégé personality in receipt of mentoring and career success', *Academy of Management Journal*, 37, 3, 688–702.

Wanous, J. P. (1980). *Organisational Entry: Recruitment, Selection and Socialisation of Newcomers* (Philippines: Addison-Wesley).

West, J. and Lyon, K. (1995). 'The trouble with equal opportunities: The case of women academics', *Gender and Education*, 7, 1, 51–68.

Williams, C. P. and Savickas, M. L. (1990). 'Developmental tasks of career maintenance', *Journal of Vocational Behaviour*, 36, 166.

Wilson, R. (2003). 'How babies alter careers for academics', *The Chronicle of Higher Education L*, 50.

6
Doing Senior Management

Jenny Neale

6.1 Introduction

This chapter looks at the dynamics of senior managers in their universities. It focuses on how women and men work together in university senior management teams, how they are perceived, whether there are differences in management styles and whether having women in senior management positions is considered to make a difference.

As already discussed in the Introduction, those interviewed for the current WHEM study were members of their university senior management team and thus operating as academic leader and managers. That is, while their top level positions in the university were designated management positions, they were required to exhibit the traits of both manager and academic leader. Therefore both aspects will be explored in this chapter.

Those in leadership positions are expected to behave in certain ways. Kouzes and Posner (2007, p. 5) suggest that there are five functions of leadership: model the way, inspire a shared vision, challenge the process, enable others to act and encourage the heart. Furthermore, it is argued (Kouzes & Posner 2007) that leadership is about establishing trusting and friendly relationships between colleagues and the organisation's value system (Chesterman 2004).

On the other hand leadership is continually being defined along the lines of 'think manager, think male' (Miller 2006, p. 6). This has implications for women in the workplace as '[t]he women manager is defined as a specific gendered subject position by the contingently determined context' (Priola 2007, p. 29). For women this means that they are continually judged because of their gender and, for example, if a problem becomes too difficult to manage their 'subject position is seen as feminine, thus soft, weak and emotional' (Priola 2007, p. 29). This form of stereotyping can hinder women's progression through the workplace hierarchy, as they are constantly being thought of as timid and passive, traits that go against those qualities predominantly associated with leadership (ILO 2007). However, the increasing number of women appointed to senior positions suggests another aspect that needs to be considered: the so-called glass cliff. Research has indicated that women are over-represented in appointments to precarious leadership positions and are thus set up to fail, reinforcing gendered stereotypes (Ryan & Haslem 2005; Ryan & Haslem, 2007, Haslem & Ryan 2008).

The gendered stereotypes frequently used in the workplace were formed through observations of successful role models, and those have historically been male (ILO 2007). These observations have become 'prescriptive beliefs,' which determine how things should be – for example leaders should behave in an active, assertive manner – rather than 'descriptive beliefs' which say how things are rather than how they should be. Women thus have to deal with a clash of perceptions, between the roles of 'woman' and 'leader' (Eagly & Sczesny 2009). This means that women may find their own sense of identity is not easily adapted to their context and they may position themselves as an 'outsider on the inside' (Gherardi 1996 cited in Priola 2007, p. 30).

6.2   Perceptions of senior managers

For the reasons discussed above, the present research found considerable differences in the way the senior managers consider they are perceived by their colleagues. Some focus on personal attributes that are seen to either enhance or detract from the way that the job is done, while others comment on the way in which they are seen to actually carry out the job.

> Male colleagues see me as helpful, non-threatening, thoughtful, as 'having a vision' and putting things into operation that no-one else has done. In comparison, female colleagues have given me positive feedback, noting how they appreciated the time I take to listen, offer solutions and have recognised how things have improved.
>
> (NZ man 25)

> Both men and women appreciate that I am determined but soft-spoken.
>
> (SWE woman 6)

Both male and female managers perceive that their colleagues consider they have a number of valuable attributes. Approachability, efficiency and trustworthiness are all valued, though generally men are seen as agenic – the 'doers' – while women are seen as 'communal' and relating to people (Eagly & Sczesny 2009, p. 23), and there is an assumption that men are agenically competent (Eagly & Carli 2007). In some countries, male respondents see these agenic qualities being recognised.

> [I am] somebody who has a vision for where they want it to go, somebody who is fair, somebody who makes decisions. People will say they don't always like them but they like the fact that I make decisions, [that I am] somebody who is transparent and puts all the cards on the table.
>
> (IRE man 10)

> Colleagues see me as someone who is highly manipulative in the positive sense of getting things for the Faculty and working in a large, complicated business.
>
> (NZ man 15)

> I was seen by all as the leader who would only make decisions and take actions to benefit the University, who could solve problems.
>
> (TR man 11)

In contrast, one Irish man comments on the drawbacks for him associated with displaying a communal style:

> I would think for the most part trustworthy, approachable, have their interests at heart. Maybe at times, they would like me to represent what they see as clearly academic interests more forcefully than I am able to do. I spend a lot of time negotiating between positions rather than pushing through a particular position.
>
> (IRE man 8)

On the whole, these senior managers believe that their female and male colleagues see them in a similar manner, whether it is positively:

> I doubt that perceptions of me by male and female colleagues differ. There is a job to be done. I am happy to work with all of them. I like to keep it pretty simple. My portfolio is very competitive externally. So if we are to get the job done, we have to work together.
>
> (AUS man 8)

You build your own reputation every place you go as Chair and Head of this area. I think I would have a strong reputation among everyone, men and women.

(IRE woman 13)

[I] do not see any gender differences at all in the behaviour of men and women colleagues and hope I'm respected by both for my knowledge and what I do.

(SA man 5)

Or less favourably:

Moving from a male grammar school, I am possibly seen as very male oriented by staff.

(NZ man 3)

There is no gender in my work life. I am a manager. I do not feel any difference between male and female managers. If I were a male they would again be jealous about me.

(TR woman 2)

6.3 Gendered expectations of behaviour

Being different does not stop when women and men achieve senior-management positions. Women are considered 'other' when measured against the standards and norms set by men (Wilson 2005), and there are different expectations and behaviours for them (Mavin 2006; Neale and Özkanli, 2010). Remaining outsiders because of the gendered style of management reinforces this as a different experience for women (Bagilhole & White 2006). While women do not necessarily consider themselves to be different, men ascribe to them different, and at times, somewhat inferior qualities (Wilson 2005), as evidenced in the current WHEM research (see also Chapter 4):

Women can be more assertive due to insecurity and for this reason sometimes become more pro-active. Another difference is that women often want assurances about decisions but are then prepared to discuss and put things forward for consultation. In comparison men 'get on and do it' and are indifferent to encouragement and consultation processes.

(NZ man 25)

I would say males are more target driven, let's set the target here and see how we can manage it and go for it. The female approach would be, what is the end game: you don't have to put numbers but have a feel for what it might be and we can work on that then. Female colleagues tend to personalise it more; if we have a disagreement it is a personal disagreement, with male colleagues it is a job we do and we disagree with this one and we move on.

(IRE man 21)

Women leaders can have difficulties being accepted because they are confronted with differing expectations. Prescriptive gender stereotypes see them having to meet both female and leadership roles. Wolfram and Mohr (2007) indicate that gender-role discrepant female leaders (that is, those exhibiting autocratic styles) are less respected than gender-role discrepant male leaders (that is, those exhibiting democratic styles). Thus, men are rewarded for being democratic while women are not, because this is a 'taken for granted' attribute of women leaders. Further, they suggest that followers with traditional gender role attitudes are prone to have comparatively little professional respect for female leaders. Several participants in the present study suggest that women are more likely to 'micro-manage', possibly related to a need to ensure they meet the standards that are expected of them:

I would say females are probably more directive, from my experience and more generic: 'I want this done' ... they micro-manage. The males tend to have the same expectations but they let you get on with it and do it. Females tend to micro-manage, perhaps because people have such harsh expectations of females.

(AUS woman 7)

Our current VC is a woman who can be very assertive and decisive, even dogmatic. She does not want to put a foot wrong, so follows rules rigidly even if no longer appropriate.

(SA woman 1)

And a New Zealand man echoes their sentiments:

The typical working style of men and women managers is that women are more process conscious and formal than men. Women bosses are more inclined to look to doing things differently. That may be because they're in such a minority they feel they have to make some difference; nevertheless position can affect that.

(NZ man 25)

When women do hold senior leadership positions, they often have a feeling of isolation:

> Being at this level is very lonely. I am the only woman among [several] Pro Vice-Chancellors and it is a very competitive environment. You live or die by your own decision, and can't be friends now with other heads of schools. You're too busy being rivals with other Pro Vice-Chancellors ... especially the fight over finite resources. This is particularly difficult as a woman, since the other PVCs think women will be a pushover and can be ignored, and when I come in from left field it takes them by surprise and worries them every time.

(NZ woman 7)

The gendered discourses within university settings promote women as being the 'dependable mother figure' (Thomas & Davies 2002, p. 381), where they become associated with the 'housework' of education (Worden & Groombridge 2003). Women often become locked into the maintenance and emotional work within the university, facing greater difficulty in establishing their credibility and capability (Neale & White 2004; Thomas & Davies 2002; Rhodes 2003). Alternatively, when women do seek and gain leadership roles, and push aside the 'nurturing' role, they are often perceived as being 'bossy' and domineering', as their 'toughness' is seen to be a liability (Rhodes 2003, p. 9). As a participant in the present study put it: 'One comment you hear about female managers is that they're bossy – just means they're demanding and you wouldn't say that about males' (NZ man 3).

Studies have described a traditional gendered leadership style, in which male managers are more likely to be autocratic and employ a command and control style of leadership (Miller 2006). Both women and men tend to characterise women generally as being more inclusive, collaborative, cooperative, flexible and participative, as well as better at consensus building and having strong communication skills (Chesterman 2004; Eagly & Carli 2007). This is reflected in the present study:

> I have a pure woman management style; I try to use my woman skills that I naturally have. I prefer diplomatic style, warm relations,

more friendly, authority through charisma, not through harsh measures.

(TR woman 2)

Women are more reflective than men. Men don't think through the ramifications of what they are doing. When women disagree it is more subtle. I have worked with a female boss in my university career. She was a fantastic organic leader, but embedded certain ideas and let you own them. Male leaders tend to be more overt. Female senior managers have a greater social dimension to their working style, and are more concerned with consensus and making people feel comfortable.

(AUS man 21)

Women's often different management style produces some ambivalent responses. Where management is combined with a range of consultative techniques, a shared ownership of decisions is more likely (Chesterman 2004). However, women's more consultative style can be seen to have some drawbacks. This type of management is often criticised by others because of the expectation that women will take on the pastoral work 'as this was equated with familial discourses of "women's work"' (Thomas & Davies 2002, p. 387). A gendered division of labour results, in which women managers may be responsible for 'feminine' tasks such as equity, administration and staff support (Yeatman 1995). Further, Morley (2003) and Deem (2003) report that when women are 'allowed' to enter management in order to take on the responsibility of domestic arrangements of audit, this leaves the male colleagues free to focus on their own priorities. Moreover, as Cikara and Fiske (2009) point out, men see co-operation by women as consent, further reinforcing their mores, as evidenced by the following comments from the present study:

I think men tend to be more narrowly focussed and women are more broadly focussed. Women can be more sensitive to the emotional underplay of a situation than men, and that has a big plus and sometimes a minus. It can both eliminate and cloud.

(AUS man 11)

Some time ago a colleague of mine said that 'your office looks like a confessional'. I've replied to him that he was getting the wrong picture, because what happens is that we women have a different sensitivity for certain issues. And I feel this because when there are problems, regardless of their nature (political, financial, social), in a general way my colleagues tend to approach me to talk about this.

(PT woman 10)

Women and men do work differently. Women give a different perspective to issues, women have more empathy. Men don't sympathise with students.

(SA man 7)

Women leaders draw on feminine discourses to critically reflect on and critique the highly masculinist subject positions offered in leadership (Alimo-Metcalfe 2004; Thomas & Davies 2002). This is viewed as an 'alternative self' where supportive transformational styles of leadership are adopted (see Introduction): 'Women prefer to lead in ways that are consensual, [and] empowering, encouraging participation and team work' (Miller 2006, p. 15). A respondent in the present study pointed out that 'Men are very transactional, women are very transformational but women need to be better at working with each other' (IRE woman 5). Eagly and Carli (2007) indicate that in transformational leadership, the leader establishes themself as a role model by gaining the follower's trust and confidence, stating future goals, and planning how to achieve them to innovate and empower followers. Both men and women in the present study see these communal leadership qualities being enacted by women, and consequently these are the attributes by which colleagues differentiate women senior managers from their male counterparts:

Gender skills are still alive. Women provide skills around resolution of conflict, how to deal with it quickly, and to know what is going on for individuals and for the organisation. It is so undervalued and yet it is critical for an organisation's health.

(AUS woman 13)

Women are likely to see things differently: relational aspects and the facts of the situation, rather than just the 'big picture'. More likely to have a sense of how things will be seen by the organisation.

(NZ man 13)

A more pragmatic approach is also appreciated:

Sometimes, when I'm with my colleagues and I ask: 'so, how is it going to be? How are we going to decide?' Maybe they don't ramble and maybe it's me who is too fast and pragmatic, but I notice they are more complex, not only concerning top management issues but also with other topics. In daily activities, women are much more pragmatic than men.

(PT woman 10)

Those qualities which are linked with masculinity, such as being assertive, forceful and authoritative are the same qualities that some women and men in senior management adopt and apply to their leadership positions (Currie et al. 2002; Rhodes 2003). As one senior woman in the present study indicates, she is seen as 'the only one in Directorate with any balls ... applauded for being action focussed and not just a talker ... [with a] reputation for being a doer' (UK woman 2). Changes in university management have increased pressures on staff that may reinforce a traditional male model of work, while industrial relations changes have decreased the transparency of pay setting schemes, thus increasing the possibility for discrimination (Strachan et al. 2008). Participants in the current study suggest that the ways in which some men work remain problematic.

Working with men things move a lot more slowly, there's a lot more care in terms of not offending other male colleagues, cloaking sectional interests and opinions in a low key neutral kind of pseudo objectivity, which is difficult to challenge. In working with women there is a much greater focus on the task to be done, the job in hand.

(IRE woman 1)

Women are less concerned with the personal accolades, more concerned with the job. They are not in the political dance for leadership that you find with men. With men there is a tension that is absent from the same conversation with women. Women pay such incredible attention to detail, they lead by example and they always show concern for people. Men are political or they are bullies. Women are more focussed on the task than their ego. But they set things right to do with the task without the tension that men create. Women remain mindful of people.

(SA man 6)

On the whole women are less bothered about status, territoriality and positional issues, are more prepared to listen and be down-to-earth. Women are more prepared to get to the real core of an issue and work together to get a solution. When there are more women in a senior management team [there is] less male stereotypical behaviour. Not sure men understand that women are not impressed and don't want to take part in those competitive games.

(NZ woman 12)

Some women are able to opt into the masculine nature of the academy and demonstrate a general compliance with the masculine norms of the university culture (Thomas & Davies 2002). These can work to render the individual a 'successful organisational subject, someone who is "fit" to join the ranks of management' (Thomas & Davies 2002, pp. 390–1). This indicates that senior women are able to recognise the attributes of traditional masculinist behaviours, and are willing to take them on in order to fit into the role of a senior manager in the tertiary sector (Mavin 2006), as the following respondent illustrates:

There is also pressure to become more like men: more combative in management style. Women who don't do this are seen as weak or unable to perform. Many women are wary of entering senior management because of an unwillingness to accede to these very stereotypes. I am never going to please everyone, it's really difficult when people are really hostile.

(NZ woman 2)

If women are largely seen as 'other' in a male-dominated environment – emotional as opposed to rational – this can create contradictions for the identities of those women who do gain entry, having previously been undervalued, disempowered and dismissed as non-rational (Morley 1994; Wager 1998; Wyn, Acker & Richards 2000). Women's leadership styles may therefore bring them into conflict with organisational norms (Brooks 2001), and a lot of women will be at a loss in navigating senior management unless they re-socialise themselves in terms of work practices and identities (Blackmore & Sachs 2000). However, this can be challenging:

There's definitely a difference in management styles between men and women. Women will hold a grudge for 20 years. Men will go toe to toe and then it's done. With women you need to negotiate and that works all the way down the line. However, I try not to let gender get in the way and am taken aback when I get a gendered response. I accept men for what they are without parodying them, but by coming across as comfortable in my own skin. One difficulty facing women is that there is a certain expectation of what constitutes a leader, and they have to forge a different image.

(NZ woman 7)

Morley (1999) notes that women's seniority was often perceived as a betrayal and compliance with management's regulatory functions, where a commitment to feminism was called into question. The wider use and acceptance of feminist managerial styles, with such notions as the power to empower others; negotiation of institutional goals and processes; and facilitative leadership, could strengthen and motivate women and decrease the stresses that might otherwise be felt (Deem & Ozga 1997).

Women may be held to a higher standard of competency than men (Eagly & Carli 2007). In the present study, there were some negative comments about how senior managers are viewed. For example, while most Turkish senior managers indicate that they are seen positively by their colleagues and gender was not an issue, one woman did say that:

Both male and female colleagues seem quite positive. But most of the time women did not want me as a senior manager. At the same time, males do not prefer female colleagues.

(TR woman 24)

However, several Turkish men hold negative female stereotypes and comment that: 'Women academicians need help from male academicians. They complain too much' (TR man 17); 'I believe female managers are more emotional' (TR man 5); 'Female administrators tend to be more fixed-minded, less flexible and they talk too much' (TR man 11); and 'Sometimes women are more rigid' (TR man 13). Further, a UK woman academic remarks that she is 'seen as competent, pleasant, too nice therefore limited' (UK woman 7) and a New Zealand woman has some reservations about why her male colleagues are supportive: 'I do wonder whether they wanted me in the job because they thought that I would be able to be manipulated' (NZ woman 26).

Acting like a man or not being tough enough, are twin hazards for women leaders who have to negotiate between the communal qualities such as a concern for others that people prefer in a woman, with agentic qualities such as assertion, dominance, individualism, ambition and control that people think leaders need to exhibit to succeed (Eagly & Carli 2007, p. 123). Those men who continue to believe that a good leader possesses mainly masculine attributes resist women's authority more as they perceive women in senior management as a direct challenge, competing with them for power and authority (Mavin 2006; Eagly & Carli 2007). Comments by women respondents in the current study exemplify this male resistance: 'The men find it a struggle reporting to me as a woman' (AUS woman 19); 'There are some people who are very uncomfortable with having a woman in a senior role' (IRE woman 23); 'Male colleagues see me as a bit formidable; a bit frightening but with good judgement' (NZ woman 19); 'Seen as powerful and a threat by senior men' (UK woman 1); and 'Probably also seen as frightening by the men' (UK woman 13). O'Connor (2010, p. 9) suggests that use of the word 'frightening' is 'evocative of both women's perceived power and yet their unacceptability'.

6.4   Women acting like men

Most of the characteristics conventionally associated with leadership are at odds with the traditional characteristics associated with women. Priola (2007) suggests that when some women position themselves as managers, they have the tendency to enact more masculine types of behaviours because women in male-dominated fields are often given the message that they need to conform to a masculine image of leadership (Eveline 2004). This is reflected in the present study:

> Came from 60s, 70s, 80s [when] only blokes ran the universities and there are still staff that think it should be. Women do feel the need to adopt a male style – part of it is because it's the line of least resistance and that's the way universities do things and most effectively but I don't let them forget that I'm a woman.
>
> (NZ woman 23)

> They feel under pressure; they work a bit more, a bit harder, they have to kind of adopt the male approach – aggressive, target driven.
>
> (IRE man 21)

Women who are seen to be more traditionally feminine are deemed to be not sufficiently masculine; that is, not tough, decisive or competent enough and too weak, uncertain or ineffectual. Women who adopt an agenic mode of leadership are criticised for being too masculine; that is, dominant, highly competent or self promoting and not feminine enough and not warm, selfless or supportive enough (Eagly & Carli 2007,

p. 187). Women have to provide strong information that counters these stereotypes to show that they are qualified for such positions, but this deviation from the norm can attract a backlash and, interestingly, dominant behaviours can be interpreted as less dominant when displayed by women (Cikara & Fiske 2009). Whereas agenic men are perceived as competent, as discussed earlier, for women this is a negative characteristic as they are labelled as aggressive, not assertive. As one respondent in the present study points out: '[It is] difficult for women who have to be not too male and not too female' (UK woman 8).

Not only do women consider that they must try to conform to a traditional masculine style, they also often feel the need to avoid any nurturing or caring behaviour, for fear of being criticised as too 'soft' (Priola 2007; Rhodes 2003). For some women, 'buying in' to the competitive nature of the university is their only alternative (Thomas & Davies 2002, p. 386), and 'becoming more male than men' has been recognised as being an issue for female senior academics (Mavin 2006, p. 80), as reflected in the present study:

> A number of women at the university have adopted male behaviour styles to get ahead and this is problematic for all concerned. They become not genderless, but sexless and they become very scary to men.
>
> (SA man 3)

This style of leadership demands a 'ruthless', single-minded approach to work where relationships and collaboration are replaced with an individualistic, output-focused academic one (Thomas & Davies 2002, p. 387). Thus, women can be seen to lack the typical attributes of good leaders and are then criticised when they display these attributes.

Without a critical mass of other women to affirm the legitimacy of a participative style, women usually opt for whatever style is typical of the men (Eagly & Carli 2007, p. 126), as several respondents illustrated:

> Women can feel the need to adopt male management styles and I think its unfortunate but maybe it's inevitable because there are so few role models around.
>
> (IRE woman 14)

> Definitely think that a lot of women think they have to act like men to get ahead. Probably it's a lack of female role models but it is

almost something in the system that forces you. We know that we will be more successful if we fit the mould and we will get further if we make fewer waves.

(SA woman 11)

Some of the senior managers thought this behaviour occurred because it was judged as the only way to 'get on':

There is pressure for women to adopt a 'male style' of management. Changing the culture of the current 'extremely conservative male model' of senior management will be a long-term task, probably it will take 10 years to change it.

(NZ man 5)

Very often women tend to adopt a more masculine style in order to stand firmly to their position and compete with men. But this is a masculine stereotype, because now always one can verify this stereotype in men's behaviour.

(PT man 21)

However, this pattern may be changing:

There have been women who have tended to adopt a male management style. It is becoming less common now, but there are still women who think they have to behave like men as managers.

(AUS woman 1)

Nevertheless, Turkish senior managers generally consider that management is management and there is not a gendered perspective involved:

In the management team, there shouldn't be any need to adapt to a certain management style of the relevant gender.

(TR man 5)

Adapting a style is not valid. There is a science of management. The women in senior management have to study management.

(TR woman 7)

There is no difference between the roles and expectations of male and female Rectors. They use the same managerial tools.

(TR man 14)

Several other respondents also consider that adopting male management styles is not an issue:

> I don't think women adopt male (masculine) styles. Women I know have their own style but not stereotypical. I know men whose decision-making styles I'd emulate because they're effective.
>
> (NZ woman 22)

> Some of them take an unusually strong approach to certain matters, but if they are confident in their own abilities and their own management capabilities in my experience they don't do that.
>
> (IRE man 9)

> Women do not feel the need to adopt a male management style any more. I would have seen it more 15–20 years ago.
>
> (AUS woman 7)

6.5   Women supporting women – or not

Women expect their women managers to display stereotypical female behaviours, and if they do not they are judged more harshly than are men in similar positions. Therefore, other women are not natural allies, because women in senior management roles have destabilised the normative gender expectations (Mavin 2006, p. 72), and thus become 'exiles' from their sex. As senior managers, they need to prove they are capable of doing the job in a masculine-gendered workplace, where they have to continually learn to survive. There are issues for them around being more visible than their male counterparts are, so either they try assimilation, as a survival strategy, or they become marginalised. There is also the expectation from other women that they will promote and progress women in management issues, while not becoming a man or 'Queen Bee' (Mavin 2006, p. 77), defined as someone who did it by themselves, enjoys being unique and denies that there is any systematic discrimination. The complex way in which a privileged gender-order is an embedded, socially constructing everyday experience for women (Mavin 2006, p. 85), encourages and exacerbates differences between women in order to prevent opposition in the form of an ordered coalition of women's interests.

> Women demand a lot from other women. You should never enter into a discussion that says 'well she is alright BUT'. And then there is

a lot of negative stuff ... I have women as support ... there are others who are more negative.

(SWE woman 7)

Some women in the present study feel the pressure of not meeting the expectations of other women, as also noted earlier in Chapter 4:

Once in senior management a lot of people do see you differently and it is hard to maintain networks and friendships. Sometimes women can be quite nasty to each other, the attitude seems to be 'I've done it hard and expect you to do it the same way'.

(NZ woman 11)

The expectations on women in top positions are different, they are an extra burden ... seen as a representative of all women. Women place a heavier burden on other women than men do.

(SA woman 15)

About the women, I actually think that very many of them are anti-feminist for some strange reason ... It is as if they think it is embarrassing to be a woman. Everyone should hide it. Sometimes it can be very difficult to collaborate with women.

(SWE woman 5)

My male colleagues see me simply as an administrator; my female colleagues see me as a woman and an administrator. When I became a candidate for the job of the Rector the severest criticisms I received, including comments on my lifestyle (I am single) and my gender, were voiced by my women colleagues.

(TR woman 1)

One woman went even further, saying that 'I think we teach men through our posture, the way we behave, because I'm anti-feminist and I think feminism leads nowhere' (PT woman 10).

There are women who believe that their female colleagues see them in a more favourable light than their male colleagues. Contrary to the position outlined above, they see that the differences they exhibit gain the support of other women, as discussed in Chapter 4:

I think probably female colleagues have a higher opinion of me than my male colleagues have, which is an interesting thing to say.

But I am relatively understated. I don't tend to grandstand or to empire build.

(AUS woman 9)

Other women stress this aspect of women's support saying that 'Women are more open, listen better and are more supportive on the whole' (UK woman 7) and they are 'seen as supportive, co-operative and collegiate' (UK woman 1).

6.6   Making a difference

While some women do get promoted to senior positions in universities, many who achieve this leadership role are considered to be 'token' women (Bagilhole 2000), a symbolic source of leadership. Once in senior academic positions these women are made ineffectual. Men are able to maintain their values and ideas as the dominant group while women are merely appointed to the job as a way of solving the dilemma of diversity, and thus are given no group voice (Bagilhole 2000). As a respondent in the present study notes:

Absolutely it makes a difference having women in senior management. We end up with more than one perspective. Quite often a woman's perspective is quite different. I don't believe in legislated diversity and equality in university committees. When you do that a few women end up on a ridiculous number of committees and it is to their disadvantage. Yes, they are tokens and they know it.

(AUS male 15)

It makes decisions better if you have people with different experiences, so that they can throw light from their perspective, the perspective that after all you have with you if you are a man or a woman.

(SWE man 3)

White (2005) suggests that while the presence of women in senior positions does not necessarily further the position of the majority of women, it could be argued that the presence of 'token' women may have symbolic importance, as these individuals are then able to show others that women are capable of reaching senior positions. This relates to one of the tenets of self-efficacy, defined as the belief in one's ability to be successful at a task or in reaching a pre-determined goal (Bandura 1997). Bandura (1997) identifies four sources of information by which self-efficacy beliefs are formed, including vicarious learning (that is watching someone else perform a task). Betz and Hackett (1997) argue that women, as a result of their sex-role socialisation, lack strong expectations of personal efficacy around career-related behaviours and consequently do not realise their potential. They have less access to the four sources of information identified by Bandura (1997). In particular, they lack exposure to female role models, which denies them information via vicarious learning. Women in senior management may therefore be seen as a '"beacon of hope" for women' (Mavin 2006, p. 72) and as role models for other women. This is voiced in the present study:

> [I've] not played a conscious gender role but by just being a woman in the position and 'doing your job' it helps other women.
>
> (SA woman 11)

> By and large female colleagues are very pleased to see women in senior roles ... somebody who has managed to get into a senior position and has done it while raising a family and doing other things and hence fairly useful as a role model.
>
> (IRE woman 23)

> Having women in senior management does make a difference. Men know we're there, and women bring a different perspective. They may not think they're a patch on them, but they see women performing these roles.
>
> (NZ woman 1)

> It does make a difference having women in senior management. They are still seen as iconic roles. It says to junior females, 'if you choose to go into senior roles, you can'.
>
> (AUS woman 16)

One man was 'optimistic now that women have been appointed to the senior management team, more women will be encouraged to apply' (NZ man 5).

There were also benefits for students in having women in senior positions as 'it makes a difference to students particularly women students. I think it changes their world view if they see that women take positions of equal responsibility to men' (IRE woman 14).

However, one woman thought that 'at this level any difference was rarely related to gender' (NZ woman 26), a position supported by several others:

> Having women in senior management positions does not make a huge difference except that it is good to have a female perspective on certain issues.
>
> (IRE man 9)

> [All] it should do is add a layer to decision making that is reflective of peoples' backgrounds, experiences, personality and these are far more important, whether you are male or female so you bring that with you. It is embedded, endemic.
>
> (IRE man 12)

A Swedish respondent indicates that 'of course there is a difference depending on what university management there is; but whether that has anything to do with whether you are women and men, that I cannot say' (SWE woman 1).

6.7   Working together

Given the perceived gender differences in management and leadership styles, women and men indicate different preferences about the composition of the senior management group in which they work, and different levels of comfort with working with members of the opposite sex. Some senior managers consider that there is really no difference based on gender. As one man indicates: 'a professional approach is more important' (NZ man 20) and a woman points out: 'The job's pretty structured so little difference shows' (UK woman 15). Another woman elaborates on this, saying:

> I see no difference in working with women at my level in comparison to working with men. I don't perceive that the difficulties are gender related, they are related more to individual characteristics that are non-gender related.
>
> (IRE woman 2)

However, some women prefer working with women because of the particular attributes they display in a senior management setting:

> I prefer to be among women. The odd male is alright, but if they outnumber you too much it becomes a 'them and us' situation. They can gang up on you, and lobby behind the scenes.
>
> (UK woman 16)

Women are more willing to air issues than men; for example, around work/life balance. Women are more strategic and operational. They are more conscious of implications of decisions made on staff.

(AUS woman 18)

If it's only women it is a more casual, friendlier type of discussion around the issue. The structure of the conversation is a bit different, more of a willingness to embrace new ideas, to push the boat out, to do something different.

(IRE woman 14)

With an all-woman team you don't have to worry about egos: it is easier, less formal ... Blokes being blokes, they didn't listen to what you said.

(NZ woman 23)

I prefer working with women because [in our culture] women are task-oriented, they are problem-solvers, they communicate more effectively, and they contribute more toward reaching a consensus. Men communicate poorly, and are more interested in asserting their power rather than addressing the problem at hand.

(TR woman 1)

Men also appreciate the strengths women bring to senior management, asserting that their communal style adds a further dimension to the process. They also find women more supportive and easier to relate to:

I probably value working more with teams of women than men. I find them focussed and their points of view creative and divergent. They are more able to contextualise decisions in terms of their impact on people.

(AUS man 2)

On average I find women easier to work with than men. Women are more open to criticism of their ideas and of amendments of them in order to turn them into ideas that would work.

(IRE man 7)

On the other hand, some respondents prefer to work with men:

I grew up with two brothers so I am very comfortable in the company of men, more so than women.

(SA woman 17)

I am more comfortable in a predominantly male management team. Academically I prefer males, for administrative positions I prefer females. Academic thinking is a bit male thinking. Males have higher IQ. For administrative jobs EQ [emotional quotient] is more important.

(TR woman 2)

I rather prefer to work with men ... men are different. When there are many women together the final output isn't that good. I think there's a kind of rivalry, competition.

(PT woman 19)

6.8   Doing it differently

In general it would appear that women's view and style of leadership is different to that of men: characterised by a willingness to share power and information, with high regard for people, as well as tasks, and more of a focus on collaboration and communication (Joyner & Preston 1998). Further, the attributes generally associated with female management are multi-tasking, supporting and nurturing, people and communication skills, and teamwork (Priola 2004). While doing it differently may be problematised, at the level of the individual in such a position this is not necessarily the case. Bringing a different ethos and perspective to the top positions was appreciated by both women and men in the present study. Different types of behaviour are manifested when women are part of the management group:

It does matter; all-male clubs are always a problem, I know you can't generalise, but women bring different perspectives; it's a different ethos, if it's mixed [there are] different ideas and perspectives.

(IRE woman 4)

Having women in senior management does make a difference. It is hard to articulate why it does, but if it prevents that footy club mentality developing that is really important. There is a different way of viewing the world and that perspective is important, and is subtle but distinct.

(AUS man 5)

Rapport-building especially is easier among women who value directness. Senior male management by comparison have ego problems, an element of competition and not wanting to share. Sometimes men are not as good at that pausing, reflecting, listening. Some men have status issues.

(NZ woman 2)

As Eagly and Carli (2007) suggest, women manage differently, but some of these differences are quite subtle. They tend to blend agency with communion rather than using a 'command and control' style, which works well in a range of settings. As already discussed, women can be sufficiently directive and assertive to be good leaders, while still retaining their expected warmth. This style also helps build social capital, as people like working with friendly assertive leaders and appreciate their goal directed energy, as indicated in the present study:

> It definitely makes a difference having female senior managers. They have a different approach, a different emphasis, a greater sensitivity to the emotional content of situations.

(AUS man 11)

> More women would be a net benefit. It would broaden the base of experience and expertise and provide other women with a role model. It would also be good for the blokes to deal with different styles.

(NZ woman 2)

> I don't think it will automatically lead to a different steer, lead to different decisions necessarily but it will certainly make a difference to the institution. It is important for the University to be seen as an institution that values women. Universities have lagged behind. Voices and language are male.

(IRE woman 14)

6.9 Moving on

In the changing environment of university cultures away from the more traditional masculinist model, transformational leadership, more commonly adopted by women, is increasingly being used as an effective leadership style and is considered to be the most effective in current conditions (Chesterman 2004; Doherty & Manfredi 2006; Miller 2006; Eagly & Carli 2007; Van Vugt, Hogan & Kaiser 2008; Eagly & Sczesny 2009).

A critical mass of women at senior levels creates an environment where a range of management styles is accepted. Women exhibit several different styles of management, such as innovation, building of relationships, valuing of staff and students, and discouraging competitive behaviours (Chesterman, Ross-Smith & Peters 2003). As more women take up leadership roles, beliefs that women do not resemble leaders are changing, as it is recognised that they have the characteristics required for the job (Eagly & Carli 2007). When people repeatedly and consistently observe women fulfilling non-traditional roles, they alter their stereotypes to reflect the qualities demanded by these roles. There have been changes in expectations of how leaders will behave with the inclusion of more communal characteristics, such as fostering followers' commitment and the ability to contribute creatively to their organisations (Eagly & Sczesny 2009, p. 33). The acceptance of diversity is reflected by those senior managers in the present study who prefer working in a mixed or balanced senior management team:

> During my administrative capacity I worked very extensively with both sexes. Almost half of the Deans were females. Almost half of the administrative staff working under my supervision was female, so were academicians. So, I always felt equally comfortable working with both sexes.
>
> (TR man 10)

Some managers feel uncomfortable being in an environment where they are an absolute minority, sometimes based on previous experience and sometimes based on self-knowledge:

> I'm more comfortable in a balanced team, definitely not in a predominantly male [one] as has been the case in the past.
>
> (UK woman 1)

> Slightly uncomfortable in an all male environment – always conscious that certain dimensions to the University are not always represented by an entirely male group ... women bring a slightly different perspective on some issues which is missing in an all male environment.
>
> (IRE man 9)

> Would not like to be in an all-women team as I worked in a girls' school. I prefer diversity in terms of decision-making; there is a bland homogeneity without different ages, genders, and diversity. Women can be conservative.
>
> (NZ woman 17)

Participants express a range of views about the benefits of balanced senior management teams, particularly the opportunity to draw on different viewpoints and approaches to dealing with issues:

> I do prefer a mixture because you get a more rounded set of views. Even to be able to remind men that the world is not male or that there are different considerations is a really valuable thing to do.
>
> (AUS woman 9)

> I believe in multifaceted teams. Men may come with very specific issues and they want to see those specific issues dealt with. Women may come with specific issues but take a broader context, which may become more important. You end up dealing with specifics but you have a much better contextualisation of where those specifics are emanating from.
>
> (IRE man 12)

> The balance in perspective is important. Sometimes all women teams get bogged down in details. All men teams miss the subtleties of the situation.
>
> (NZ woman 4)

Interestingly one woman prefers to work in a mixed gendered team because she feels that a mixed team 'moderated men's ego and women's tendency towards bitchiness' (NZ woman 26).

6.10   Conclusion

Different ways of behaving are attributed to gender, and while individual women may not conform to these stereotypes, the group ascription remains. Conversely, individual men may not behave in the expected stereotypical manner. Sinclair (1998, p. 37) argues that the expectation for leaders to be a certain type of person – a tough, heterosexual male exhibiting 'heroic masculinity', is an outdated concept (see also Chapter 7). However, a male bias can be difficult to overcome as males assume leadership and can patronise women (Van Vugt, Hogan & Kaiser 2008).

Men as well as women benefit from thinking about how gender shapes leadership style (Van Vugt, Hogan & Kaiser 2008, p. 25). As is evident in the current study, the importance of empathy and networking skills, and of valuing collaboration and cooperation over hierarchical management, is supported by many man as well as women (Chesterman, Ross-Smith & Peters 2003; Van Vugt, Hogan & Kaiser 2008).

Synergistic leadership theory (SLT), the framework developed by Irby et al. (2002), provides a way of examining and reflecting on the feminine voice in educational leadership by including organisational structure, leadership behaviours, external forces, and beliefs, attitudes and values (Leonard & Jones 2009). Rather than a hierarchical structure, it suggests that each factor equally affects the success of the leader in context, as well as their organisation; and, being gender-inclusive, it acknowledges that women exhibit leadership behaviours that differ from traditional male leadership (Irby et al. 2002).

There is some evidence that 'think manager, think male' (Miller 2006, p. 6) is no longer the absolute norm. Our eight-country study of senior managers in universities indicates that while both men and women buy into stereotypes, the agenic versus communal style of management is not sufficient to explain how management is conceptualised. Drawing on the factors posited by Irby et al. (2002), managers appreciate that neither they nor their colleagues generally fit comfortably at either end of the continuum. Rather, they see men and women choosing from a range of possibilities in terms of management style, and they realise the benefits of complementarity. In the final analysis, the majority of those interviewed see that having both women and men as members of the senior management team make for better decisions as more perspectives are considered and particular strengths compensate for areas of identified weakness.

References

Alimo-Metcalfe, B. (2004). 'Leadership: A masculine past, but a feminine future?' *Gender and Excellence in the Making*, (Brussels: European Commission), 161–8.

Bagilhole, B. (2000). The myth of superman: A feminist investigation of academic careers, paper presented to 2nd European Conference on Gender Equality in Higher Education, Zurich.

Bagilhole, B. and White, K. (2006). 'Making it to the top? Towards a gendered skills analysis of senior leadership and management positions in UK and Australian Universities', in C. Chesterman (ed.), *Change in Climate: Prospects for Gender Equity in Higher Education*, Proceedings of ATN WEXDEV Conference (Adelaide: ATN WEXDEV), 1–17.

Bandura, A. (1997). *Self-Efficacy: The Exercise of Control* (New York: Freeman).

Betz, N. E. and Hackett, G. (1997). 'Applications of self-efficacy theory to the career assessment of women', *Journal of Career Assessment*, 5, 4, 383–402.

Blackmore, J. and Sachs, J. (1999). *Managing Diversity or Managing for Diversity in the Corporate University* (Melbourne: Australian Association for Research in Education).

Blackmore, J. and Sachs, J. (2000). 'Paradoxes of leadership and management in higher education in times of change: Some Australian reflections', *International Journal of Leadership in Education* 3, 1, 1–16.

Brooks, A. (2001). 'Restructuring bodies of knowledge', in A. Brooks and A. Mackinnon (eds), *Gender and the Restructured University* (Buckingham: Society for Research into Higher Education and Open University), 15–44.

Chesterman, C., Ross-Smith, A. and Peters, M. (2003). 'They made a demonstrable difference: Senior women's efforts to redefine higher education management. Research outcomes for the project: Senior women executives and the cultures of management', *McGill Journal of Education,* 38, 3, 421–35.

Chesterman, C. (2004). Not doable jobs? Exploring senior women's attitudes to leadership roles in universities, paper presented at Women's Higher Education Network Conference (Bolton UK).

Cikara, M. and Fiske, S. T. (2009). 'Warmth competence and ambivalent sexism: Vertical assault and collateral damage', in M. Barreto, M. K. Ryan, and M. T. Schmitt, (eds), *The Glass Ceiling in the 21st Century: Understanding Barriers to Gender Equality.* (Washington: American Psychological Association), 73–96.

Currie, J. Thiele, B. and Harris, P. (2002). *Gendered Universities in Globalised Economies.* (Oxford: Lexington Books).

Deem, R. and Ozga, J. (1997). 'Women managing for diversity in a postmodern world', in C. Marshall (ed.), *Feminist Critical Policy Analysis: A Perspective from Post Secondary Education* (London and New York: Falmer), 25–40.

Doherty, L. and Manfredi, S. (2006). 'Women's progression to senior positions in English universities', *Employee Relations*, 28, 6, 553–72.

Eagly, A. H. and Carli, L. L. (2007). *Through the Labyrinth: The Truth about How Women Become Leaders* (Boston: Harvard Business School Publishing Corporation).

Eagly, A. H. and Sczesny, S. (2009). 'Stereotypes about women, men and leaders: Have times changed?' in M. Barreto, M. K. Ryan and M. T. Schmitt (eds), *The Glass Ceiling in the 21st Century: Understanding Barriers to Gender Equality* (Washington: American Psychological Association), 21–48.

Eveline, J. (2004). *Ivory Basement Leadership* (Crawley: University of Western Australian Press).

Haslam, S. A. and Ryan, M. K. (2008). 'The road to the glass cliff: Differences in the perceived suitability of men and women for leadership positions in succeeding and failing organisations', *The Leadership Quarterly* 19, 530–48.

International Labour Organisation (ILO) (2007). *Equality at Work: Tackling the Challenges. Report under the follow-up to the ILO Declaration on Fundamental Principles and Rights at Work* (Geneva: ILO).

Irby, B. J., Brown, G., Duffy, J. A. and Trautman, D. (2002). 'The synergistic leadership theory', *Journal of Educational Administration*, 40, 4, 304–22.

Joyner, K. and Preston, A. (1998). 'Gender difference in perceptions of leadership role, performance and culture in a university: A case study', *International Review of Women and Leadership*, 4, 2, 34–45.

Kouzes, J. and Posner, B. (2007). *The Leadership Challenge*, 4th edn (San Francisco: Jossey-Bass).

Leonard, N. and Jones, A. (2009). 'Synergistic leadership theory. 21st century theories of educational administration', *International Journal of Educational Leadership Preparation,* (Educational Modules and Materials, Virginia Tech).

Mavin, S. (2006). 'Expectations of women in leadership and management – Advancement through solidarity?' in D. McTavish and K. Miller (eds), *Women in Leadership and Management* (Cheltenham: Edward Elgar Publishing Limited), 71–88.

Miller, K. (2006). 'Introduction: Women in leadership and management: Progress thus far?', in D. McTavish and K. Miller (eds), *Women in Leadership and Management* (Cheltenham: Edward Elgar Publishing Limited), 1–10.

Morley, L. (2003). Sounds, silences, and contradictions: Gender equity in commonwealth higher education, Clare Burton Memorial Lecture Australia http://www.atn.edu.au/wexdev/news/burton2003.htm

Morley, L. (1994). 'Glass ceiling or iron cage: Women UK academia', *Gender, Work and Organisation*, 1, 4, 194–204.

Morley, L. (1999). *Organising Feminisms: The Micropolitics of the Academy* (New York: St. Martins Press).

Neale, J. and Özkanli, Ö. (2010). 'Organisational barriers for women in senior management positions: A comparison of Turkish and New Zealand Universities', *Gender and Education*, 22, 5, 547–63.

Neale, J. and White, K. (2004). 'Achieving the right balance: A comparative case study of senior academic women in Australia and New Zealand', *International Journal of Knowledge, Culture and Change Management* 4, 959–67.

O'Connor, P. (2010). 'Is senior management in Irish universities male dominated? What are the implications?' *Irish Journal of Sociology*, 18, 1, 1–21.

Priola, V. (2004). 'Gender and feminine identities: Women as managers in a UK academic institution', *Women in Management Review*, 421–30.

Priola, V. (2007). 'Being female doing gender. Narratives of women in education management', *Gender and Education*, 19, 1, 21–40.

Rhodes, D. (2003). 'The Difference "Difference" Makes', in D. Rhodes (ed.), *The Difference 'Difference' Makes: Women and Leadership* (Stanford: Stanford University Press), 3–50.

Ryan, M. K. and Haslam, S. A. (2005). 'The glass cliff: Evidence that women are over-represented in precarious leadership positions', *British Journal of Management*, 16, 81–90.

Ryan, M. K. and Haslam, S. A. (2007). 'The glass cliff: Exploring the dynamics of the appointment of women to precarious leadership positions', *Academy of Management Review*, 32, 2, 549–72.

Sinclair, A. (1998). *Doing Leadership Differently* (Carlton South: Melbourne University Press).

Strachan, G., Peetz, D., Bailey, J., Broadbent, K. and Whitehouse, G. (2008). 'Gender equity in universities: should we be worried?', in P. Stanton and S. Young (eds), *Workers, Corporations and Community: Facing Choices for a Sustainable Future* (The Association of Industrial Relations Academics of Australia and New Zealand http://www.mngt.waikato.ac.nz/airaanz/)

Thomas, R. and Davies, A. (2002). 'Gender and new public management: Reconstituting academic subjectivities', *Gender, Work and Organization*, 9, 4, 372–97.

Van Vugt, M., Hogan, R. and Kaiser, R. (2008). 'Leadership, followership and evolution', *American Psychologist*, 63, 3, 182–96.

Wager, M. (1998). 'Women or researchers? The identities of academic women', *Feminism and Psychology*, 8, 2, 236–44.

White, K. (2005). 'Surviving or thriving in academia: Women, teaching, research and promotion in Australian universities', in V. Maione (ed.), *Gender Equality in Higher Education* (Milan: FrancoAngela), 391–406.

Wilson, F. (2005). 'Caught between difference and similarity: The case of women academics', *Women in Management Review*, 20, 4, 234–48.

Wolfram, H. J. and Mohr, G. (2007). 'Professional respect for female and male leaders: Influential gender-relevant factors', *Women in Management Review*, 22, 1, 19–32.

Worden, S. and Groombridge, B. (2003). 'Values, visions, strategies and goals: Is coaching a viable pathway?' in B. Groombridge and V. Mackie (eds), *Re-searching the Research Agendas: ATN WEXDEV 2003 Conference* (Perth: Learning Support Network Curtin University of Technology), 175–85.

Wyn, J., Acker, S. and Richards, E. (2000). 'Making a difference: Women in management in Australian and Canadian faculties of education', *Gender and Education*, 12, 4, 435–47.

Yeatman, A. (1995). 'The gendered management of equity-oriented change in higher education', in J. Smyth (ed.), *Academic Work: The Changing Labour Process in Higher Education* (Buckingham: Society for Research into Higher Education and Open University Press), 194–205.

7

Where Do Women Fit in University Senior Management? An Analytical Typology of Cross-National Organisational Cultures

Pat O'Connor

7.1 Introduction

Universities present themselves as gender-neutral meritocracies, concerned with the transmission and creation of scientific, objective knowledge. However, it is now widely accepted that they are in fact gendered organisations (Brooks 2001; Collinson & Hearn 1996; Currie, Thiele & Harris 2002; Deem, Hilliard & Reed 2008; Hearn 2001; Morley 1994, 1999). In this chapter the focus is on the broader organisational culture, focussing particularly on its gendered character as seen through the eyes of senior academic managers.

It has been suggested that 'organisational culture is a function of leadership' (Parry 1998, p. 93). The concept of 'organisational culture' is a contested one. Alasuutari (1995, p. 25) suggests that it refers to a 'collective subjectivity' 'a way of life or outlook'. Wajcman (1998) argues that cultures are produced and reproduced through the negotiation, sharing and learning of symbols and meanings. McIlwee and Robinson (1992) suggest that it is reflected in day-to-day activities and interactions. Smircich (1983) and Bagilhole et al. (2007) suggest that organisational culture is a dynamic process that can be conceived as something an organisation *has*, something an organisation *is*, and something an organisation *does*. In the context of management, the concept of organisational culture has been used to refer to a complicated fabric of management myths, values and practices that legitimise women's positions at the lower levels of the hierarchy and portray managerial jobs as primarily masculine (Deem 2003; Bagilhole 2002; O'Connor 1996; Benschop & Brouns 2003), with Acker (1998) asserting that organisational culture reflects the wishes and needs of powerful men. Such work has suggested that the barriers women face in universities include those related to male definitions of merit; a 'chilly' organisational culture premised on male lifestyles and priorities; and a culture where senior positions are seen as 'posts of confidence' (Bond quoted in Brooks 2001, p. 24; Currie & Thiele 2001; Hearn 2001) and are premised on 'the way masculinity is constructed as a care-less identity' (Lynch & Lyons 2008, p. 181; see also Grummell, Devine & Lynch 2008; Bailyn 2003; Acker 1998).

In this context, changing women's position in universities requires changes to gendered culture as well as other kinds of change. For Hearn (2001, p. 70) the most important aspect of this is 'changing men and men's position in universities and their cultures'. Men as he sees them are 'a social category associated with hierarchy and power ... Management is a social activity that is also clearly based on hierarchy and power ... Academia is a social institution that is also intimately associated with hierarchy and power'. In this situation, 'Women's place' is defined by men and is a subordinate one. While 'ignoring difference, acting as equal' is often 'an important strategy for women ... it leaves patriarchal cultures intact' and is inherently fragile since at any moment women's status as honorary males may be withdrawn (Cockburn 1991).

As discussed in Chapters 2 and 4, academic senior managers who report directly to the Rector/VC/President are likely to be appointed by him in a managerial system, while in a collegial system they are likely to be nominated by largely male constituencies (O'Connor & White 2009). There has been a good deal of discussion about whether the organisational culture in collegial or managerial systems is more helpful for women. Deem (1998, pp. 48, 50) noted that managerialism makes explicit the low profile administrative and caring roles that have typically been carried out by women (Brooks 1997). However Deem (1998, p. 66) also argues that a managerial culture is incompatible with 'concerns about equity and feminist values' (see also Ozga & Walker 1999; Kerfoot & Knights 1996; Knights & Richards 2003). Similarly, Currie and Thiele (2001, p. 108) argue that although certain aspects of managerialism, such as equity targets, assist a few women to move into senior positions, most women, like most men, are 'likely to be proletarianised' by it. However, regardless of the collegial or managerial status of the organisational culture, Husu (2001b, p. 172) concludes that 'women's under-representation among academics and gender inequalities in academia appear to be persistent and global phenomena'. Hence, in this chapter the focus is on the gendered aspects of the wider organisational culture.

7.2   Sinclair's typology

Sinclair (1998, p.19) identifies a typology of such culture at senior management level:

1. *Denial*: that is the absence of women in such positions is not seen at all and/or is not seen as a problem
2. *Problem is women*: that is women should adopt male attitudes or life styles
3. *Incremental adjustment*: that is allowing access to a small number of women who are seen as a low risk to the established culture
4. *Commitment to a new culture*: that is commitment to fundamental cultural change and/or the identification of specific ways of producing that change

This schema is used to classify gendered organisational cultures in this cross-national study. However, the denial category is redefined to include both denial and the identification of processes used to maintain a culture that perpetuates male dominance and that is identified as a pro-male culture.

7.2.1   Denial and/or the identification of a pro-male culture

Connell (1987) is among those who suggest that it is in men's interests to deny the existence of gendered patterns or to see them as 'natural', 'inevitable' or 'what women want'. In their Australian and American study, Currie and Thiele (2001) find that men are most often in what the authors called the denial category, as reflected in the perceived lack of importance attaching to gender, or in suggestions that discrimination 'doesn't happen anymore' (see also Kloot 2004). There are costs for women in identifying gendered processes, not least of which is the fact that women do not want to depict themselves as 'victims of misfortune or injustice', or to open themselves up to the possibility of being professionally discredited or perceived as ungrateful (Husu 2001a). There is evidence to suggest that women are less likely than men to deny the importance of gender. In Harris, Thiele & Currie's (1998) study, the system is depicted as gender neutral by those who see it as 'reasonable': male professors, in particular, stress that 'there is no sex discrimination in university or academic life' (Harris, Thiele & Currie 1998, p. 259). On the other hand, those who see the system as flawed (and women academics are the majority of these in that study) are critical of what they see as institutional traditions that favour middle-aged men and 'people in the know', and of patterns of direct and indirect discrimination that favour those in the 'old boy's network'.

Deem (2003) finds two thirds of the women manager-academics in her UK study claim that women are treated differently to men in their universities. Furthermore, more than two-thirds of the women manager-academics in that study, as compared with 44 per cent of their male counterparts, think that gender affected their careers. Similarly, Bagilhole (1993) finds that three quarters of the women in her UK study consider that there is discrimination against women in their university. However, among the Turkish and Portuguese respondents in the present study, although both men and women deny the importance of gender, there are contradictions in their responses, with gender being simultaneously ignored and valorised (see Chapters 4 and 6). Similarly Healy, Ozbilgin & Aliefendioglu (2005, p. 257) highlight the fact that although women at professorial level in Turkey face 'structures of gendered discrimination yet the perception of gendered disadvantage was not high among our respondents'. The majority of the Turkish men and women in the present study suggest that there are no specific barriers to women's advancement in their University: 'There is none' (TR man 3); 'barriers for promotion are the same for men and for women' (TR woman 7); and a Portuguese respondent asserts: 'I've never felt mistreated or neglected because of being a woman' (PT woman 2). In this context, although the Rector is seen as extremely powerful, his role in relation to the gender profile of senior management is irrelevant, since there is no perceived discrimination: 'The Rector is very powerful legally. He is omnipotent. In Turkey there is no prejudice against women in senior management' (TR man 8).

Among the Portuguese participants there is a general sense that the academic environment in higher education itself is likely to be 'a more neutral environment' (PT man 22) in gender terms than the wider society: 'I don't think that in the university, there is this feeling of harming someone's academic career just by the fact of being a woman' (PT man 15): 'We are in a highly masculine society, we can't ignore that. But I think that higher education, despite all, is more neutral and indifferent to gender issues' (PT man 22).

Probert (2005, p. 70) stresses the importance of specifying the practices involved in perpetuating a pro-male culture. Men's relationships with other men are widely seen as a key factor in perpetuating such patterns (Hartmann 1981). This phenomenon is referred to in various terms that are variants of homosociability (Lipman-Blumen 1976; Hearn 2001; Kanter 1977/1993; Witz & Savage 1992; Husu 2001a and

2001b; Collinson & Hearn 2005; Blackmore, Thomson and Barty 2006). The essence of this process involves selecting leaders 'with familiar qualities and characteristics to one's self' so that leaders effectively '"clone" themselves in their own image', 'guarding access to power and privilege to those who fit in, to those of their own kind' (Grummell, Lynch & Devine 2009, p. 333; see also Witz & Savage 1992). Van den Brink (2009, p. 224) notes that in The Netherlands 'men tend to help their own sex in an unintentional "matter-of-fact" way', with obvious consequences as regards the way in which gatekeepers and support systems operate (see also Bagilhole & Goode 2001; Yancey Martin 1996; O'Meara & Petzall 2005).

In the present study, respondents from the UK, Australia, New Zealand, Ireland, Sweden and South Africa implicitly refer to homosociability as a key factor. For the UK respondents, collegiality is 'a convenient cloak for forms of male sociability and patriarchal exclusion'; 'men still prefer to work with men', with references to senior management as 'a boys club':

> Definitely the old boys' network still exists. They like promoting people like themselves. They are not willing to take what is seen as a risk with women, who are seen as different.
>
> (UK woman 16)

Among the New Zealand respondents there is a suggestion that, when there are more men than women on a promotion panel: 'There is a natural tendency for them to go for [candidates] who are the same as them' (NZ man 13), indicating the way in which homosociability is reproduced and even seen as 'natural' although it is recognised that 'they [women] may also perceive overt bias' (NZ man 5). Among the Australian respondents it was suggested that

> One barrier for women is that when recruiting someone for a position, you have a particular sort of person in mind ... If you are a male, you might see very masculine behaviour as ideal for a manager.
>
> (AUS woman 1)

Among the South African respondents reference is made to 'the boys club' as the main barrier to the advancement of women ('although it will be denied') and senior appointments being 'an opportunity to pay back my buddy' (SA man 8). Among the Swedish respondents male networks were simultaneously seen as natural and problematic and requiring intervention:

> I think the male networks are an obstacle. I don't think a lot of men
> sit around and plan to favour other men ... But we do have a greater
> part of our acquaintances of the same gender. Most people do, don't
> they? Since those in leading positions are mostly men, then their
> networks are mostly men.
>
> (SWE man 8)

This is compatible with the trends emerging in Currie and Thiele's
study (2001) where among their Australian and American respondents
pro-male attitudes of varying degrees of intensity are also perceived,
particularly by women. Similar kinds of patterns emerge with the Irish,
and to a lesser extent, the Australian respondents:

> Most of the men that I work with, the bottom line is that they would
> be much more comfortable to be working with men. They vaguely
> put up with you, accept that you have a right to be there, but if it was
> up to themselves they are more comfortable around men.
>
> (IRE woman 15)

Gherardi (1996) suggests that this reflects a positioning of women as
effectively 'guests' within a male world in a context where they are
simply not accepted as an equal. Such views are very strongly articulated by the Irish respondents: 'You think: are we in the twenty-first
century or in the eighteenth? There is chauvinism to the Irish psyche'
(IRE woman 13):

> One thing you can never be in this job is one of the boys ... [there is]
> a certain place that other male colleagues can go with regard to one
> another that you won't go.
>
> (IRE woman 23)

Parker and Jary (1995) suggest that conformity characterises higher
management in universities (see also Goode & Bagilhole 1998). Harris,
Thiele & Currie (1998, p. 142) also find in their Australian study that
what are seen as the organisational attributes of success include
those who 'don't rock the boat' and who show 'a certain deference
pattern', whereas 'if you speak up and you do things ... that are seen
to be threatening, you don't get ahead'. Madden (2005, p. 6) notes that
'Direct language, disagreement ... were less well received from women'.

Irish and occasionally Australian respondents considered that being outspoken is problematic: 'They have a vision of senior female managers as ones who do not speak' (AUS woman 16); 'You are supposed ... not to be outspoken on things you feel very strongly about; it is a very male domain' (IRE woman 4). Gherardi (1996, pp. 194, 196) also refers to the 'outsider who ... refuses to conform to local traditions, who asks embarrassing questions':

> Sometimes you can find yourself looking at things slightly differently. If you do that quite a lot ... you can get pigeon-holed as the person who will always have a contrary view.
>
> (IRE woman 14)

Hey and Bradford (2004, p. 697) also refer to the 'antagonism of misogyny disguised as rational public discourse' (see also Morley 1999). Deem (1999) and Whitehead (1998, p. 209) draw attention to the ways that keeping 'emotions under wraps' is seen as important, reflecting the priority still attached to 'the man/manager as the rational, controlled and logical agent'. Indeed Morley's (1999, pp. 84, 86) respondents see the organisational culture in the academy as aggressive (see also Goode & Bagilhole 1998). References are also occasionally made in the present study to an aggressive management culture and, particularly in the UK, Ireland and Australia, one that is seen as effectively hostile to women: 'Men don't like female voices ... There is an openly aggressive, anti-female environment in senior management and they don't even realise it' (AUS woman 16). Reference is made by the UK respondents to a 'macho management culture' (UK woman 1); an 'aggressive male management style' (UK woman 8) and 'a testosterone fuelled agenda' (UK woman 17). In one Irish case so real is the possibility of physical violence that it is officially recognised: 'I was personally threatened. I was experiencing bullying by people who had been on senior management ... I was shouted at, screamed at, threatened' (IRE woman 6).

The tension between leadership and gender roles (Eagly, Johannesen-Schmidt and van Engen 2003) is referred to by the South Africans and it is suggested that it is a lose/lose situation for women:

> Sometimes the requirement is to be aggressive or competitive and if you cannot do that by virtue of your socialisation, then it is not in your favour and if you are able to do it, you get judged negatively, so it is a double whammy.
>
> (SA woman 14)

Currie and Thiele (2001) also find that low profile, nurturing and housekeeping tasks are given to women, which do not facilitate their subsequent visibility and success, thus raising questions of the differential value that is attached to activities undertaken predominantly by men/women (see also Kloot 2004; Bagilhole 1993). As one respondent notes: 'There is a habit of giving high teaching loads to women' (AUS woman 1). Among Irish and New Zealand respondents there are occasional references to the fact that (as in Harris, Thiele & Currie's 1998 study), things are improving, in a context where all-male boards had been accepted in the recent past. There are references to 'lack of transparency in the procedures: no clear criteria for promotion' (UK woman 15) and to other issues involving procedures and criteria:

> One barrier is a very cumbersome and bureaucratic process ... I think women are put off by the increasing focus on research, because they are in those discipline areas that don't have a strong research background.
>
> (AUS woman 9)

Overall, then, the denial of the importance of gender within the academy is most likely to characterise the responses of the Turkish and Portuguese respondents. Among the Irish, UK, Australian, New Zealand and South African respondents, there are references, particularly by women, to a pro-male culture, which is reflected in homosociability and in subtle ways of privileging men and marginalising women.

7.2.2 'The problem is women ... and their attitudes and priorities'

Morley (1994, p. 194) identifies early the danger of constructing women 'as a remedial group with the emphasis on getting them into better shape in order to engage more effectively with existing structures' (see also van den Brink 2009). More recently, Morley (2005, p. 115) notes that 'We need a theory of male privilege rather than female disadvantage'. However, many of the senior managers in the present study, particularly men, refer to women's own attitudes, which they see as limiting possibilities as regards change, thus implicitly depicting women as 'the problem'. Such explanations have an element of validity, reflecting as they do 'the psychological effects of living in a sexist society' (Husu 2001a, p. 38). To some extent this can be seen as effectively 'blaming the victim'. However, insofar as such attitudes reflect deeper constructions of femininity, they can be seen as constituting cultural limits to the possibilities for change (see Grummell, Devine & Lynch 2008).

The men in both Bagilhole and Goode's (2001) study of academics and in Davies-Netzley's (1998) wider study of Chief Executives, attribute their success to individual qualities, thus reflecting and reinforcing an ideology of individualistic success: 'individualism is the myth while male support systems are the reality' (Bagilhole & Goode 2001, p. 162). In the present study there is widespread evidence both of depicting women's own attitudes as 'the problem' and of stressing their greater domestic and family responsibilities. There are even elements of seeing women as the problem in Australia, Sweden and South Africa, but in these cases such attitudes tend to be located within an appreciation of the nature of the wider cultural and social context.

It is widely recognised that women are poor at marketing themselves and taking credit for their achievements, such patterns reflecting cross-cultural norms surrounding modesty concerning individual achievements (Eagly & Carli 2007; Yancey Martin 1996; Bagilhole & Goode 2001; Doherty & Manfredi 2006; Davies-Netzley 1998), and contrasting with what Collinson and Hearn (1994) call the practical enactment of careerist masculinity. These kinds of attitudes appear particularly but not exclusively among the Irish, New Zealand and South African respondents:

> When you kick a goal, what do you do? You dance around and hug everyone. You make sure that everyone recognises that you scored a goal ... Those that weren't at the match you say: "I will buy you a drink". They [women] weren't comfortable playing those games.
>
> (IRE woman 5)

> Women do not claim enough credit. They just get on and do the job with very little fanfare. So they are not strategic enough about their personal branding.
>
> (SA woman 13)

Both men and women refer to women's feelings of not 'being valued' (IRE man 12): 'women do not even try because they don't believe they are good enough, probably as a result of socialisation' (SA woman 10); 'Women often don't appreciate their own worth and don't push' (NZ woman 23); 'women are a bit more modest when it comes to holding up their own merits ... and saying "I'll take it. I am good and I can do it"; a little more self critical' (SWE man 3). Bagilhole and Goode

(2001, p. 169) find that women have a 'misguided faith in the idea that high quality work and demonstrated commitment would be recognised and rewarded', and they want 'to achieve in their own right and through their ability'. They suggest that this is 'not just naivete', but rather that it reflects a rejection of academic politics (Bagilhole & Goode 2001): 'Promotion is a game. They [women] did not see it as a game and they thought the rules were unfair' (IRE woman 5):

> They [women] just won't believe that men, and those who further men, work very much together. They really lobby. We as women don't understand that we have to go in and act ... you think it is tiresome.
>
> (SWE woman 7)

References are made by the Australian and New Zealand respondents (both men and women) to women not applying for positions in the same proportions as men and/or doing so at a later stage: 'Women want to be sure and not be rejected, and are averse to risk, whereas men will chance their arm' (NZ woman 19); 'Women clear the bar by a great deal when they apply ... women wait until they are certain they can get over the bar' (AUS man 21). Among Irish and South African respondents, women's insufficient career planning features as an explanation (see also Thomas & Davies 2002):

> Males had planned ... what they would need to do, how much funding, PhDs, publications ... where females seemed to just keep doing these things [and thought that] I will at some point put it together and I will be promoted – much more passive.
>
> (IRE man 12)

It is striking how often individual 'private troubles', in a South African context, become presented as 'public issues' (Wright Mills 1970). Thus, for example, an awareness of systemic processes is evident in explaining women's lack of advancement; their difficulty in breaking into established networks and being 'politically savvy at institutional level' (SA woman 11): 'all marginalised groups do not always understand processes' (SA woman 13).

For Acker (1998), as for Bailyn (2003), the gendered subculture in organisations ultimately rests on the fact that economic structures have priority over all other structures. This is ultimately premised on 'the way masculinity is constructed as a care-less identity' (Lynch & Lyons

2008, p. 181). At the other extreme familial constraints are identified and accepted by both Turkish men and women. In a number of studies (Deem 2003; Currie & Thiele 2001), it is particularly men who are likely to see women's academic careers as negatively impacted on by childcare. In the present study, among the Irish, Portuguese and the New Zealand respondents and to a lesser extent the Australians and South Africans, it is particularly men who think that family responsibilities must be a barrier: 'This is what is the barrier for women ... family is a huge issue' (IRE man 18); 'Ladies are the ones to give birth to children as well as the ones who take care of them ... men can help in raising them, but for now, things are like this' (PT man 14); 'The barriers ... are women's different life experiences; taking time off for child rearing and bearing and career breaks are an issue' (NZ man 8); 'Career interruptions are still a major barrier for women. To the extent that women have time out of the workplace, it does create an extra hurdle' (AUS man 11). In Sweden and to a lesser extent in South Africa there was a reflective problematising of family as 'normal obstacles – no I should not say normal – the frequent obstacles that exist in society with the difficulties in combining career and family' (SWE man 3). A senior woman commented:

> I don't think it is home and children and such, like everybody says ... What prevents us is that we live in a patriarchal society where what women do is not valued in the same way as what men do. Where people find it hard to see that a woman may be a good leader ... that men are scared of women. Or that they don't have any respect for women.
>
> (SWE woman 5)

The Australian and Swedish respondents also occasionally link patterns to a wider societal or situational context: 'There is a culture that women do not relocate because their partners will not move' (AUS man 21); 'Some of the most successful women here have retired husbands or stay-at-home husbands' (AUS woman 12):

> The barriers come with the holistic roles that women have – family demands, interrupted careers, managing motherhood. How their career interruptions are perceived by promotion panels ... there are societal expectations that put women in complex and challenging roles.
>
> (AUS woman 10)

Interestingly the South African respondents think it is possible to transcend these difficulties, through familial support as well as through mentoring and systemic change.

Overall, then, much is made, particularly but not exclusively by men, of women's lack of career planning and poor ability to market themselves and their domestic and family responsibilities across the countries in the present study. Such explanations implicitly or explicitly define women as 'the problem' and so obviate the need to look at intra-organisational culture and procedures in explaining these patterns. However in the case of the Australian, Swedish and South African respondents, these explanations are likely to be located in a wider situational or societal context reflecting a recognition of the cultural construction of gender, including family responsibilities (Ely & Padavic 2007).

7.2.3 Incremental adjustment

Husu (2006, p. 5) stresses that gate keeping has a 'dual nature'; it 'can function as exclusion and control, on the one hand, and as inclusion and facilitation on the other'. Chapter 5 differentiates between advancement into the academic professoriate and into senior academic management. Admission to the professoriate is typically presented as being purely meritocratic, although van den Brink (2009) very seriously challenges that assumption. But, typically, to be considered for academic senior management, professorial status is seen as a prerequisite, thus inevitably restricting the available pool of women because women are under-represented at this level (see Chapter 2).

In the incremental ideal type, some women are admitted, not least to legitimise the system, but they remain 'outsiders on the inside' (Moore 1988 in Davies-Netzley 1998). Thus, they are never quite accepted: 'By choosing men as insiders, they are relegating women to outside status even when intentional gender bias is absent' (Bagilhole & Goode 2001, p. 171). In this context, as Kanter (1977/1993) notes, women are under considerable pressure to uphold the existing structures and culture and, in particular, not to support other women: 'The price of being one of the boys is being hard on the girls'. Several New Zealand respondents focus on helping individuals in a context where the culture is seen as an 'extremely conservative male mode ... You can't legislate for change ... [instead] try and help individuals ... cultural change will take time' (NZ man 5), although there was a suggestion that things were changing:

The sciences continue to have a very chauvinistic climate ... [However] the further you go up, the less likely you are to get that kind of behaviour ... There are still traces of prejudice and a lack of role models.

(NZ woman 1)

There are occasional references to women's 'insider outsider' position reflected in the differential perception of men's and women's failure: 'If women fail this is seen as being much worse than if men fail and this could affect the situation for all women' (NZ woman 22). There are references to women being excluded from the inner senior management team, and to not getting paid the same salary and bonuses as male senior managers (AUS woman 20). Blackmore (2002, p. 437) refers to a '"glass escalator" that facilitates male academics (and managers) moving up higher and faster'.

In Ireland, there are some academic men (but no women) in senior academic management positions who are not at professorial level and this is completely ignored by the respondents. On the other hand, some Irish men present themselves as well-intentioned and frustrated by the absence of 'suitable women' for senior academic management positions, saying of the absence of women: 'It's more through lack of opportunity and lack of potential candidates within the system than any design' (IRE man 9). There is also a suggestion that being in senior management is ultimately not in women's interests (Connell 2005):

> We have a number of good women doing a great job ... but I wouldn't want to pull them out of what they are doing ... to pull them into the management area, even from their own career path point of view they are better off ... doing their own research, publishing papers, getting money in, getting very well known in their own area.

(IRE man 19)

This seems to reflect a kind paternalistic 'heroic masculinity' (Kerfoot & Whitehead 1998, p. 451) insofar as it purports to protect women, while at the same time reflecting and maintaining men's own positional power. Similar kinds of attitudes are occasionally referred to by South African respondents: 'it is still a very paternalistic set up' (SA man 12) and this is seen as being reflected in describing women always as 'young and promising' (see also van den Brink 2009).

As noted in Chapter 6, in New Zealand, Ireland, Australia and the UK, the presence of women in senior management is to varying degrees seen as important in terms of potentially influencing young people for the future and so contributing to incremental change (Bagilhole

1993): 'It says to junior females "if you choose to go into senior roles, you can"' (AUS woman 16); 'They have to see people in these positions for them to think "I might do that"' (IRE woman 14); 'there are [glass] ceilings all over the place. They have to be corrected [and to do this we] need role models' (IRE man 12). Among the New Zealanders there is a strong feeling that having women in senior management makes a difference in terms of showing men that women are capable of undertaking these tasks: 'Men know we are there' (NZ woman 1); and that 'it signals that this is a viable career option for women' (NZ woman 22). This kind of change is essentially incremental and poses little threat to the current status quo.

Among New Zealand participants, references to incremental change are most obvious. The dominant culture is explicitly recognised as, to varying degrees, are the challenges this poses for those who are in a minority position. On the other hand, Irish and Australian respondents suggest that women 'would be better off' accepting that they would remain outside it. Thus New Zealand, Irish, UK, and Australian respondents see the presence of women in senior management as important in terms of potentially influencing young people in the future, reflecting an incremental approach to change.

7.2.4　Commitment to a new culture

Sinclair (1998) suggests that the essence of this commitment is recognition of the importance of fundamental change in the university organisational culture. Such tendencies are most obvious with the South African and to a lesser extent the Australian and Swedish respondents insofar as gender is taken seriously as a systemic issue. Probert (2005, p. 64) argues that in Australia 'policies in support of equal employment opportunities and affirmative action have been effective', although her focus on the almost equal representation of men and women on the executive of the University of Western Australia is very much on best practice.

The South African respondents are unusual in referring to the University as 'a highly political space' (SA man 6). Experiences in a racial context in South Africa transfer in some cases to a gender context: 'the structure of gender and the structure of race are everywhere in the way that the University is organised' (SA man 3). They are reflected in assertions that: 'Issues of gender sensitivity are important ... we cannot treat them [women] as second-class citizens' (SA man 7). However, race supersedes gender: 'If I cannot get a black person, at least it must be a woman' (SA woman 13); 'Race definitely overrides gender in selection decisions' (SA man 6); 'In our country we see first race and then gender– It is a double whammy for a black woman' (SA woman 10).

The South African participants see the culture as a predominantly white male one; it is a 'tough environment for women' who have to spend a 'lot of emotional energy to think consciously and strategically about what position they are going to take over an issue, whereas men have only to think about the issue' (SA man 3). In this context it is noted that 'institutional cultures are not women friendly', with the barriers to women's advancement being seen as 'very rigid philosophies, ideologies, beliefs and practices that are male dominated and are inherently women unfriendly' (SA woman 15); 'There are institutional cultural factors, discrimination (explicit and implicit) in selection processes' (SA woman 14). It is stressed that the VC and the Deans should provide active leadership in improving the gender equity profiles of their faculties, with the VC in particular expected to be: 'A direct supporter of gender equity and that gender equity (with targets) form a central part of the Dean's key performance areas' (SA woman 15).

The barriers to women's advancement include references to 'a history of not promoting women, not enough change agents who were black or female' (SA woman 10); 'We need stronger policies. Then we need proper monitoring of implementation with consequences for non-performance' (SA man 8). However, because of racial sensitivities, there is a striking willingness among South African VCs to 'make a rigorous and conscious effort to appoint demographically representative individuals even if it takes much longer' (SA woman 13). to reject short lists if they are 'demographically unacceptable' (SA man 12); and to challenge the recommendations of selection committees which had not changed their composition, as they 'remain in their comfort zone of appointing people like themselves (i.e. white males)' (SA woman 10).

For Australian and Swedish respondents what is most striking is the taken-for-granted acceptance of the legitimacy of specific attempts to change the organisational culture:

> The VC restructured the Executive Group and added two positions to it with the express purpose of getting two women in the group. It was very much an affirmative action initiative on the part of the VC.
>
> (AUS man 5)

> On two occasions the previous female VC quite deliberately gave two women the chance to act in senior management roles for substantial periods of time ... so that they had sufficient track records

to apply for the positions when they came up. That was a deliberate intervention that was successful.

(AUS woman 9)

The colleges elect ... the Rector decides. If it is very even she may decide to take the woman if there has never been a woman before ... There is a policy to have a woman as Pro-Rector if the Rector is a man and vice-versa.

(SWE woman 5)

He [the Rector] said that he wanted a female Pro-Rector ... there is of course such a policy concerning leadership positions that you are supposed to look for women where it is male-dominated.

(SWE woman 1)

Blackmore (2002) outlines the changes occurring in Australian universities and highlights their negative gender consequences. In the present study, there are suggestions that the 'push' in Australia in the 1990s regarding gender equity has eased off, with some respondents specifically referring to the fact that there were more women in senior management in the past and that 'now it is predominantly male' (AUS man 8). However, others note that in particular universities the proportion of women in senior management still is 'a corporate indicator' (AUS woman 9). Hence, although contra-tendencies are recognised, the Australian participants suggest that there is still a commitment to a new culture. Similarly although there are particular areas that are seen by Swedish respondents 'as unbelievably male dominated' (SWE woman 2) there is typically an acceptance of the need for change in organisational culture. Such change includes implementation of specific measures for women such as, for example, 'a power package for gender equality' (SWE woman 1), including research grants for women in minority positions who are at risk of exploitation; additional supports for women who are near professorial level (SWE man 8) and a leadership and coaching programme for women. It also includes a taken-for-granted acceptance that an active commitment to gender balance necessitates rigorous vigilance: 'You have to co-ordinate if you are to maintain gender equality in these positions ... The Deans always forget to consult with one another and then in the last minute they have to make a replacement, for otherwise there will be four men standing there' (SWE man 9).

There is also a strong suggestion, particularly by the Australian, but also to some extent by the Swedish and South African respondents, that such changes reflect the presence of women in senior management in these countries and their role in keeping a focus on gender: 'the gender balance issue is invisible if you don't keep reminding them' (AUS woman 13); 'It is an advantage to have a woman Rector who is alert to gender issues' (SWE woman 6); 'We have a strong equity focus here because of our female VC' (AUS woman 10); 'Women Rectors care about gender equality in all management positions ... all decisions must go through a gender scrutiny' (SWE woman 4); 'Being at the table as a senior manager keeps people honest; people correct themselves ... we want to have women doing this' (AUS woman 14). Thus the presence of women is typically seen as impacting on attitudes, including preventing 'that footy club mentality developing' (AUS man 5) and 'bringing in the human element ... what are the important issues to people in the organisation' (AUS woman 13). Furthermore, the taken-for-granted presence of women in senior management in Australia is reflected in the observation that

> To make a comment on whether women in senior management make a difference, you would have had to be in an organisation where they weren't there, so therefore it is difficult to make a comment.
>
> (AUS woman 7)

Interestingly in contexts where the systemic nature of the problem of organisational culture is recognised, there appears to be a greater willingness to refer to variations between women: 'It probably matters which women you have got' (AUS woman 20):

> There are different types ... of women in these positions. There are those who are not very gender conscious or gender interested ... But then there are women who have taken their stand ... and are working with gender issues very much.
>
> (SWE woman 1)

There are a small number of references by the South African and Swedish women to some women's negative attitudes: 'Women place a heavier burden on other women than men do' (SA woman 14); and to women 'who do their best to discourage and sabotage the efforts of other women' (SA woman 15); 'I am disappointed in many women. There is no network, no solidarity, nothing. There is, rather, competition and exploitation' (SWE woman 5). Some men also suggest that women are not supportive of each other: 'the female participants were not more positive towards the female applicants than the male ones were; rather the opposite ... if there was a difference at all' (SWE man 3). There are occasional suggestions by the South Africans that the problem lies with black men rather than with white men, exemplifying a kind of 'othering' of hostility and a fracturing of patriarchy along racial lines that is reminiscent of a colonial perspective. These same phenomena are also occasionally evident among Australian respondents: 'where there are more women on the panel, the tougher it is for female applicants' (AUS man 17); 'Some of the men have terrific qualities in relation to gender, others go by the book' (AUS woman 3).

Among the Irish respondents, organisational culture characterised by gender discrimination (Husu 2001a, p. 334) is occasionally seen as 'old-fashioned' (IRE man 9); and 'Universities have lagged behind; the voices and the language are mostly male still' (IRE woman 14). In that context the presence of women in senior management is seen as most legitimate in a discourse that stresses diversity, representation and equality:

> If you are a team player why would you not have women in the team? senior and junior? ... We talk a lot about access or disabled, disadvantaged... and it is a bit strange when people don't think [that] 50% of the people are men 50% are women.
>
> (IRE man 11)

However, reservations about the extent to which gender issues are salient are expressed by some respondents, particularly women: 'It would be nice to think that there is some consciousness of it, I'm not so sure that there is' (IRE woman 23); 'in relation to gender, I just wonder are they gender blind? They don't see it as an issue' (IRE woman 15). For UK respondents, although gendered barriers to women's promotion are identified, 'men were perceived as the rightful owners of management positions' (UK woman 8), and gender is not seen as part of the agenda of the VC: 'He [VC] doesn't have gender on his agenda' (UK woman 16); 'The gender profile is not seen as an issue' (UK woman 17). Even in Sweden there were occasional suggestions that an earlier momentum is not being maintained: 'the big effort was done about ten years ago' (SWE woman 5); 'Perhaps we have not come so far in twenty years after all. It is the same arguments that come back; new persons with the same arguments' (SWE woman 7).

Thus, not only among the Turkish and the Portuguese, but also among the Irish respondents there is very little evidence of any willingness to think about new procedures to bring about that change. Indeed there is a good deal of ambivalence regarding the use of the President's/ VC's great power in Ireland and New Zealand to create gender balance in the senior management team, with gender presented as very much a residual issue: 'It is important, all things being equal, that decisions that are at the margins they should go in the direction of gender balance' (IRE man 20); 'I think he [the President] is interested in equality issues … [but] I don't think he would say to the Director of HR we need to get another woman on Senior Management' (IRE woman 13). Some tentativeness also appears among the New Zealand respondents, although it is clear that some New Zealand VCs are 'very pro-equity and diversity' and interested in actively increasing the women in their management team. However, even these consider that they 'could not push too hard with regard to Heads of Department in case there was a backlash' (NZ man 20). For others, 'political correctness' is seen as getting in the way 'of engaging properly with gender and leadership issues' (NZ man 21).

Overall, then, a commitment to a new culture is most evident in the South African and to a lesser extent the Australian and Swedish respondents. Among the Irish and the New Zealanders a kind of tentativeness is identified reflecting an unwillingness to actually commit to the creation of a new culture. These findings reflect Fletcher's (2002, pp. 3–4) observation that: 'the transformative potential of new leadership practices is being co-opted, silencing its most radical challenges to workplace norms about power, individual achievement, meritocracy, and the privileging of managerial and hierarchical knowledge'.

7.3   Summary, explanations and conclusions

This chapter describes variation in organisational cultures at senior management level focussing on the gendered dimension. Denial of the importance of gender in universities is most obvious among the Turkish and Portuguese respondents. In Chapter 4 it was shown that these countries are most likely to have universities that are collegial rather than managerial. On the other hand, a commitment to a new culture is most apparent in South Africa, Sweden and Australia – and the latter in particular is moving strongly towards managerialism.

As in Currie and Thiele's (2001) research, women in the present study more often refer to systemic factors while men are more often in the denial category. The organisational culture that is depicted, particularly by the women respondents in the UK, Australia, New Zealand and Ireland, is one where men are, for the most part, generally comfortable working with other men, and which is conformist and homosocial. In most of the countries in the present study, there is some evidence of depicting women as 'the problem', either because of their attitudes or because of their perceived domestic and family responsibilities (although the systemic source of such problems is particularly likely to be referred to by the Australian, Swedish and South African respondents).

Such patterns are also identified in other studies (Whitehead 2001), although they sit uneasily with the fact that the proportion of women in senior management at less prestigious institutions is considerably higher than in universities even within the same country (O'Connor 2007; Bagilhole & White 2008). Incremental change is most obvious among the New Zealand respondents. However, although there is widespread acceptance that the VC/President can determine the gender profile of the senior management team, in New Zealand and Ireland there is a marked reluctance to actually do this, with references being made to lack of potential candidates and a paternalistic attitude that women are 'better off' not being in management.

In understanding such variation, it is suggested that the role of the state is critical. The overall context of the Irish state is described as patriarchal (O'Connor 2008). Thus the state structures in Ireland that interface with universities provide little support or encouragement for gender change at senior management level (O'Connor & White 2009). In contrast, in South Africa, although gender is subordinated to race, the state is seen as having a very clear responsibility to transform the white male organisational culture within universities; while in Sweden the state is supportive of measures to actively promote gender equality. Similarly in Australia, the importance of state policies and particularly the role of femocrats in the 1990s in advancing a feminist perspective has been crucial in creating a commitment to a new culture there, although there were suggestions that this was waning.

In addition specific situational factors are also seen as important (Healy, Ozbilgin & Aliefendioglu 2005). Such factors may inhibit or facilitate challenges to the organisational culture. Thus, for example, in Ireland senior manager-academics are most likely to be internal: 'It's cheaper for them not to go out' (IRE woman 13) and the tendency towards cultural continuity is exacerbated by 'a lack of any tradition of mobility between institutions' (IRE man 19), thus reducing the existence of possible change agents from outside the system. A similar pattern exists in Turkey (Neale & Özkanli 2010). In contrast in Australia and South Africa, possibilities for advancement are seen as lying in a move 'out and up', a factor that is arguably not unrelated to the greater commitment to a new culture in university senior management in those countries.

Overall, however, with the exception of the denial of the importance of gender by senior managers in Turkey and Portugal, and a commitment to a new culture particularly in South Africa, Australia and Sweden, the similarities in this cross-national study are more striking than the differences, with homosociability and the perception of women as 'the problem' for various reasons occurring across all of the countries.

References

Acker, S. (1998). 'The future of "gender and organizations": Connections and boundaries', *Gender, Work and Organisation*, 5, 4, 195–206.

Alasuutari, P. (1995). *Researching Culture: Qualitative Method and Cultural Studies* (London: Sage).

Bagilhole, B., Powell, A., Barnard, S. and Dainty, A. (2007). *Researching Cultures in Science, Engineering and Technology: An Analysis of Current and Past Literature* (Research Report Series for UKRC No.7).

Bagilhole, B. (2002). 'Challenging equal opportunities: Changing and adapting male hegemony in academia', *British Journal of Sociology of Education*, 23, 1, 19–33.

Bagilhole, B. and Goode, J. (2001). 'The contradiction of the myth of individual merit, and the reality of a patriarchal support system in academic careers', *The European Journal of Women's Studies* 8, 2, 161–80.

Bagilhole, B. (1993). 'How to keep a good woman down: an investigation of the role of institutional factors in the process of discrimination against women academics', *British Journal of the Sociology of Education*, 14, 3, 261–74.

Bagilhole, B. and White, K. (2008). 'Towards a gendered skills analysis of senior management positions in UK and Australian Universities', *Tertiary Education and Management*. 14, 1, 1–12.

Bailyn, L. (2003). 'Academic careers and gender equity: Lessons learned from MIT', *Gender, Work and Organisation*, 10, 2, 137–53.

Benschop, Y. and Brouns, M. (2003). 'Crumbling ivory towers: Academic organising and its gender effects', *Gender, Work and Organisation*, 10, 2, 194–212.

Blackmore, J. (2002). 'Globalisation and the restructuring of higher education for new knowledge economies: New dangers or old habits troubling gender equity work in universities?' *Higher Education Quarterly*, 56, 4, 419–41.

Blackmore, J., Thomson, P. and Barty, K. (2006). 'Principal selection: Homosociability, the search for security and the production of normalised principal identities', *Educational Management, Administration and Leadership*, 34, 3, 291–317.

Brooks, A. (2001). 'Restructuring bodies of knowledge', in A. Brooks and A. Mackinnon (eds), *Gender and the Restructured University* (Buckingham: Society for Research into Higher Education and Open University), 15–45.

Brooks, A. (1997). *Academic Women* (Buckingham: Open University Press).

Cockburn, C. (1991). *In the Way of Women: Men's Resistance to Sex Equality in Organisations* (London: Macmillan).

Collinson, D. L. and Hearn, J. (2005). 'Men and masculinities in work, organisations and management', in M. Kimmel, J. Hearn and R. W. Connell (eds), *Handbook of Studies on Men and Masculinities* (California: Sage), 289–306.

Collinson, D. L. and Hearn, J. (1996). 'Breaking the silence: On men, masculinities and managements', in D. L. Collinson and J. Hearn (eds), *Men as Managers, Managers as Men: Critical Perspectives on Men, Masculinities and Managements* (London: Sage), 75–86.

Collinson, D. L. and Hearn, J. (1994). 'Naming men as men: Implications for work, organisation and management', *Gender, Work and Organisation*, 1, 1, 2–22.

Connell, R. (1987). *Gender and Power: Society, the Person and Sexual Politics.* (Cambridge: Polity Press in association with Blackwell).

Connell, R.M. (2005). 'Growing up masculine: Rethinking the significance of adolescence in the making of masculinities, *Irish Journal of Sociology*, 14, 2, 11–28.

Currie, J., Thiele, B. and Harris, P. (2002). *Gendered Universities in Globalised Economies* (Oxford: Lexington Books).

Currie, J. and Thiele, B. (2001). 'Globalisation and gendered work cultures in universities' in A. Brooks and A. Mackinnon (eds), *Gender and the Restructured University* (Buckingham: Society for Research into Higher Education and Open University), 90–115.

Davies-Netzley, S. (1998). 'Women above the glass ceiling: Perceptions on corporate mobility and strategies for success', *Gender and Society*, 12, 3, 339–55.

Deem, R., Hilliard, S. and Reed, M. (2008). *Knowledge, Higher Education and the New Managerialism* (Oxford: Oxford University Press).

Deem, M. (2003). 'Gender, organisational cultures and the practices of manager-academics in UK universities', *Gender, Work and Organisation*, 10, 2, 239–59.

Deem, R. (1999). 'Power and resistance in the academy: the case of women academic managers', in J. Hearn and R. Moodley (eds), *Transforming Managers: Gendering Change in the Public Sector* (London: UCL Press), 60–83.

Deem, R. (1998). '"New managerialism" and higher education: the management of performance and cultures in universities in the UK', *International Studies in Sociology of Education* 8, 1, 47–70.

Doherty, L. and Manfredi, S. (2006). 'Women's progression to senior positions in English Universities', *Employee Relations*, 28, 6, 553–72.

Eagly, A., Johannesen-Schmidt, M. and van Engen, M. (2003). 'Transformational, transactional, and laissez-faire leadership styles: A meta-analysis comparing women and men', *Psychological Bulletin*, 129, 4, 569–91.

Ely, R. and Padavic, I. (2007). 'A feminist analysis of organisational research on sex differences', *Academy of Management Review* 32, 4, 1121–43.

Fletcher, J. (2002). 'The greatly exaggerated demise of heroic leadership: Gender power and the myth of female advantage', *CGO Insights*, Briefing Note 13, 1–4.

Gherardi, S. (1996). 'Gendered organisational cultures: Narratives of women travellers in a male world', *Gender, Work and Organisation*, 3, 4, 187–212.

Goode, J. and Bagilhole, B. (1998). 'Gendering the management of change in higher education: A case study', *Gender, Work and Organisation*, 5, 3, 148–64.

Grummell, B., Lynch, K. and Devine, D. (2009). 'Appointing senior managers in education: Homosociability, local logics and authenticity in the selection process', *Educational Management, Administration and Leadership* 37, 3, 329–49.

Grummell, B., Devine, D. and Lynch, K. (2008). 'The care-less manager: gender, care and new managerialism in higher education', *Gender and Education*, 20, 6, 1–17.

Harris, P., Thiele, B. and Currie, J. (1998). 'Success, gender and academic voices: Consuming passion or selling the soul', *Gender and Education*, 10, 2, 133–48.

Hartmann, H. (1981). 'The unhappy marriage of Marxism and feminism: Towards a more progressive union', in Linda Sargent (ed.), *Women and Revolution: A Discussion of the Unhappy Marriage of Marxism and Feminism*. (Boston: South End Press), 1–41.

Hearn, J. (2001). 'Academia, management and men: Making the connections, exploring the implications', in A. Brooks and A. Mackinnon (eds), *Gender and the Restructured University* (Buckingham: Society for Research into Higher Education and Open University), 69–89.

Healy, G., Ozbilgin, M. and Aliefendioglu, H. (2005). 'Academic employment and gender: A Turkish challenge to vertical sex segregation', *European Journal of Industrial Relations*, 11, 2, 247–64.

Hey, V. and Bradford, S. (2004). 'The return of the repressed? The gender politics of emergent forms of professionalism in education', *Journal of Educational Policy* 19, 6, 691–713.

Husu, L. (2006). Gate keeping, gender and recognition of scientific excellence, paper presented at XVI ISA World Congress of Sociology.

Husu, L. (2001a). *Sexism, Support and Survival in Academia: Academic Women and Hidden Discrimination in Finland* (Helsinki: University of Helsinki).

Husu, L. (2001b). 'On metaphors on the position of women in academia and science', *NORA*, 3, 9, 172–81.

Kanter, R. (1977/1993). *Men and Women of the Corporation* (New York: Basic Books).

Kerfoot, D. and Knights, D. (1996). 'The best is yet to come? The quest for embodiment in managerial work', in D. Collinson and J. Hearn (eds), *Men as Managers, Managers as Men: Critical Perspectives on Men, Masculinities and Management* (London: Sage), 78–98.

Kerfoot, D. and Whitehead, S. (1998). 'Boys' own' stuff: masculinity and the management of further education', *Sociological Review*, 46, 3, 436–57.

Knights, D. and Richards, W. (2003). 'Sex discrimination in UK academia', *Gender, Work and Organisation*, 10, 2, 213–38.

Kloot, L. (2004). 'Women and leadership in universities: A case study of women academic managers', *The International Journal of Public Sector Management* 17, 6, 470–85.

Lipman-Blumen, J. (1976). 'Towards a homosocial theory of sex roles', *Signs*, 3, 15–31.

Lynch, K. and Lyons, M. (2008). 'The gendered order of caring', in U. Barry (ed.), *Where Are We Now?* (Dublin: Tasc Publications), 168–84.

Madden, M. E. (2005). '2004 Division 35 Presidential Address: Gender and Leadership in Higher Education', *Psychology of Women Quarterly*, 29, 3–14.

McIlwee, J. S. and Robinson, J. G. (1992). *Women in Engineering: Gender, Power and Workplace Culture* (Albany: State University of New York Press).

Morley, L. (2005). 'Sounds, silences and contradictions: Gender equity in British Commonwealth higher education', *Australian Feminist Studies* 20, 46, 109–18.

Morley, L. (1999). *Organising Feminisms: The Micropolitics of the Academy* (New York: St Martin's Press).

Morley, L. (1994). 'Glass ceiling or iron cage: Women in UK academia', *Gender, Work and Organization*, 1, 4, 194–204.

Neale, J. and Özkanli, Ö. (2010). 'Organisational barriers for women in senior management positions: A comparison of Turkish and New Zealand Universities, *Gender and Education*, 22, 5, 547–63.

O'Connor, P. (2008). 'The elephant in the corner: Gender and policies related to higher education', *Administration*, 56, 1, 85–110.

O'Connor, P. (2007). 'Still changing places: Women's paid employment and gender roles', *The Irish Review*, 35, 64–78.

O'Connor, P. (1996). 'Organisational culture as a barrier to women's promotion', *The Economic and Social Review*, 3, 187–216.

O'Connor, P. and White, K. (2009). Power in the universities: Sources and implications, paper presented to 6th European Conference on Gender Equality in Higher Education, Stockholm.

O'Meara, B. and Petzall, S. (2005). 'Vice chancellors for the 21st century? A study of contemporary recruitment and selection practices in Australian universities', *Management and Research News*, 28, 6, 18–35.

Ozga, J. and Walker, L. (1999). 'In the company of men', in J .Hearn and R. Moodley (eds), *Transforming Managers: Gendering Change in the Public Sector* (London: UCL Press), 107–20.

Parker, M. and Jary, D. (1995). 'The McUniversity: Organisation, management and academic subjectivity', *Organisation*, 2, 2, 319–38.

Parry, K. W. (1998). 'The new leader: A synthesis of leadership research in Australia and New Zealand', *The Journal of Leadership Studies*, 5, 4, 82–105.

Probert, B. (2005). 'I just couldn't fit it in: Gender and unequal outcomes in academic careers', *Gender, Work and Organisation*, 12, 1, 51–72.

Sinclair, A. (1998). *Doing Leadership Differently* (Carlton South: Melbourne University Press).

Smircich, L. (1983). 'Concepts of culture and organisational analysis', *Administrative Science Quarterly*, 28, 3, 339–58.

Thomas, R. and Davies, A. (2002). 'Gender and new public management: Reconstituting academic subjectivities', *Gender, Work and Organization*, 9, 4, 372–97.

Van den Brink, M. (2009). Behind the scenes of science: Gender practices in the recruitment and selection of professors in the Netherlands, PhD Thesis, Nijmegen University.

Whitehead, S. (2001). 'Women as managers: a seductive ontology', *Gender, Work and Organisation*, 8, 1, 86–107.

Whitehead, S. M. (1998). 'Disrupted selves: Resistance and identity work in the managerial arena', *Gender and Education*, 10, 2, 199–215.

Wright Mills, C. (1970). *The Sociological Imagination* (Middlesex: Pelican).

Wajcman, J. (1998). *Managing Like a Man: Women and Men in Corporate Management* (Oxford: Wiley and Sons).

Witz, A. and Savage, M. (1992). *Gender and Bureaucracy* (Oxford: Blackwell).

Yancey Martin, P. (1996). 'Gendering and evaluating dynamics: Men, masculinities and managements', in D. L. Collinson and J. Hearn (eds), *Men as Managers, Managers as Men: Critical Perspectives on Men, Masculinities and Management.* (London: Sage), 186–209.

8
Towards Interventions for Senior Women in Higher Education

Barbara Bagilhole and Kate White

8.1 Introduction

This book has analysed gender, power and management in higher education across eight countries. It explored the significance of women being part of, rather than excluded from, university senior management, albeit in a minority position with all the implications of this status. The complex processes that impact on women in male-dominated occupations were explored through the different chapters. These include the relationship for women between paid work and their continuing responsibility for unpaid caring work, internal labour markets that can present structural obstacles and barriers, and a cultural environment where women have to deal with issues around patriarchy. Also relevant were power bases and issues of marginalisation and exclusion, and being very visible at times as one of very few women, but also invisible sometimes when trying to be heard and make changes (see Bagilhole 2002 for a full discussion of these issues in academia and other male-dominated occupations). The background to the study undertaken by the international collaborative Women in Higher Education Management (WHEM) Network, how the Network was developed, the selection of countries and the logistics of the study were outlined.

The focus on power in this book was on positional power (Handy 1985), and power vested in expertise – that is power as vested in the position of Rector/VC/President and power accruing to senior managers from their academic expertise. As the role of the top university position increasingly moves to being a CEO, following the managerial model as in the private sector, it is clear that positional power has become more important. However, in this study senior managers considered their academic expertise as an additional source of legitimacy.

Management and leadership were also key foci of this book and adopted Taylor and Machado's (2006) distinction that leadership is a process of influencing decisions and guiding people, whereas management involves implementation and administration of institutional decisions and policies.

This is the first multi-country study to examine the dynamics of women and men working together in HE senior management teams. It analysed the impact and potential impact of women as HE senior managers on both organisational growth and culture, within the context of the gendering of academic careers, in circumstances where – in most countries – the career trajectory more typical of academic men continues to be considered the usual path into senior management.

Chapter 1 provided the broad context for the study, by examining the gender profiles of each country and the influence of the European Union (EU) on the legislative framework for labour-force participation of women, given that four of the eight countries in the study – Ireland, Portugal, Sweden and the UK – are member states. These countries had more comprehensive EO frameworks than those that were not in the EU. The role of the EU as a catalyst for national legislation has been to ensure that member countries focus on reconciling the competing demands of paid work and family life. Some have been more successful than others. For example, Sweden stands out in its development – prior to joining the EU – of a concept of reconciling paid employment and private life that is based on equal parenthood and the dual-breadwinner family. In contrast, the Irish government still considers child care as a family responsibility, and the UK's policies concentrate on women's predominant responsibility in the caring role.

In the non-EU countries, especially Australia and New Zealand, the development of EO frameworks has been much more overtly influenced by national politics. For example, generally when Labour governments have been in power there has been more commitment to EO. In contrast, South Africa has a much broader EO framework to address discrimination in the workplace, which is dominated by the agenda to redress racial inequality. Turkey remains the least developed in terms of EO policies and legislation, with none at all.

Chapter 2 indicated some differences in the organisation of research and HE between those countries based on the British model and those in continental Europe. However, there was no clear connection between collegial and managerial systems and the recruitment of women to senior management. Rather, the general discourse and equality laws on gender were more important for women accessing positions of power than the organisational model of universities. The chapter noted male dominance in the collegial system with male informal networks and homosociability likely to exclude women from leading positions; and in the managerial system where gender equality depends on the views of central management. These views resonate with the findings in Chapter 7. In reviewing the question posed in the introduction about the factors in women's under-representation in HE senior management, this chapter argued that they were mostly related to broader political considerations. It concluded that the future of women leaders in HE depended on pressure from public opinion and political forces that may induce their colleagues and top management to include women in decision-making positions.

As discussed in Chapter 3, an innovative methodological approach was taken. While each thematic chapter included data from all of the participating countries, the interviews were carried out by the investigator in each country, who then summarised them. The advantages were that each interviewer had a broad understanding of the HE system and major policy debates in their particular country, and of legislative changes that impact on the operations of the university sector, and therefore it was possible to explore some topics on which it is difficult to obtain robust statistics.

8.2   Main findings

Some critical issues have emerged from this research in relation to career paths, changes in leadership roles, gendered stereotypes of leadership, demands of senior management roles, and the dynamics of gendered leadership teams.

Chapter 4 identified an increasing tendency for leadership to reflect a CEO perspective, and to become simultaneously more oriented to the university's external environment. However, the way this may impact on gender relations inside academia was far from clear. Using Le Feuvre's (1999) typology, the chapter found that senior managers did not make use of a single theoretical gender perspective. Rather, their experiences were based on the paradoxical nature of gender. On the one hand, traditional stereotypes were reinforced with the persistence of patriarchal cultures, but were also presented as an opportunity to enhance women's positions. On the other hand, institutionalisation of new gender relations, presenting men and women as interchangeable, was not consistent with the persistent under representation of women in top positions. In this sense, senior managers' discourses revealed the coexistence of a myriad of complex factors that constrain women's progress in universities, evident in the dialectic confrontation between traditional and new visions of gender relations in HE. These factors suggest that there is no straightforward answer to the question posed in the introduction about whether or not collegial and managerial models differently impact on the opportunities for female managers and leaders in universities.

Chapter 5 identified a common academic career path for senior managers, starting as a lecturer and working through the ranks with promotion largely dependent on research output. This is the path most usually followed by those who eventually lead universities and was also weighted against women getting into senior management. It has been demonstrated in this and other studies that women are actively excluded from powerful networks that influence appointment procedures and access to funding and resources (Wroblewski 2010; Faltholm & Abrahamsson 2010; Husu 2004). Moreover, these networks gate-keep to preserve the power of the dominant group (van den Brink 2009). Although most participants in this study did not initially plan to attain a senior leadership position, they were responsive to opportunities to advance. Most had supportive colleagues or superiors who actively encouraged or invited them to apply for more senior positions. Clearly, mentors and strong professional networks facilitated career advancement in academic circles. Importantly, this social capital was easier for men to acquire than women given the obvious gate-keeping that took place in certain circles, as described above. It was clear that there were greater expectations of women in senior management, on the one hand, and the loneliness, stress on relationships, loss of social life, and loss of privacy and freedom that they faced on the other. In these circumstances women often needed to go outside the university for mentoring and support.

The chapter concluded that the different competencies valued directly related to the position of each country on the organisational culture matrix (see Figure 4.1), and charted the collegial/managerial and internal/external orientation of universities.

The only universal competency was a strong academic research record, which women were likely to achieve later in their career than men, because of their additional care-giving responsibilities. However, once in a senior management position the rewards were significant. Opportunities to interact with stimulating people across sectors, and the power to effect positive change with lasting impact for future generations, were highly valued by the leaders of research. Therefore, thinking back to the question raised in the introduction about the skills required for effective leadership and management, apart from a strong research record, the skills or competencies in each country were influenced by whether or not top senior managers were considered 'primus inter pares' or whether, under a managerialist model, they had moved to being CEOs.

Chapter 6 examined the dynamics of senior managers in their universities. It found that different ways of behaving were regarded as gender based despite the fact that both individual women and men might not behave in the expected stereotypical manner. Nevertheless a male bias could be difficult to overcome as males in leadership roles could patronise women (Van Vugt, Hogan & Kaiser 2008). The chapter argued that men as well as women benefit from thinking about how gender shapes leadership style (Van Vugt, Hogan & Kaiser 2008, p. 25), and that many men as well as women in this study supported the importance of such attributes as collaboration and cooperation over hierarchical management.

The chapter concluded that while both men and women buy into stereotypes, the agenic versus communal style of management was not sufficient to explain how management was conceptualised. Managers appreciated that neither they nor their colleagues generally fitted comfortably at either end of the continuum. Rather, they saw men and women choosing from a range of management styles and realising the benefits of complementarity. Returning to the question posed in the Introduction, it has been suggested in this chapter that women and men can have different management styles and this complementarity of styles has an influence with strengthening senior management. In considering the further question of whether or not having women in senior management impacts on decision-making in HE, it was clear that having both women and men in senior management teams produced better decision-making.

Chapter 7 described variation in organisational cultures at senior management level, focussing on the gendered dimension. In reviewing the questions in the Introduction about whether or not having women in senior management impacts on the organisational culture, whether or not collegial and managerial models differently impact on the opportunities for female managers and leaders in universities, and the power of Rectors/VCs/Presidents and their impact on the gender composition of senior-management teams, this chapter found that in Turkey and Portugal, where universities are more collegial, the importance of gender was denied. On the other hand, a commitment to changing the gendered culture was most apparent in South Africa, Sweden and Australia, with the latter in particular moving strongly towards managerialism. Interestingly, Australia does not rate highly on the Global Gender Gap Index discussed in Chapter 1, which suggests that the commitment to a new culture identified in this chapter is measuring trends that are not being taken account of in the indices.

The chapter found that the organisational culture depicted, particularly by the women respondents in the UK, Australia, New Zealand and Ireland, was conformist and homosocial with 'men generally being more comfortable to work with other men'. In most countries women were depicted as 'the problem', either because of their attitudes or because of their perceived domestic and family responsibilities. The chapter asserted that such patterns sit uneasily with the fact that the proportion of women in senior management at less prestigious institutions was considerably higher than in research-intensive universities, even within the same country (O'Connor 2008; Bagilhole & White 2008). Although there was widespread acceptance that the VC/President can determine the gender profile of the senior management team, in New Zealand and in Ireland there was a marked reluctance actually to do this.

In understanding such variation, the chapter suggested that the role of the state was critical. For example, in Ireland, state structures that interface with universities provide little support or encouragement for gender change at senior management level (O'Connor & White 2011). Whereas, in contrast, in South Africa, although gender as an issue is subordinate to race, the state was seen as having clear responsibility to transform the white male organisational culture within universities. In addition, specific situational factors could inhibit or facilitate challenges to the organisational culture. Thus, for example, in Ireland the tendency towards cultural continuity was exacerbated by lack of mobility of senior management between institutions, thus reducing the existence of possible change-agents from outside.

The chapter concluded that the similarities between countries were more striking than the differences, with homosociability and the perception of women as 'the problem' consistently recurring.

The challenges for women common to all the countries studied are outlined below.

8.3   Issues for developing interventions

Despite the marked differences in political and legal context in the various countries in this study, as outlined in Chapters 1 and 2, there is a remarkable similarity in the numerical predominance of men in senior management in HE. This leads to continuing challenges for women wishing to enter senior management positions and for those already in such roles, as discussed later.

8.3.1   Changes in leadership roles

The study identified changes in the way leadership roles were developing in HE in the different countries. However, it was not clear how this affected the dynamics of gender relations. There were no homogeneous or linear patterns evident in the research, when analysing the identity of senior managers or reflecting on the experiences of women and men in these positions.

In analysing recent changes in senior management roles, it was possible to identify a tendency for leadership increasingly to reflect a business model – with the top position being similar to that of a CEO in the private sector – and simultaneously, more oriented to the HE external environment, including the corporate sector. While the way this may impact on gender relations inside academia was far from clear, it was evident that the women in this study – and some of the men – were looking towards new leadership models as the old ones were deemed to be ineffective. These respondents disliked the macho, boys'-club style of management teams. The key question is why women and the men who are uncomfortable with the authoritarian leadership of Rectors/Vice-Chancellors/Presidents do not challenge this behaviour. It is clear that when women are assertive, they risk being labelled troublemakers. But the more interesting question is why the men in management teams do not challenge leadership styles that they find unacceptable.

8.3.2   Gendered stereotypes of leadership

While most of those interviewed held stereotypical views on leadership roles, which might be interpreted as the persistence of patriarchal cultures constraining women's progress, others saw leadership as an opportunity to enhance women's position. There was also a sense that some characteristics of university senior management were not gendered, reflecting earlier findings that characteristics such as integrity, emotional intelligence, confidence, and resilience appear to have less obvious gender dimensions (Bagilhole & White 2008). Moreover, where characteristics were more strongly identified with one gender rather than the other, they were not necessarily exclusively manifested by either.

8.3.3   Demands of the job

Once in the senior management role, significant sacrifices were made by both women and men in most countries in terms of relinquishing individual research interests, personal freedom and family or leisure time, as identified in Chapter 5. Long hours were characteristic at these career levels, as was frequent travel. Given the internal or self-surveillance (Foucault 1985) that senior managers learnt as academics, they were prepared to accept from the outset of their careers these unreasonable demands of the job and the negative impact on work/life balance. Thus the gendered nature of care-giving responsibility, in all the countries included in this study, made achieving a senior position that much more difficult for women. Nevertheless, this research has questioned the demands of these jobs. Are senior management roles, and particularly the top jobs, 'doable'? Many mentioned the costs involved, such as losing any private life and being constantly under public scrutiny. Then there were the unrealistic hours, the external pressures from government, and the extremely competitive HE environment, especially in Australia, South Africa and the UK.

The study found that different competencies were valued in different university and country specific cultures. But it should be noted that the power for women to effect change in management positions can be at odds with holding on to their core values. And what do they do when they reach the tipping point, where power has become more important than being comfortable with their management style?

8.3.4   Dynamics of gendered teams

An analysis of the dynamics of women and men working together in senior management teams in HE has been presented. If more women are to be encouraged to take on senior management roles, it is important to note the different experiences of women in university management. The study found that different ways of behaving are regarded as gender based. While Sinclair (1998) argues that the expectation for leaders to be a certain type of person is an outdated concept, the assumption of male leadership remains. Moreover, women continue to be excluded from influential networks that are essential to career development (van den Brink 2009; Sagabiel, Hendrix & Schrettenbrunner 2010; Benschop 2009). Interestingly, the importance of empathy and networking skills (Faltholm & Abrahamsson 2010; Husu 2004; Sagabiel, Hendrix & Schrettenbrunner 2010; Benschop 2009), and valuing collaboration and cooperation over hierarchical management is supported by many men as well as women (Chesterman et al. 2003; Van Vugt, Hogan & Kaiser 2008), as is evident in the current study. Returning to male infused models of leadership, it is noted that these were at odds with the attitudes of some of the men in this study, which raises the question of how do top male leaders manage to enforce heroic masculinity on their management teams.

It should be noted that the positive traits identified as specific to women in university senior management tended to reproduce the stereotypical association with 'soft' management (Carvalho & Machado 2009). As managerialism is usually identified with 'hard' management, this can represent a threat for women in the managerial university model (White, Carvalho & Riordan 2011).

8.4   Towards developing interventions

8.4.1   Why interventions

- Many women aspiring to senior positions in academia – which this research has demonstrated is an important stage of the career path to management – are actively excluded from powerful networks that would provide the social capital needed to succeed. Not surprisingly, then, the representation of women in senior academic staff remains consistently low. For example, across most EU countries it is less than 20 per cent (OECD 2006).
- The study has demonstrated that having more women in senior management teams confirms that women are valued, that there is better decision-making and therefore there are better outcomes for the university. Thus increased representation of women in HE management has the capacity to achieve change through a dual agenda of 'interventions that will advance gender equality objectives while *simultaneously* serving the organisations' instrumental goals' (Ely & Meyerson 2000, p. 591).
- Having more women in senior management teams can in some circumstances modify the more extreme aggressive and competitive male behaviour, although it is necessary to question why men who, as this research demonstrated, do not endorse such behaviour remain silent. Nevertheless, having more women might also encourage the other voices in management to be heard.
- Having more women in senior management sends a strong positive message to staff and students that women are an integral part of the institution.

8.4.2   Where should interventions happen

- Attention should be paid to women's lack of mentors and exclusion from professional networks that are crucial to gaining sufficient social capital to achieve and succeed in management positions. Women who are considering applying for senior management positions in their own university should be assisted to access suitable internal and external mentors. Preferably, the institution will establish a formal mentoring program and also a peer networking program that includes being informed of the rules of the game (Benschop & Brouns 2003). Given high workloads of senior academic women including extra pastoral care (Barrett & Barrett 2011), the institution must provide time release from teaching in order for these interventions to be effective, and also to show their commitment to women's career development.

- Role modelling for women further down in the organisation is essential. But what kind of women do we need as role models? It has been established in this research that women managers are more effective as role models when they do not adopt a tough, aggressive masculine stance but demonstrate leadership styles with which they are comfortable. However, in this role modelling they can be stymied by a lack of effective networks. Given the isolation they often experience, even from male peers, they are reliant on networks of women in less senior positions or outside the university. In strengthening these networks, they can provide strong role modelling in university management, although there was evidence that women in management sometimes had difficulty discussing issues with other women in 'lower' positions.
- Both women and men could benefit from considering how gender influences leadership styles: understanding that gendered stereotypes of leadership can be used in different ways, including enhancing women's progress, and could be utilised to enable women to explore effective styles in university management. Men as well as women in this research emphasised the particular strengths of women in university management teams. However, at the same time, singling out women's particular or 'special' leadership competencies is not necessarily the way forward. Fletcher (2002, p. 2) calls this the separate spheres phenomenon in which the social world is separated into two spheres of activities that are separate, unequally valued and sex-linked. Thus many women, comments Fletcher (2002, p. 3), 'experience the so-called female advantage as a form of exploitation, where their behaviour benefits the bottom line but does not mark them as leadership potential'.
- There is often a disconnection between what universities say is required for effective leadership and what is rewarded. Universities are increasingly developing competency frameworks of what they expect from managers, but they tend to appoint managers who do not model the competencies that they promote. In this book we have identified that some senior managers in managerial universities say

that they value the collaboration and communication that women bring to management teams, but there is a tendency to reward 'hard' managerial leadership, which is aligned with the traditional trans-actional leadership style. Universities need to build on the competencies that respondents in this research consider are essential for effective university management. Universities need to be challenged to focus on developing and making explicit a much broader set of competencies that are not gender specific. They and HE policy makers need to challenge the notion that HE senior managers are recruited on the basis of international excellence in academic research careers. The reality in several of the countries in this study, as discussed above, is that an academic skill set is not necessarily appropriate or useful for effective management in highly specialist roles, especially at Pro-Rector/PVC level, and that increasingly non-academic experts are being recruited into these positions.

- Achieving broader acknowledgement and understanding of the advantages and strengths of gender diverse management teams could be used as a catalyst to lever institutional change. But we need to keep in mind Fletcher's (2002, p. 2) questions: 'Why, if there is general agreement on the need for new leadership practices, are the practices themselves not more visible in the workplace? Why, if these models are aligned with the feminine, are not more women being propelled to the top? And why, if there is transformational potential in these new models of leadership, are organisations not being trans-formed?' Part of the answer may rest with the findings of our research that, while men in senior management understand the strengths of gender diverse teams, in some countries they lack the courage to embrace new leadership practices (see Chapter 7). As a consequence many women regard university management as a hostile environ-ment and are not attracted to leadership roles, with the outcome that the transformational potential of new leadership models is not realised. Therefore, interventions are also necessary for men who are currently in management teams so that they can give voice to their dissatisfaction with what they consider are outdated models of leadership.

- Women and men need to fully understand the breadth and com-plexity of senior management jobs and their huge time demands, which work to the detriment of work-life balance. But, at the same time, they need to challenge the orthodoxy that these jobs are man-ageable and sustainable in their present form. We need to under-stand the link between the heroic masculinity model of leadership and impossible jobs. There are strong synergies between narrow perceptions of the leader and 'not-doable' jobs. While transactional leadership, in the final analysis, is regarded as the leadership style that achieves results, it remains an unattractive approach for women, and therefore continues to exclude women from leadership roles.

• Universities need to envisage new ways of leading. It is clear from this research that new leadership styles need to be explored and tried, as universities tend to be immersed in set leadership styles, or promote newer styles but in reality cling to old models. While Binns (2006, p. 306) finds it difficult to envisage a 'social world in which gendering "patterns" do not (re)produce masculinised or feminised identities', she offers a view of leadership as a 'multilayered' practice 'that constantly overspills its discursive boundaries to form new identities and practices' (Binns 2006, p. 307). Proposed strategic interventions to encourage more women to apply for leadership roles should therefore explore the possibilities of new identities and practices in leadership, rather than take a deterministic view that gendered patterns are immutable.

While this chapter has not explored the content of such interventions, it found that the principles used by HERS-SA in South Africa in its approach to professional development were useful (HERS-SA 2010, adapted from Willis and Daisley 1992). These are:

Women only: as experience has shown that women's groups explore issues at a deeper level when participants realise that their issues are taken seriously and significant support exists for them within the group. Some of the topics that emerge in discussions are likely to be gender-specific and require a secure environment for thorough exploration. This approach is pro-women, not anti-men.

Self-nomination: professional development interventions frequently demand a great deal from the participant, from self-examination through to making significant changes in one's approach to both personal and work life. Therefore, women should choose to participate.

Holistic approach: interventions should recognise that work is one element of the multiple roles that women balance. Therefore, interventions should accommodate these various demands on participants' time, and also encourage women to relate the material and discussions to their own circumstances, knowing that life experiences beyond the work place are perceived as valid.

Confidentiality: participants should be encouraged to share real examples of their work experiences rather than to speak about hypothetical cases. Therefore, confidentiality is essential. All those in the group, including the facilitator, must respect this principle.

While supporting the principle of women-only programmes, the Network considers that additional interventions are required for men in university management teams who wish to explore new models of leadership.

The next phase of the Women in Higher Education Management Network project is to develop and evaluate interventions for women seeking to move into university senior management roles as well as those currently in these roles.

References

Bagilhole, B. (2002). *Women in Non-Traditional Occupations. Challenging Men* (Basingstoke: Palgrave Macmillan).

Bagilhole, B. and White, K. (2008). 'Towards a gendered skills analysis of senior management positions in UK and Australian Universities', *Tertiary Education and Management*, 14, 1, 1–12.

Barrett, L. and Barrett, P. (2011). 'Women and academic workloads: career slow lane or Cul-de-Sac?', *Higher Education*, 61, 141–55.

Benschop, Y. (2009). 'The micro-politics of gendering in networking', *Gender, Work and Organisation*, 1, 2, 217–37.

Benschop, Y. and Brouns, M. (2003). 'Crumbling ivory towers: Academic organising and its gender effects', *Gender, Work and Organisation*, 10, 2, 194–212.

Binns, J. (2006). The possibilities of relational leading: rethinking gender, power, reason and ethics in leadership discourse and practice, unpublished PhD, University of Western Australia.

Carvalho, T. and Machado, M. (2009). Gender and shifts in higher education managerial regimes, paper presented to 6th Gender Equality in HE Conference, Stockholm.

Chesterman, C., Ross-Smith, A. and Peters, M. (2003). 'They made a demonstrable difference: Senior women's efforts to redefine higher education management. Research outcomes for the project: Senior women executives and the cultures of management', *McGill Journal of Education*, 38, 3.

Ely, R. and Meyerson, D. (2000). 'Advancing gender equity in organisations: The challenge and importance of maintaining a gender narrative', *Organisation*, 7, 589–608.

Faltholm, Y. and Abrahamsson, L. (2010). 'I prefer not to be called a woman entrepreneur' – Gendered global and local discourses of academic entrepreneurship, paper presented to the Gender, Work & Organisation Conference, Keele University.

Fletcher, J. (2002). 'The greatly exaggerated demise of heroic leadership: Gender power and the myth of female advantage', *CGO Insights*, Briefing Note 13, 1–4.

Foucault, M. (1985). *The Use of Pleasure* (New York: Pantheon).
Handy, C. (1985). *Understanding Organisations*, 2nd edn. (Harmondsworth: Penguin).
HERS-SA (2010). www.hers-sa.org.za/development/htm. Retrieved 15 September 2010.
Husu, L. (2004). 'Gate-keeping, gender equality and scientific excellence', in *Gender and Excellence in the Making*, (Brussels: European Commission), 69–76.
Le Feuvre, N. (1999). 'Gender occupational feminisation and flexibility', in R. Crompton (ed.), *Restructuring Gender Relations and Employment. The Decline of Male Breadwinner* (Oxford: Oxford University Press), 150–78.
O'Connor, P. and White, K. (2011). 'Similarities and differences in collegiality/managerialism in Irish and Australian universities', *Gender and Education* (forthcoming).
O'Connor, P. (2008). 'The elephant in the corner: Gender and policies related to higher education', *Administration*, 56, 1, 85–110.
OECD (2006). *Women in Scientific Careers: Understanding the Potential* (Paris: OECD).
Sagabiel, F., Hendrix, U. and Schrettenbrunner, C. (2010). How women scientists at the top change organisational cultures, paper presented to the ISA World Congress of Sociology, Gothenburg.
Sinclair, A. (1998). *Doing Leadership Differently* (Carlton South: Melbourne University Press).
Taylor, J. and Machado, M. (2006). 'Higher education leadership and management: from conflict to interdependence through strategic planning', *Tertiary Education and Management*, 12, 2, 137–60.
van den Brink, M (2009). Behind the scenes of science: Gender practices on the recruitment and selection of professors in the Netherlands, PhD thesis, University of Nijmegan.
Van Vugt, M., Hogan, R. and Kaiser, R. (2008). 'Leadership, followership and evolution', *American Psychologist*, 63, 3, 182–96.
White, K., Carvalho, T. and Riordan, S. (2011). 'Gender, power and managerialism in universities', *Journal of Higher Education Policy and Management* 33, 2, 179–86.
Willis, L. and Daisley, J. (1992). *Developing Women through Training* (London: McGraw Hill).
Wroblewski, A. (2010). Barriers to women on their way into top positions in Austrian universities: How gender biased are application procedures for university professors? Paper presented to the ISA World Congress of Sociology, Gothenburg.

Appendices

Appendix 1: Women in Higher Education Management Network – protocol for sharing material

It was agreed that

- Individual researchers were free to use the country-specific data they collected in whatever way they wish;
- If writing a single-authored paper using data from another country, researchers must consult the person(s) whose data was used. These other researchers needed to know what was quoted and the context;
- If using data from all countries in a paper or journal article, the draft must be circulated to all the members of the group;
- There was a need to update each other when we presented conference papers or published articles using our own data or data of others;
- There was a need to always acknowledge the WHEM Network when making presentations;
- Once data had been used in a conference paper or journal article it was in the public domain;
- If a member of the Network used data of other researchers to write a conference paper or journal article, they needed to negotiate with the other researchers about whether or not it should be a single or co-authored paper. If a piece of research used the whole data set, all investigators would be co-authors. The person who undertook the substantial research for the paper/article should be first author, but a footnote on the first page must acknowledge all the countries and investigators. Alternatively, co-authors should be acknowledged by the term 'in association with';
- The model developed for writing the Perth paper in 2008 (where all investigators contributing data were acknowledged as co-authors) would hold up for a year or so. But as research from the project was published, investigators would be able to quote from these papers because they would be in the public arena;
- If any investigator was unhappy about others using their data, they must in the first instance raise the matter with the person concerned. The project coordinator would be happy to assist in these negotiations; and
- All WHEM researchers would sign up to this formal protocol.

Appendix 2: Women in Higher Education Management Network Interview Schedule

Senior University Managers

Getting into – and on in – senior management ALL

- How do you define senior management in your university?
- Did you experience any difficulties in becoming a senior manager?

- In retrospect did you consider management as a career path or was it unplanned?
- What factors or people were most supportive in getting you into your current/last management position?
- What factors or people were most supportive in your current/former tasks in senior management?
- Has being in senior management affected your work/life experience? If so, in what ways?
- What do you see as the advantages and disadvantages of being in university senior management?
- Where do you see your career in five years time? Why do you say that?

Doing senior management in your current/last position <u>ALL</u>

- How do you think you are/were seen by your male colleagues? And your female colleagues?
- (If male) Are you more comfortable in an all-male management team or a predominantly female one? (If female) Are you more comfortable in an all-female management team or in a predominantly male one?
- Based on your experience, what sort of things are different about working with women at your level in comparison with working with (other) men? What about working for a female boss compared to working for a male boss?
- Do you think women in senior management feel the need to adopt male management styles? Does this vary according to discipline?
- Are you aware of areas/disciplines where academic women are most likely to be found in your university? What do you see as the characteristics of these areas?
- What do you think women see as the barriers to promotion in your university?

For Rectors/VCs/Presidents only

- What has been your experience of selection panels for senior management appointments?
- Have you appointed academic and/or non-academic women to your management team? Why/why not?
- What have been your observations about the working styles of female and male managers?
- Do you think that women prefer to work with men or women or both? Why do you say that?
- Is there anything that someone in your position could do about the current predominantly male management culture?
- Does having women in senior management positions really make a difference, or not? In terms of management decisions? What about to faculty? Students?

Broader management culture <u>ALL</u>

- What do you see as the typical career path into senior management at your university?
- Describe a typical Rector/VC/President in your university.

- What kinds of characteristics do you think are valued in senior management in your university? What about personal qualities and skills?
- Describe the appointment process of senior managers in your University. Are there key bodies or individuals who influence the process?
- What is the balance of males and females in senior management in your University? How many of these women are academics?
- How powerful do you think Rectors/VC/Presidents are in relation to faculties? What do you see as their key contribution to an organisation? What about as regards the gender profile of senior management?

Index